W9-BYH-519

THE

BEST

GAME

YOU

CAN

NAME

ALSO BY DAVE BIDINI

On a Cold Road
Tropic of Hockey
Baseballissimo

FOR YOUNG ADULTS
For Those About to Rock

DAVE BIDINI

THE BEST GAME YOU CAN NAME

McCLELLAND & STEWART

Library and Archives Canada Cataloguing in Publication

Bidini, Dave
The best game you can name / Dave Bidini.

ISBN 13: 978-0-7710-1459-8
ISBN 10: 0-7710-1459-7

1. Hockey–Canada. 2. Hockey players–Canada.
3. National Hockey League. I. Title.

GV848.5.A1B52 2005   796.962'0971   C2005-903151-4

The lines on page vii from "Hockey Players" by Al Purdy from *Beyond Remembering: The Collected Works of Al Purdy*, 2000, appear courtesy of Harbour Publishing.

The lines on page 66 are from "Nothing Else Matters" by James Hetfield and Lars Ulrich. Copyright © 1991. Reprinted by permission of Creeping Death Music. All Rights Reserved.

The lines on page 94 from "The Shooting of Dan McGrew" appear by courtesy of the Estate of Robert Service. Copyright © 1910

We acknowledge the financial support of the Government of Canada through the Book Publishing Industry Development Program and that of the Government of Ontario through the Ontario Media Development Corporation's Ontario Book Initiative. We further acknowledge the support of the Canada Council for the Arts and the Ontario Arts Council for our publishing program.

Typeset in Centaur by M&S, Toronto
Printed and bound in Canada

This book is printed on acid-free paper that is 100% recycled, ancient-forest friendly (100% post-consumer recycled).

McClelland & Stewart Ltd.
75 Sherbourne Street
Toronto, Ontario
M5A 2P9
www.mcclelland.com

2   3   4   5   6   09   08   07   06   05

FOR LO

"And how do the players feel about it
this combination of ballet and murder?"

— Al Purdy, "Hockey Players"

CONTENTS

PLAYERS

Frank Beaton:	New York Rangers, 1979–80
Curt Bennett:	Atlanta Flames, 1972–78
Harvey Bennett, Jr:	Philadelphia Flyers, 1976–78
Perry Berezin:	Calgary Flames, 1986–89
Sam Bettio:	Boston Bruins, 1949
Yuri Blinov:	Team U.S.S.R., 1972
Bruce Boudreau:	Toronto Maple Leafs, 1976–83
John Chabot:	Pittsburgh Penguins, 1984–87
Yvan Cournoyer:	Montreal Canadiens, 1963–79
Joe Daley:	Winnipeg Jets, 1972–79
Brad Dalgarno:	New York Islanders, 1985–96
Don Edwards:	Buffalo Sabres, 1976–82
Tim Ecclestone:	St. Louis Blues, 1967–71
Nick Fotiu:	New York Rangers, 1976–79
Alexander Gusev:	Team U.S.S.R., 1972
Todd Hartje:	Sokol Kiev, 1990
Anders Hedberg:	Winnipeg Jets, 1974–78
Pat Hickey:	New York Rangers, 1975–80

Harry Howell: New York Rangers, 1952–69
Igor Kravchuk: CSKA Moscow, 1987–92
Jeff Jackson: Quebec Nordiques, 1987–91
Mike Laughton: Oakland Seals, 1967–71
Steve Larmer: Chicago Blackhawks, 1981–93
Bob Lorimer: New York Islanders, 1976–81
Steve Ludzik: Chicago Blackhawks, 1981–89
Frank Mahovlich: Toronto Maple Leafs, 1957–68
Seth Martin: Canadian National Team, 1960–67
Al McDonough: Pittsburgh Penguins, 1971–74
Walter McKechnie: Toronto Maple Leafs, 1978–80
Mike Pelyk: Toronto Maple Leafs, 1967–74
Eddie Mio: Edmonton Oilers, 1978–81
Ron Murphy: Chicago Blackhawks, 1957–64
Mark Napier: Montreal Canadiens, 1978–84
Larry Playfair: Buffalo Sabres, 1979–86
Dean Prentice: New York Rangers, 1955–67
Alexander Ragulin: Team U.S.S.R., 1972
Jim Schoenfeld: Buffalo Sabres, 1972–82
Gord Sherven: Edmonton Oilers, 1983–85
Derek Smith: Buffalo Sabres, 1975–82
Fred Stanfield: Boston Bruins, 1967–73
Garry Unger: St. Louis Blues, 1970–78
Rick Vaive: Toronto Maple Leafs, 1979–87
Ryan Walter: Montreal Canadiens, 1982–92
Bugsy Watson: Pittsburgh Penguins, 1968–74

COMMENTATORS

Art Berglund:	Executive, USA Hockey
John Brophy:	Coach
Dan Diamond:	Writer
James Duplacey:	Former Curator, Hockey Hall of Fame
Gary Green:	Coach, Broadcaster
John Halligan:	New York Rangers, NHL, media
Richard Harrison:	Poet
Bartley Kives:	Writer
Igor Kuperman:	Journalist
Igor Mukhin:	Writer
Vladimir Mozgovoy:	Writer
Chuck Molgat:	Writer
Karl-Eric Reif:	Writer
Mike Smith:	Former NHL General Manager
Lou Vairo:	Coach, Executive, USA Hockey
Eric Zweig:	Writer

MORNINGSTARS 2004

Craig Barnes
Cheech
The Chizzler
Dutch
Andy Ford
Tom Goodwin
Brad "Howie" Hardman
Tom Paterson
Alun Piggins
Mark Robinson (The Winterbird)
Schmiddy
Johnny Sinclair
Steve Stanley
T
Chris Topping
and
me

1 | A FROZEN RIVER OF STOUT

If it's true that the best time for sports is when you're eleven, I've discovered that it's also pretty good when you're forty. My athletic renaissance came on the heels of turning thirty-four, which is how old I was when I lit out to discover world hockey. Later, and older, I spent an entire summer dogging an Italian baseball team up and down the Boot. One evening while I was in Nettuno – my Italian baseballing town – I paced with some agitation behind the town's seawall, holding my cellphone and listening to my friend Ozzie from his couch in Etobicoke, Ontario. He was shouting the names of undrafted NHLers: "Thomas Vokoun? Available, I think. Comrie? Gone. Brisebois? You really wanna pick Brisebois?"

Purple waves licked the beach not twenty feet from where I was standing under the bright Roman moon, pondering the kind of quibbler that must have perplexed Marcus Aurelius or Cicero or any number of Latin thinkers who'd paced this same long stretch of sand:

"Anson Carter gives us depth, sure, but if Brian Boucher's around, you know we can never have too much goaltending."

Ozzie paused while a Sputnik orbiting hundreds of miles overhead ensnared our transcontinental frequency in static, then volleyed a thought about the unpredictability of a young American goaltender. Would Boucher ever supplant Sean Burke as number one in Phoenix, he wondered, and, hey, what was Italy like anyway. I told him that Italy was fine, just fine, then pressed on with the matter at hand: to draft our fantasy league team with a handful of other hockey freaks.

Arguing eggheadedly over draft picks during the sweet soft hours of an Italian evening — to say nothing of spending what should have been prime holidaying time catching fungoes — is proof that sports means as much to me now as it ever did at age eleven. Which is saying a lot. As a boy growing up in suburban Toronto, my life was a hockey card collection, a gas station stamp book, a Team Canada poster, an Export 'A' Leafs calender, Gordie Howe's name scribbled in blue ink on the back of a beer mat, Tiger Williams at Kingsway Motors, a pair of Marlie greys, a front tooth knocked out by Martin Dzako's street hockey follow-through. I was just as obsessed as the next scamp with the gladiators of ice, but my friend Murray Heywood went one step further. When Murray was eight, his brothers would invite their friends over to watch the kid put on a show. He'd leave the room while they put a hockey card on the kitchen table, obscured except for the players' eyes. They'd call Murray back into the room. He'd guess right every time.

The players Ozzie and I drafted onto our fantasy team were the adult equivalents of a hockey card collection. We obsessed over them as we once obsessed over the flat, sugar-dusted squares stacked stat-to-stat in shoeboxes and lunch tins. A fondness for the outdoor rinks and skating ponds and scraps of ice that collect in the ravines, creeks, and parking-lot potholes of my kid-dom returned after a long, post-adolescent, soul-clearing wander into the land of art, love, dope, movies, and the strains of Killing Joke. Hockey had been drummed out of my heart, head, and hands by demanding coaches, aggressive peers, and a natural tightening of life, to say nothing of the siren of rock and roll. It had led me away from sports, but it had taken me back there again. In rinks like Bill Bolton, Moss Park, DeLaSalle, St. Mike's, Scadding Court, Dufferin Grove, McCormick, and Wallace Emerson — each pad seated near the heart of the city — I rediscovered the game.

This rebirth of sporting love is common among youngish Canadians who, on the other side of twenty-five, suddenly see hockey as being more than just the domain of guys in mullets weaned on White Snake and Extra Old Stock. A collection of these enlightened folk can be found every Easter weekend at the Exclaim! Cup hockey tournament, a yearly play-down sponsored by *Exclaim!*, a national music magazine that is to *The Hockey News* what Thurston Moore is to Michael Hedges. The tourney takes place over four days and features twenty-four musician teams whose players, like me, fell out of, then back in, love with the game. Members of the Fruit, Dufferin Groove, Wheatfield Souldiers, Victoria Humiliation, Vancouver Flying Vees, Edmonton Green Pepper All-Stars, and all the other teams know that while the

dividing line between art and sport is thick, the E! Cup proves that the geek and the goon can co-exist, even flourish in a single body.

During the tourney, rinkside rock bands serenade the crowd with everything from "More Than a Feeling" played in twenty-second *kerrangs* to the occasional hippie drum-jam extended for as long as it takes the referee to collect players for a faceoff. It's the Vans Warped Tour meets the Allan Cup Finals. At the evening socials (coined the "Hockey Hootenany" by the organizer, Morningstar Tom Goodwin), the teams become bands again, executing the kind of cultural switcheroo that never would have happened back in my high-school days, not when left wingers were beating the snot out of safety-pinners on local football fields. For their performance at the '04 Hootenany, the Montreal entry, organized by Ninja Tune records, debuted a work by

British electronic music king Amon Tobin: a remix of the *Hockey Night in Canada* theme. The tune – transformed by Tobin's thunderous beats and growling industrial textures – became a celebration of hockey without the macho cruelty, art without the arrogance.

The E! Cup began as a challenge match between the Sonic Unyon Pond Hockey Squad (Sonic Unyon is a Hamilton label that's put out records by Frank Black, Sianspheric, and Mayor McCA, who also happens to be Ric Seiling's nephew) and my team, the Morningstars, which has suffered three straight Cup losses after winning the first three. Much has changed since the inaugural E! Cup, the most notable difference being that which has kept us at arm's length from sporting glory: talent. In the first year of the tourney, there were only two teams. We defeated the Unyon in a shootout final, earning us the right to skate the circumference of the rink alongside a fellow dressed like a giant beer (Guinness was the event's co-sponsor). Back then, life was sweet and the 'Stars were winning, drunk on the magic of timely twine-benders and a river of glorious stout. But soon, the other teams got good.

Partly because of our three titles, partly because I'd travelled the world wearing the home reds, partly because my book about those travels was a success, and partly because certain players just couldn't stand to see someone else skating with a giant beer, the Morningstars became the most gunned-for team in Toronto rec hockey. One team, Boom, was formed with the express purpose of tipping us from our perch. We started losing. By 2004, we had lost three consecutive semifinals and had grown weary and battle-worn with age. We were faded icons. We drew some pride not from our stickhandling but from the fact that we sold more merchandise than any other team. We tried to feel flattered that ours was the team most often cited in derisive slogans and the troop-rallying cries of rival clubs. One team, the Jokers, whose membership includes the bizarre CanRock array of Stompin' Tom Connors, Jr., Tyler Stewart, Seán Cullen, and Orin Isaacs, presented a short film as part of their Hootenany performance in which Gary Bettman, no less, mocked the Morningstars' chances at repeating as Cup champs. (Tyler, because of his musical caché, had been given an all-access pass to roam the NHL dressing rooms, filming at will.) In one scene, Chris Pronger, under the banner GUNNING FOR BIDINI, speculated on what he would do should he ever meet yours truly in the corner. He was gonna wax me, he said, which didn't sound like it was supposed to tickle. Only DOA's punk potentate, Joey Shithead, defended the 'Stars in the short film, rising from his chair during a bogus segment of TSN's *Off the Record* to declare, "Nobody's gonna beat the Morningstars," before slumping back in his seat.

Without the burden of a championship defence on my mind during the '04 E! Cup, I spent my time savouring those fine, floating details of the game's inner architecture. While I pondered the similarities and differences of being in love with hockey at ages eleven and forty, I remembered those figures in my card collection and realized, after a long, contemplative chew on my gummy mouthguard, that we now had something in common: none of us played in the NHL. What struck me as really weird was that these former dervishes of the ice now spent their days worrying about mortgages, car payments, and cable bills, while yours truly had recently been paid to travel the world whacking around a puck for book and film. The sense of who played hockey for a living had become terribly blurred.

Another thing: My friend Chris Brown, ex-keyboardist for Barenaked Ladies and Bourbon Tabernacle Choir, leads a sublime and ridiculous life. The last time we spoke, he'd just come back from a reception at the Swedish embassy in honour of B.B. King. Chris counts Neil Young and Wayne Gretzky as friends, and two years ago, he was asked to go to Wyoming to play with the New York Rangers Oldtimers, even though he's neither old nor from New York (nor is B.B. King Swedish, so there you go). He continues to be friendly with many of the Rangers, and often refers to Rod Gilbert – of the famed Ratelle-Gilbert-Hadfield line – as "Uncle Rod."

After hanging out with the Rangers' old-timers, Chris told me that he realized how much professional players in the 1960s and 1970s were like musicians: both took long bus rides, earned sparse incomes, spent endless time in bars, stayed in countless bland hotels, ingested a mountain of bad food, and played to half-full houses. All of a sudden, I felt closer to players who once seemed as unknowable as the cosmos. Using a single game from the tournament as my framework, I decided to collect these stories in an effort to draw a line between their lives and mine, as citizens of Planet Hockey. All I had to do was pick up the phone and ask the rink-roughened voice on the other end whether it was Bugsy Watson or Anders Hedberg or John Brophy I was speaking to. And wouldn't you know it?

I was.

JEFF JACKSON: I came from Dresden, Ontario, population 2,600. There was a river that ran through town – the Sydenham River – which froze in the winter, so we played pretty much every day. My backyard turned into a rink naturally too, and if we weren't playing in either spot, we were at the arena. We won almost every tournament we entered because we played so much hockey. There was one player who'd made it from Dresden: Ken Houston. He played for Atlanta, Calgary, and a few other teams. When I was growing up, he was the guy who gave me hope that I could go somewhere in the game. When you're from a small town, the rest of the world seems so far away and unreachable, whether you're gifted or not. So the fact that Ken used to come home every summer was special. He'd stop by and play grass hockey with us – we'd have two games going on the lawn in front of the high school – hang around, tell stories.

Years later, when I made it to the NHL, my first ever shift was against him. I lined up on left wing and he was on right wing for an exhibition game at Maple Leaf Gardens. Before the faceoff, he cracked me on the pads with his stick and said, "All right. Go get 'em kid." On my second shift, I was carrying the puck around the net feeling like a million bucks. My head was down, and when I looked up, there he was. I heard him holler, "Keep your head up, kid!" and then he came at me.

MIKE LAUGHTON: The International Hockey Clinic came to Nelson, British Columbia, when I was sixteen years old. Andy Bathgate, Glenn Hall, and Metro Prystai were there. It was exciting to see them in person, and have them help me with drills. Andy Bathgate could shoot the puck like a bullet. There was a red sign in the bleachers above the net, and he asked if I wanted him to hit it. Someone said, "You couldn't hit that sign with two hundred pucks, Mr. Bathgate!" but he hit it with his first shot. Just seeing him do something like that made us believe in the fantastic. It confirmed that what we'd seen on television was, in fact, real.

TIM ECCLESTONE: I was in Kansas City playing for the Blues' farm team when Scotty Bowman called my coach, Doug Harvey, and asked for a defenceman. Doug said, "Give Ecclestone a try. He's playing as good as anybody else." So I flew up to New York City. I'd hardly ever been on a plane before and it was my first time in the Big Apple. Needless to say, I was overwhelmed on the cab ride coming in. I had no idea what to do. I showed up at the old Madison Square Garden about two hours from game time with sticks, skates, and a bag of about a week and half's worth of clothing. So, I went around to the side door of the rink and told the attendant that I was there for the game. He said, "Man, this is New York City. We see a lot of stuff here, but nobody's ever tried this one on us before." He said that if I was for real, I'd better try the players entrance around back. When I finally found the dressing room, Scotty introduced me to the guys, then gave me the best seat in the house: right beside the spare goalie at the end of the bench, opening and closing the gate. On about the third shift, somebody went down, and Scotty threw me out there.

LOU VAIRO: When my dad was a kid, he used to play hockey with the heel of a shoe as a puck, sticks cost fifty cents, and they'd play manhole cover to manhole cover. But there wasn't a single rink outside of the old Madison Square Gardens on 48th, which had a figure-skating rink above it, with no boards. One day, when I was eight or nine, I was playing baseball outside with friends when this thin, sallow-cheeked guy pulled up in a beat-up old car with Cellophane windows and AI EXTERMINATING hand-painted on the door. The guy got out and said, "Have you guys ever thought about playing hockey, or roller hockey?" We hadn't. He had a hockey stick and a roll of black friction tape, and he shot it against the wall of the nearby supermarket. We were so impressed that he could lift the roll of tape off the ground, we all tried it; none of us could do it. He started a team. We lived in a section of Brooklyn called Canarsie, and he named the team the Canarsie Rangers. We all got roller skates, and eventually fashioned enough equipment: construction workers' gloves, that sort of thing. We'd go to the dump and find an old couch or chair and take out the cushioning to make pads. For shinguards, we used magazines. The blocker was an old black-and-white schoolbook with duct tape around it. This was how we did it. Then we got permission to flood the schoolyard so we could play by the light of the moon. My mother couldn't stand to watch me play. One time, she was sitting outside the rink waiting to take me and my brother Jerry home. She thought the game was supposed to be over, so she asked one of my friends where we were. He told her, "They're in sudden death, Mrs. Vairo." She fainted in the street. She didn't know what he meant.

PAT HICKEY: I was drafted in the eighth round of the junior draft by the Hamilton Red Wings. I showed up to camp to find seventy-five other players on the ice. I phoned my dad crying my eyes out, but he said, "Son, just do one more day." The next day,

I called and said, "Dad, there are forty-five guys better than me!" He told me the same thing, "One more day, son." The fourth day I called him back and said, "You know what, Dad? There's nobody here who can do what I can do."

IGOR KRAVCHUK: We played street hockey as kids, but instead of shoes, we wore skates, and instead of ice, we skated on snow that was pressed down really hard. I can't recall how I got into the game, but I do have a memory of walking out into the yard, chopping down a small Christmas tree, cutting off all the branches and twigs, and then bending the end into the shape of a blade. In my town – Ufa, in the Ural Mountains – you were lucky to get a proper stick, because whenever they put a new shipment on the shelves, they'd be sold out in five minutes. If you weren't lined up outside the store on that morning, it was back to the woods with the axe.

ANDERS HEDBERG: The local professional team, Modo, were always trying to recruit me. I lived in a little village and used to tell them, "I'm happy here playing with my youth team, but thank you." I could bike to Modo every now and then and see a game, and that was good enough for me. Pro hockey wasn't that big in Sweden in the 1960s, so I didn't see it as a career. I thought I'd go to university and become a teacher. Finally, when I turned sixteen, I tried out for the senior team, and I made it. But the first day of play was also the final game of the TV Puck – a huge Swedish tournament for the country's youth teams. Modo wanted me to play in their season opener, but I told them: "I have to play with my peers, my friends." They said, "No, it's silly.

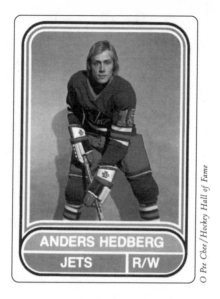

ANDERS HEDBERG
JETS   R/W

O Pee Chee / Hockey Hall of Fame

You've made our elite team. You're playing with us." I defied them and said that I was going to play with my friends. The press began trumpeting this story and it became quite a sensation. So Modo had no choice; they arranged a small plane to pick me up after my youth game. Because the TV Puck was broadcast all around Sweden, the whole country looked in to see who this sixteen-year-old was, demanding to play in his youth game as well as with the big club. We played at one o'clock in the afternoon and I ended up scoring five goals. I flew thirty minutes from Sundsvall to Modo, and at six o'clock, I took to the ice for my first professional game. Thankfully, I scored in that game too, beating Leif "Honken" Holmquist, one of the greatest Swedish goaltenders of all-time. It was quite a day, but I still didn't think I'd end up playing on a line with Bobby Hull in Winnipeg, not in my wildest dreams.

RYAN WALTER: I left home at fifteen to play junior hockey in Langley, British Columbia. I was playing tier two when most kids were still in bantam. My uncle told me I shouldn't be leaving home so young, but my parents thought it was okay as long as my grades stayed high. My first year went well – my grades actually went up, and I scored twenty-six goals – and in my second year I was called up to Kamloops to play against Victoria in the first round of the WHL playoffs. In the first game, I drove outside with the puck and had the defenceman beat while heading to the net when he took his stick and sliced me down at the skates. I hit the post with my knee and ripped everything. I had two pieces of cartilage removed, and both cruciates and the interior and exterior ligaments were badly damaged. Everything was torn and mangled. At the end of the operation two doctors took my parents aside and told them that I'd be fine for walking, but that I'd never skate again. I was sixteen and cocky and I refused to believe what they were saying. In rehabilitation, I had to work harder than I'd ever worked in my entire life. I never went through more pain than I went through trying to get the knee back to where it was supposed to be. In the end, I think that having to do this set me apart from other players in my peer group who had similar talent. I had to push harder than they did. I had to learn about resilience and resolve very early on. Afterwards, bloody noses or cuts were nothing to me.

GARY GREEN: I came from a farm in Tillsonburg, Ontario. Colin Campbell was my best friend. He was a townie, I was a farm boy. In the winter I'd shovel the driveway at five, my mom would put the coffee on, and then she'd take me to the rink in town. The rink manager would open the doors and we'd skate in the dark. My mom hung out in what was called "the warm room." Colin and I would skate, then we'd referee until noon, go back to his folks' place for lunch, play hockey out on Lake Lister, public skate some more on the rink, then referee in the evening. Colin eventually got drafted by Peterborough, where he played for Roger Neilson. I used to hitchhike with my skates to see him. Roger would let the guys go out on the ice in the middle of the night. He'd sleep on the trainer's bed while Bob Gainey, Colin, and I would play. We never went out or ran around town drinking. All we did was play hockey. On game days, I'd watch the team play, then Colin would take me back out to the edge of the 150 Highway and drop me off, where I'd hitchhike home again.

PERRY BEREZIN: My goal as a boy wasn't to make a million dollars playing in the NHL, it was to play for the University of Alberta Golden Bears under Clare Drake. He was an institution, a little man with a lot of respect. My focus was totally on college. I got drafted by the Great Falls Americans in the WHL, but I only went to two training sessions before I left. I didn't even tell them I was leaving, I just left. I was so terrified that I'd lose eligibility for college that I bolted. It was pretty rude of me just to disappear, but my mind was elsewhere. I wanted a scholarship. There was something about earning a scholarship that was very important to me. I never thought about going to the NHL until I got there. The summer I was drafted, I was working in a parts warehouse in Fort Saskatchewan. When I got the call from CBC Television telling me that I'd been drafted by the Flames, I was working alongside this guy named Phil, who'd made a bomb and had asked me to help him detonate it. So I told them, "Well, okay then, but I've gotta get back to the warehouse." These days, guys fly to the draft when they're the eighth or ninth pick. I was touted anywhere from a first- to third-round pick, and while I don't think you'd want your kid to be as clueless as I was, I knew that if I continued to work hard, I'd eventually stumble onto something.

When I got called up to the Flames during my second year in college at the University of North Dakota, we were playing on the road against the University of Wisconsin Badgers. I got on the elevator of the hotel to head to the rink and it stopped at a floor where two older guys got on: Cliff Fletcher and Al McNeil. I had no idea who they were, even though they'd drafted me. I'd never had contact with them, which is preposterous when you think of what draft picks go through these days. After the game, they pulled me aside and told me, "We think you're ready to play in the NHL." They told me to get an agent, because they wanted me to join the Flames once the season ended. I was totally stunned. But even then, I was thinking, Aw, it'll probably not happen. Something will go wrong.

RON MURPHY: My first pair of skates were white — my sister's skates. Everybody used to laugh at me when I'd hit the ice. We had a pond that we skated on — me, Herbie Dickenson, who lost an eye with the Rangers, and my brother, Bill, who played in the International League with Ohio — and it was on this patch of ice where I learned the game. I made a few local teams in Ancaster [Ontario], but ended up hitchhiking to Grimsby when I was a kid. I wasn't getting along with my old man. We lived with his mother and it wasn't a very good situation, so I just packed up my kit bag one day and never went back. A guy by the name of Normie Warriner got me a job in a factory. So I played in Grimsby for a while. Eventually, a scout came down from Guelph and asked me to come up and play junior, but I told him that I had no money, which was true. He said that they'd get me a place and get me situated, and before you knew it, I was in Junior A with Harry Howell, Andy Bathgate, Ronnie Stewart, Aldo Guidolin, Louie Fontinato. I'd grown up on Fiddler's Green in Ancaster, where there was only one house on the road, so Guelph seemed monstrous to me. We used to go to a place called the Green Rooster, or sometimes the Dairy Queen, which we'd hit maybe a little too often. We won the Memorial Cup in 1951 and then, one day, Alfie Pike, our coach, came up to me and said, "Murph, get yourself a trunk, 'cause you're gonna need it." I guess I looked at him kind of funny, but then he said, "We're putting you on a train, son. You're going to play in New York City."

2 | DOUGHNUTS BY THE MORNING LIGHT

Good Friday 2004 – the second day of the tournament – started not with the usual chaos of knee-high children, pots of coffee brewed and drained, newspapers flown open across the kitchen table, but with silence. Sunlight flooded our west Toronto street, the first taste of spring after the crunching months of winter. Cats crawled from under front porches, branches hung heavy with birds, and as I climbed into my car my hockey experience began, the kind of humming pre-game reverie that every sportsman lives for. Peace. Solitude. Freedom of Thought. *Quality time with your nerves and stomach.*

Just as the final out of the World Series and the sky's first snowflake are signs that the beginning of the hockey season is upon us, April's bloom and Easter chocolate signify the coming of hockey's second season – the playoffs – and, for me, the E! Cup. The warmth of this Good Friday made Toronto look as if a dropsheet had been pulled away to reveal a forgotten trea-sure, lending the day a glimmer above the obvious promise that a game holds for a player eager to take to the ice. Before I left, my wife, Janet, found me in the doorway and said, "Do what you have to do," freeing me from the kind of familial guilt known to many slaves of the game. On more than a few occa-sions, sport has got the better of me. Once, I dragged Janet and our newborn daughter away from a festive Christmas gathering at the University of Toronto for a Morningstar "practice," booked on an icepad north of the city. Janet wanted to know just whatthefuck I thought I was doing. I had no answer for her, other than, "It's a Morningstar practice. It's important!" She promptly stopped the car, dropped me curbside, and I had to hail a cab to the rink. I looked back for reassurance that things weren't really all that bad, only to lock eyes with my daughter, who was wondering why her father was suddenly standing alone on the street corner, holding his stick and looking like a lost explorer with a flagless pole.

My route to McCormick Arena — one of the tournament's three rinks — took me down an alley of garage faces and bent backyard fencing onto Dovercourt Avenue, one of Toronto's north-south arteries. I idled there a moment then turned south and headed to College Street. I'm saying this not to impress you with my knowledge of the city's grid, but because my neigh-bourhood is a place of hockey, for Sean Burke, Gabby Boudreau, and Manny Legace all began their hockey lives just a few blocks away from here.

Having produced an army of players, Toronto is abundant with hockey lore. I'm convinced that every Torontonian is connected to someone who once played in the NHL. Either your father-in-law's cousin's daughter married the son of the guy who was traded along with Brad Park and Jean Ratelle to Boston for Espo (Joe Zanussi), or your friend once dated a woman whose sister once dated a Toronto Maple Leaf. This is true for me. I do have such a friend, a sports writer, who did date a woman whose twenty-two-year-old sister was dating a hockey player. His girl-friend suggested they all go for dinner. My friend inventoried the current Leafs roster in his head. Would it be Wendel Clark? Gary Leeman? Al Iafrate? Instead, the fellow who walked through the door was Bobby Baun, pushing fifty, but still going strong.

A few months before the E! Cup, my two-year-old son, Lorenzo, started talking to an elderly man in a College Street bakery. When I went to join in, I saw that it was Bobby Hull, the Golden Jet. His great full pumpkin face had softened and creviced, and as he extended his hand, it was clear that the yips of age had taken over. But his hand eventually steadied, and as we gripped paws (for me, it was like placing my fingers into a catcher's mitt), I was reminded how, in my city, the possibility always exists that you will run into a Hall of Famer doughnutting by the morning light; find Tie Domi idling outside his Eglinton Avenue barbershop; come across Paul Henderson standing at the airport's baggage carousel; or spot Brendan Shanahan socked into a booth at Apache Burger in Etobicoke. So as I motored through the cool sunshine with my hockey bag lying like a sleeping bear in the cave of my trunk, I imagined young Manny Legace in the baggy Leafs sweater his grandparents had given him, butterflying across this road that runs like a vein through the city until it ends, predictably, at yet another hockey rink.

JEFF JACKSON: While I was growing up, the Leafs were a favourite team of mine – they had Sittler, Lanny, Errol Thompson, Borje – but I was a huge Islander fan too. I was a little wary of Toronto because I remembered Sittler being stripped of the C, and Harold Ballard wanting Roger Neilson to wear a paper bag on his head. That kind of stuff doesn't get lost on a kid who watches hockey closely. I knew that Toronto wasn't thought of as the greatest of organizations. But when I started playing for them, I really thought we were turning the corner. Our team in the mid-1980s had tons of talent – Steve Thomas, Todd Gill, Russ Courtnall, Al Iafrate, Wendel Clark, Gary Leeman – a core of good guys who liked each other and worked hard at practice. Harold Ballard was always in the dressing room, usually walking around naked. We'd come in and he'd be getting a massage or having a sauna. We saw him every day. My first year, me and Russ would go to the Hot Stove Lounge and have steak sandwiches with King Clancy. After practice, he'd peek his head into the dressing room and ask in his famous Irish lilt, "Are we going for our steak sandwiches today, boys?" Harold would drop by, and he was always personable. I thought he'd be more aloof, but he was just one of the guys.

JOHN BROPHY: I'd walk into the Leafs dressing room to get ready for the day, and Harold would be there in his boxer shorts, shaving. King Clancy would drop by a little later, play the fool, and then head off to the racetrack.

WALTER MCKECHNIE: Some days, Harold would walk through the dressing room and grouse, "You know, this team would be a helluva lot better if only we had some friggin' toughness on the left side." This would be Tiger Williams's cue to leap off the bench and throw down our seventy-five-year-old owner. They'd wrestle right there in the middle of the floor, and then we'd all go for a sauna.

RYAN WALTER: My first game at the Gardens was on *Hockey Night in Canada*. I was put out on wing to start the game against Sittler, Lanny McDonald, and Tiger Williams. Before the puck dropped, Tiger stood opposite me at centre ice and he gave me this menacing look. My first thought was, Man, I'm going to have to fight Tiger Williams on national television. Tiger gave me a shot with his stick. I thought, Okay, I better be ready for this. I braced for the gloves to come off, but instead he leaned in and whispered, "Keep going, kid. You're playing some great hockey."

WALTER MCKECHNIE: While taking the pre-game skate at the Boston Garden with the Boston Bruins, Darryl Sittler, whom I knew from London, called me over and said, "Walt, watch out for this kid, Tiger Williams. He's a scrapper and he's trying hard to make the team." Because it was an exhibition game, I didn't think much of it, but on the first shift, Tiger suckered Terry O'Reilly and gave him a big black eye. Between periods, I was sitting beside Terry in the dressing room and he had a huge ice pack on. The air was blue and he was just steaming, so I said, "Geez, Taz, I should have told you. Before the game, Sittler warned me about that kid. He said that ever since the exhibition season started, he's had a fight per game." The room fell silent as Terry took the ice pack off his eye, looked up at me, and said, "Well, he's going to have two tonight."

MIKE PELYK: I was called up to the Leafs with Andy Heinz, and we were instructed to meet the team in Chicago for a game at the Stadium. When we got to the hotel, we asked the bellboy where the team was, and he said to try the country-and-western bar down the street. The bar was in the basement and everyone was there. The first player I saw was goalie Bruce Gamble, and he was hammered. The next day after practice, the guys said they wanted to take us out to the Italian Village for dinner, but Andy and I were certain that we were going to get shaved. Tim Horton was there and he was into it pretty good. It was a two-storey restaurant, and at one point, he hid on the second floor and tried jumping on a bunch of guys below him. He missed and crashed right into the revolving door. That first game, I was partnered with Allan Stanley. Every few minutes, Punch Imlach would growl, "C'mon, get out there, Pelyk!" and I was practically on the ice the whole time, facing Hull, Mikita, and Pierre Pilote, who was my boyhood idol. The next day, somebody from the team walked up and gave me fifteen dollars for meal money. I thought I'd died and gone to heaven.

BRUCE BOUDREAU: The Leafs were everything to me growing up. My dad told me that when I was six years old and someone asked me what I wanted to do when I grew up, I said, "I'm going to play for the Leafs." I never varied from that, ever. The Leafs game would come on TV at 8 p.m., but I'd be in front of the set at 6, just waiting. I had to sit through both *The Tommy Hunter Show* and *Mutual of Omaha's Wild Kingdom*, which shows you how committed I was. I thought that the Maple Leaf Gardens was where God lived. When I first started playing for the Marlie Midgets,

MIKE PELYK   DEFENSE
TORONTO MAPLE LEAFS

© Pee Chee/Hockey Hall of Fame

I'd sit on the Leafs bench just to be there. I remember Paulin Bordeleau scoring on a penalty shot for our team – the Junior A Marlies – against Peterborough in Game 7 with a minute to go. It was more of a moment than winning the Memorial Cup in Montreal that year because it was such a great, intense series. Mike Palmateer and I were pulling each other back, trying to get over the boards first, bawling our eyes out.

MARK NAPIER: When I played with Shopsy's PeeWees in Toronto, they had a little section for us down at the Gardens during Marlie games. We could get in free and watch the game. I'd hop on the subway and travel down there with my friends – it was the first time we'd ever done anything on our own – and there was a great feeling of freedom going down to the rink and looking up at the ceiling and seeing how massive it was.

Johnny Bower was always around, and when the PeeWees got a chance to practise there, Darryl Sittler and some of the other Leafs would come and say hello to the team. But that was the extent of the Leafs' participation. It wasn't like Montreal, where the greats were around all the time. I think the ill feelings started with [Dave] Keon and the players of his era. Whatever Ballard did to them, he did enough to keep them away.

MIKE PELYK: Two things conspired to ruin the Leafs: the WHA and Harold Ballard. The WHA took away Bernie Parent, leaving the Leafs with Jacques Plante. Then Jacques pulled the chute, stranding them with Gord McRae and Ronnie Low. There was no excuse for the fact that such a talented team was so thin between the pipes. Harold Ballard was a miserable, antagonistic, unhappy person. Later on, he couldn't stand looking over at Roger Neilson and his group of guys who were tight and got along great and played well. It killed Harold that he wasn't part of the gang, because he was the owner of the team. He did what he had to do to make the guys suffer for actually winning. Bringing Punch Imlach back was a joke. Doug Carpenter was a joke, John Brophy was a joke. He hired Gerry McNamara and all of these other wingnuts. It amounted to the forgotten '80s, a lost decade for the Leafs and Harold.

TIM ECCLESTONE: The only time I met Harold was when Jim Gregory introduced us. I was sitting in Jim's office when Harold walked in. Jim said to him, "Here's our new acquisition, the one I've been telling you all about." I got up, shook his hand, and Harold said, "Tom, it's nice to have you with us."

BRUCE BOUDREAU: Harold was great to me, provided he could remember my name. He called me everything from Pat Boutette to Claire Alexander.

FRANK MAHOVLICH: The Leafs didn't mean much to me until the day I saw Bill Barilko. My mom pointed him out to me as he came riding down the main street in Schumacher [Ontario] in a beautiful new car, all long and shiny, like a great ship. He wore his hair in a big wave, really slick. My mom said that he was a hockey player, a Toronto Maple Leaf, and I guess it registered at the time. Later on, when I was ten, we had a priest in Schumacher named Les Costello, who'd won the Stanley Cup with the '49 Leafs. One afternoon, I went down to the rink and watched Costello and Barilko practise in their full Maple Leafs uniforms. Costello was a flying winger who could run on his skates. He kept going down the boards trying to get around Barilko, but Barilko backed up until he could hit Costello. Eventually, he ended up knocking him out of the rink and over the boards, even though Costello had the entire rink to move around on. This was around '49 or '50. In the summer of '51, Barilko died when the plane he was on, flying back from a fishing trip, went down in the bush somewhere in the north. Eleven years later, I was at the Gardens with our team, getting ready for the big parade down Yonge Street, when I saw Syl Apps walking toward me down the hallway to congratulate me on the victory. He was about ten feet away when somebody jumped in front of him and shouted, "They found Barilko! They found Barilko's body!"

DEAN PRENTICE: When I got married in Schumacher in 1954, Frank Mahovlich was about eight or nine years old. I remember coming out of the church with my bride and seeing him standing across the street watching us. What Bill Barilko was to Frank, Pete Babando was to me. Pete played for Detroit and Boston. One night, I was hitchhiking from Timmins to Schumacher — the distance was a mile and a half — and Pete picked me up in his 1950 Chev. When the car first appeared, I thought, Wow. What a great-looking car! and when I saw it was Pete Babando driving, my jaw dropped. I hopped in and we talked hockey all the way home. It was great to sit back and listen to him, but, truth be told, I couldn't stop staring at him, this real live NHL pro driving me back to town.

3 | LOVE AMONG THE SWEATPANTS

The Morningstars' personalities are like every other team's. We have one player who feels personally scarred whenever we lose (Steve); one who provides dope for our emotional needs (Cheech); one who believes there is a province-wide refereeing conspiracy preventing the Morningstars from ever achieving hockey nirvana (T); one who bears the burden of the team's organizational necessities like a cement shawl and who's known to tell us that he's fucking had it with our shit before asking politely that we please pony up our league fees (Mark, our goalie); one psycho (Dutch); one clown (I'll take the hit); one psycho clown (Johnny Sinclair); one player who carries the weight of artist-based recreational hockey in Canada despite not yet having told anyone to go fuck themselves, except for the guy from Edmonton who appeared for a post-game E! Cup handshake with his penis hanging out, a gesture thereafter known as the "Edmonton handshake" (Tom Goodwin); one small star just past his prime (Craig); one slow star way past his prime (Andy); two stars in their perpetual prime (the Chizzler and Chris Topping); and a player, with homeless hair, known to snarl obsessively like a pirate (that would be Al).

There's also Tom Paterson, our tall, smiling centreman, who owns the Paddock tavern. When I first re-entered hockey's orbit, I resisted the game's ubiquitous beerisms, but once Tom offered his bar as the team's lager lodge, I was won over. An old Bathurst Street jockeys haunt in the 1940s, the Paddock maintains the patina of old Toronto while providing easy comfort after an evening of wood whacks and elbow food.

Many of our post-game Paddock sessions last well into the night. On a few occasions, the bar staff have bolted the doors and flipped on the house lights while we've continued our forehead-gripping hockey talk. After victories, we inevitably punctuate these sessions with trips to Morningstar Alley, which, though it sounds like something dreamed up for a Rogers and Hammerstein musical, is actually a garbaged laneway that separates a community health centre from the rear exit of the bar. It's there that we smoke dope, which is to say, Cheech's dope, and incriminate ourselves with silly hockeyish behaviour.

The Paddock is constant in good times and bad. After one particularly hurting loss, we remained at the bar until well past 5 a.m., having convinced ourselves that six-goal losses were merely the will of the hockey gods and that things would even out in time. I felt so renewed and full of hope after our session that I stumbled home confident that I could deliver on an earlier promise I'd made to my kids to take them to a National Film

Board animation workshop in the morning. Climbing out of bed — or, rather, my daughter's bed; the reasons why I ended up sleeping there are obvious — I made it as far as the kitchen, where a serving bowl happened to be in the right place at the right time. Janet — who'd savoured the notion of a morning apart from the brood — was pressed into immediate action, and as she berated me with the words *Morningstars* and *beer* and *fuckin'* and *hockey*, my daughter, Cecilia, asked why her dad was throwing up in the salad.

The time we Morningstars spend together is golden, though I'm not going to blow any more hot air than this about unity, and the coming together of strangers, and love among the sweatpants, or stuff like that, even though I actually believe in all of that poofery. Anyone who has ever played on a good team knows this, and that's why the Morningstars are typical. If there's one thing differentiating us from other clubs, it's that we are largely a team of rhythm guitarists. This was proven during a performance by Al Piggins and the Quitters when the stage was cluttered with Morningstars either slashing out chords on borrowed Gibsons or feigning Richards-Wood on air guitar. This predominance of rhymatists may explain our failure, as individual players, to achieve the kind of look-at-me! stylistic dazzle often associated with lead guitarists or supple-wristed right wingers. Only the totemic Chris Topping has any kind of explosive talent; the rest of us play on the ice just as we do in our bands: as part of its supporting cast, chordal bedrock, blending in with the drums and bass to form an alliance of sound on which soloists vault. Were we more prone to floodlit leads and narcissistic finger-tricks, as skaters we might have long ago distinguished ourselves from other rec league hockey teams. Instead, we are a stolid force, reliably mediocre and cautiously good.

Some among us occasionally dabble in the extended fret run – Al, the Chizzler, Steve, Andy, Tom Paterson, Dutch, and yours truly – but really we are all marginal scrubbers (Johnny plays bass for Universal Honey, but most bass players are frustrated guitarists anyway). I include the classically trained, new music composer Dutch on the basis of his gift to me on my fortieth birthday, a song called "Hockey Fucker," which, though it had lots of swearing, featured nary a lead break. Dutch is also, I believe, the only composer in history to have both appeared on Austrian radio's Musikprotokoll and been kicked out of a hockey game for calling the referee a "dicksmoking crossing guard." One evening after watching him cross-check an opponent in front of the net in the afternoon, I settled into my seat at Roy Thompson Hall as he strode across the stage wearing a cravat. When Dutch plays the game, all of those formative years when he was being taught Bach and Schubert by hairy-eared, ill-tempered music teachers are expressed. When we first asked Dutch to join our club, he resisted, telling us that he had a "minor temper thing" and sometimes had the tendency to "go a little squirrelly." He also said that he'd recently played competitive roller hockey in France, where he'd broken some stuff in his hand after punching a guy in a scarf. I told him that, if you're gonna punch a guy, he might as well be wearing a scarf. He agreed and started the season.

Guitarist, songwriter, and pirate fetishist Alun Piggins is my old defence partner. One evening after tumbling out of the Paddock, a few of us ended up drinking shandies at Al's. The next day, Al called Janet and asked if I was feeling all right. Actually, he asked if I was alive. She told him that I was, and he laughed nervously before confessing that the ice cubes he'd used to cool the shandies weren't pure H_2O cubes at all. They were bricks of aquarium water that Al's wife had frozen while cleaning out the fish tank.

Al won't admit it, but those shandies may have been payback for having weathered years playing on the blue line alongside yours truly. Upon joining the 'Stars, Al chose the number 71 (in honour of bucket-headed grinder Mike Foligno), but because I wear number 17, he has been required to suffer the abuse of every vengeful, dyslexic opponent screaming, "Eat this, seventeen!" as they shafted the poor Pig. All these years, Al has countered these loveless advances with a crazy-faced, wild-haired grin – and a few punches of his own. It's not as if Al hasn't seen worse – or better – in the bars of southern Ontario, where he leads the Quitters in modern-day Cotton Clubs such as Captain Billy's Spaghetti House in Dover, and the Townhouse in Sudbury. On some nights, Al has broken from the rhythmic ranks to play the odd solo, but these occasions usually come after several buckets of shandy and are no less than thirteen minutes in length, making them lead-guitar parodies, if you ask me.

Besides bringing the pirate snarl back to hockey and trying to disassemble the Morningstars one ice cube at a time, one of Al's other crusades was to convince the 'Stars to do a firefighters calendar. How this was supposed to add to our team chemistry and translate into more wins wasn't entirely clear, but Al assured us that posing half-naked would send a message to other rec league teams that we were brazen enough not to be fucked with. After kicking around the idea one evening at the Paddock, Mark, our goalie, was the first to suggest that he could indeed see himself shirtless cradling a puppy while wearing nothing but hockey pants and black-and-red pads; eighty-seven pints later, we agreed that we could see it too.

Steve Stanley is an original Morningstar, as well as one of the guitarists for the Toronto band Lowest of the Low. Steve and I are good-enough friends and close-enough teammates that he whispered to me prior to the tournament that he'd started prac- tising yoga. Worse, he said that it had changed his life, and his game. I have nothing against yoga in a vacuum, but I see no reason why yoga can't keep to itself without pervading hockey, which already possesses the same freeing qualities as the old rubbery art, with a few shots to the head thrown in for levelling purposes. By confiding this personal detail to me, Steve ran the risk of yours truly envisioning him in mauve leotards and a sweatband, an image that no hockey player should impose upon a teammate.

Still, I appreciated the intimacy of his confession because it's what teammates are supposed to be all about. However, this near- ness hasn't always been the case between us. We have a history as cross-borough CanRock rivals whose careers have closely paral- leled. Before I got to know Steve, the Lowest of the Low's first independent album, "Shakespeare My Butt," was a big hit on Toronto rock radio, back in the pre–Clear Channel days when this kind of thing was still possible. The Low's rather irrational dislike of the works of the Bard was matched in enthusiasm only by their ability to sell piles of records, resulting in a popularity among fringe-striding yowlers that outshone the Rheostatics'. But even though my band and Steve's were part of the first tide of 1990s

Toronto groups, we weren't paired live until the summer of 1993, at the Ontario Place Forum, the occasion of our first meeting.

Steve was the first person from either band to cross the distance. As you may or may not know, no matter what pretence of chumminess or good-natured one-upmanship exists among competing local bands, it's ultimately about slamming the other to the floor before fan-dancing atop their corpse. So I was slightly taken aback when Steve walked up to me in the hallway underneath the seats of the Forum and asked, "Are you going to play 'Dope Fiends and Booze Hounds' tonight?"

"We are now," I told him, pausing a minute so that an unseen, clairvoyant voice might add, "For we will soon be bound by the force of a mythic hockey team!" neither of us having any notion, at the time, that the 'Stars were just a few years from being born.

This encounter holds a certain weight for me because it happened at one of Canada's most treasured outdoor concert venues, since razed by Molson, which turned it into a concrete bunker, complete with Orwellian video screens and a large security force. The Forum was the kind of place that you never forgot once you'd gone there. Because of its peculiar design, "venue" was too vague a term for it, but "theatre" or "hall" or "concert bowl" weren't right, either. The Forum was shaped like an enormous wok, with sixty or so rows of old wooden benches fanning out from the stage to a grassy climb that loomed over Ontario Place. No other concert theatre breathed like the Forum. It allowed the swirl of nearby city life – Ontario Place, now a defunct quasi park and entertainment centre, sits at the bottom of Toronto in the cold, soupy lake – to mingle with whatever music and energy was being created beneath its tented roof. If that wasn't enough, the stage spun slowly – counter-clockwise, then clockwise – when whoever happened to be playing took the stage. Billy Bragg said of it, "I feel like the world is revolving around me and I'm at the centre. I feel like Morrissey!" Its architects wanted to create a meditative hub amid the city's developmental sprawl, giving parkgoers a chance to absorb music for the price of their park admission. Sometimes you got Celebrate Croatia in Song! night, other times you got Al Green. Asleep at the Wheel, John Prine, and B.B. King played there annually. The concerts were programmed with the venue's meditative design in mind, the possible exception being the 1981 gig that has become known as "The Great Ontario Place Riot," which featured Hamilton pop/punk legends Teenage Head, hordes of New Wavers swimming across the moat that separates Ontario Place from the mainland, and teams of moustachioed Toronto cops chasing kids with green hair, years before the local police got with the steroids and riot shields.

I saw NRBQ open for Blue Rodeo at the Forum twice. The first time was on a summer night with a cool breeze singing off the lake. For the last song of their second set, Terry Adams, NRBQ's whacked virtuoso piano player, sat at his keyboard and cycled four low, beautiful chords until the band drifted in behind him, accompanied by two of Sun Ra's horn players, whom they'd brought north for the event. Eight, nine minutes later, the spare crowd stood to salute this great band, awestruck by a song that was as subtle and perfect as the evening in which it bathed. In the runway after the show, Tommy Ardolino, NRBQ's drummer, told me that, a week before the gig, he'd held the master tapes to The Beach Boys' "Pet Sounds" in his hands. "I kissed them," he confessed, munching on a corn chip.

Having experienced the Forum this way, I was thrilled to get a chance to play there myself. The gig was part of an event called Edgefest, hosted by local radio station CFNY FM. The Low and the Rheos were co-headliners, but for whatever reason, we ended up going on last. When the Low took the stage to the wild applause of a full house, my bandmates and I stood in the runway, striking the form of one cocksure band taking in another. But we didn't watch for long. The Low were having the show of their lives.

Fans and reviewers were kind the next day, but the Low greased the stage with us. The Low's frontman, Ron Hawkins, threw himself around to the music. Steve, for his part, bopped on his shoetops and sang in a pure howl. At the end of the set, Ron lifted his Telecaster over his head and smashed it down in an explosion of splinters, setting the crowd on fire and crowning the day. During our set, I tried pulling out all the stops – hoisting a kid out of the crowd on my back, bringing on a few fans to chant the chorus of "Horses." But no matter how far we reached, we couldn't reel in what the Low had cast.

In the following years, the Rheos pressed on – losing a drummer, gaining another, making more records, touring – but the Low broke up, surprising everyone (co-leaders Ron and Steve have since mended ways, relaunching the Low ten years later). After I got to know him, Steve told me that the Ontario Place gig had been the beginning of the end. Ron had been drinking all day, and when it came time to get ready for the stage, he was drunk and wandering around half-naked. When Steve asked him if he planned on getting dressed, Ron told him, "What if I fuckin' don't?" and there was a big fight. But as we've seen, the

venom and bile that was bedevilling the Low worked in their favour, if only for one memorable night.

At our 2004 season-end Morningstar team party, Steve — possibly dizzied from the effects of yoga — stood in my backyard and recited a long poem he'd written about what the team meant to him. Afterwards, he told me: "When the Low first broke up, I felt hollow on so many levels. We came to a full stop in the middle of a torrid pace, and we didn't ease into it at all. One day, we were doing two hundred and fifty shows a year; the next day it was all over. The signs were all there, but it was still hard to see it coming. The Morningstars filled that hole. To me, one of the most important aspects of being in a band is that day after the gig when you talk on the phone and deconstruct every moment of the night before, and that's what the team did. My hockey conversations were the same conversations I'd had with my bandmates. The discussion of a failed lead break was replaced with talk of our inability to put the puck in the net, but the spirit was the same: to make the next time you went on stage (or the ice) better than the time before. To me, it's the reason why you go back to the rinks and the clubs year after year. It feeds a sense of belonging and the need to always move forward."

In the 2004 season, this sentiment was written on Steve's hockey face. It was impossible for him not to race after loose pucks without his eyes blazing, teeth bared. I'm not sure he even knew he was doing it half the time. He treated every goal against personally, as if it somehow besmirched the Morningstars' name. Suddenly, Steve's skating stride and floating-brick wristshot were no longer weaknesses, but ruses to draw the defender into a false sense of security. He dug hard on every shift, carving out a groove in the goal crease and along the boards. He was the most disappointed player when we lost, the most jubilant when we won, and in our first game of the tournament, versus Capsule Music, he'd counted for two goals. The guys were thrilled that one of the least-likely-to-score players had led what amounted to a Morningstar offensive charge. After each goal, we nearly wrenched his head off in joy.

One of the reasons why the E! Cup exists, and why so many artists play hockey, is because teams provide a consistency and a social security that a life in art simply cannot. For musicians, teams provide a haven for the impetuous, unstable lives we lead beyond the rink. Throughout all of the rich creative times and dust-sucking dry spells, a hockey team — like any good sailing crew, book club, coffee klatch, or bowling team — helps mellow the blizzard of life. We rely on teams to comfort and protect us.

I remember coming to a game once after a heart-kicking rehearsal. My bandmates and I had fought for three hours, and like any player arriving after a spousal dust-up or fight with the boss, I was a mess of misery and confusion. A few minutes into the game, I chopped the puck away from an opposing forward, who took offence by turning and slew-footing me to the ice. Not stopping there, he kicked my helmet with his skate, at which point our goalie, Mark, raced from his crease, brought his stick into the air, and tomahawked the offending forward. Instantly, I felt better. Someone was looking out for me.

LARRY PLAYFAIR: In my first year with the Sabres, Bob Nystrom gave Rick Martin a whack on the head with his stick during a game at Long Island. Nobody on the ice reacted, so I jumped over the boards and screamed at Nystrom, "You're never gonna do that again!" I gave him a shot, he answered, and we squared off. I lost the fight pretty badly, but because I'd stood up for my teammate and because the Islanders were a physical team that had pushed other teams around in their own building, it was a defining moment for me. In hockey, if you go to places where other people are afraid to go, you get respect.

JIM SCHOENFELD: Our team in Buffalo was very close socially: the old and young players, everybody's wives and girlfriends. When something good happened to someone, we shared in the joy. If it was something bad, we shared in the sorrow. Our support group was the team itself. I missed my daughter's birth because we were playing in Boston, but when I got to the airport at around one or two in the morning, the wives had decorated the place with signs saying, "CONGRATULATIONS, SCHONEY. IT'S A GIRL!" Fred Stanfield gave me his car and I drove to the hospital. The next day, we played the Habs, and then we all went out and celebrated together. For us, as a young team, that togetherness was also vital when Tim Horton died. My wife and I lived in a beach home in Fort Erie. I got the call in the morning that Timmy had died and I went out and shovelled snow from one part of the patio to the other, then shovelled it back. I took our dog for a long walk on the beach to sort out my feelings, put some sense to the whole thing. When I went down to the rink, I felt pretty good, like I'd come to grips with the situation, and though everybody was down, we had a game to play. I started the game and was on the blue line when the announcer asked people to rise for a moment of silence. It was then that I felt the grief of everyone in the building. It overwhelmed me. I was on the ice crying like a four-year-old. The next thing I know, the puck dropped, it came to me, I passed it to someone, it got dumped in, there was a whistle, and I came to the bench to change. Joe Crozier, the Old Crow, came down and put his arm around me, comforted me. Then it passed. I thought of what George Harrison said, "Life goes on within you and without you." Because we'd lost Tim, we had a renewed appreciation of each other. From that point on, everyone looked at everyone else and realized that we were not only important as hockey players to each other, but that we were all persons of value. Even in death, Horty drew that team together.

FRED STANFIELD: In Boston, we had a rule that the whole team had to get together after a game. We had to sit down, have a few cocktails, and be a team, win or lose. Somebody would name a place and we'd go. Bobby Orr had a place – the Brass Rail. Whoever was in there respected us, gave us space. Bobby Orr picked up a lot of tabs. Some teams and players like to get away and talk about other things to get their mind off the game, but with us, it was hockey, hockey, hockey. When I played, if you were going through a tough time, your teammates would be behind you 100 per cent. I don't know if it's the same now. Guys would tell each other not to get down. Nobody was afraid of losing their job. It was all for the team and your teammates, 100 per cent of the time.

BRAD DALGARNO: One day in the back of the bus, Ray Ferraro and I were sharing thoughts about how things were going. They weren't going great for me; I had no identity inside and outside of the team. So Ray suggested that we invent a character for me – Night Train – a hard-partying guy who'd had a couple of DWIs and liked to rip it up. Of course, I was the opposite of this guy. Me and Pierre Turgeon would go back to our rooms after games and order pizza. We were like a little old couple. But the guys picked up on Night Train, and it started to become tangible. It changed things. For some reason, there was a different acceptance level for Night Train than there'd been for Brad Dalgarno. Night Train started going out and having beers. It changed the players' perception of me, and I realized after hanging out that you need those bonding elements that develop in the bars after the games, being together, doing stupid things.

STEVE LARMER: I lived with Steve Ludzik in Moncton when I played in the AHL. It would have made a good sitcom. There wasn't much choice about where to live because the students had taken most of the good places. We ended up with a little house that was so cold there was frost all over the electrical outlets in the morning. Suddenly, we had to do all of the things in life that had been done for us in the past. I didn't have a chequing account all year. Both of us would get our cheques, cash them, and spend the money within days. And since neither of us had ever cooked before, we nearly burned down the house a couple of times trying. We had a brainstorm one day about how we were going to do our laundry. The only possible way to keep our socks and underwear separate out of our big mountain of dirty clothes was to initial them. So, after coming home the first time from the laundromat, we went to make sense of our stuff only to realize that everything had "SL" written on it. But we got through it. It was probably the most fun that I've ever had playing hockey.

STEVE LUDZIK: Larms and I lived together in a duplex in Moncton. It was the size of a shoebox. You had to chisel ice off the electrical sockets in the morning so you could have a cup of tea. One week, you'd sleep in the bed, the next you'd have to suffer on the Y-fold couch. I remember the time my girlfriend – who became my wife – came down to see me, and I decided to make French fries. Pretty soon, the oil in the pan wasn't the only thing that started to get hot, so my attention became a little, um, diverted. When I went back to the pan, I lifted the lid and some water that had condensed from the heat dropped into the oil and caused an unbelievable explosion of fire. Because we had a

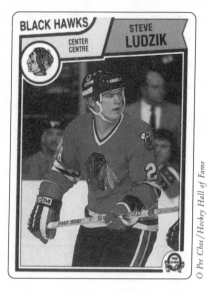

When their rookie cards came out, Ludzik and Larmer's names were switched. This is actually Steve Larmer.

O Pee Chee / Hockey Hall of Fame

cardboard ceiling, the kitchen burnt to a crisp. I turned to my girl-friend and said, "Let's get out of here; the place can burn down for all I care." Later on, Larms came in, around 2:30 in the morning. I could tell that he was inebriated because he had two cigarettes going at the same time: one in his hand, one in his mouth. I asked him, "Can you take bad news standing up or sitting down?" I brought him into the kitchen and it was like char-coal. Even worse for Larms was the fact that the next day I was called up to Chicago. We had a sander and a planer lying around and the poor bastard had to redo the whole kitchen himself.

MIKE PELYK: Eddie Johnston was the Leafs' goalie in 72–73. He helped me improve my game as much as anyone. He'd say to me in practice, "You're a way better player than what you're showing. If you start playing the way you can, I'll be the first guy to get on your bandwagon." Whenever he was the backup goalie and I'd come off the ice, he'd say, "Great shift, Mike. Don't leave anything on the ice." If I'd come down to breakfast with a hangover, he'll tell me, "Get some tomato juice and a raw egg, and you'll be fine in an hour." He looked out for me every step of the way, and whenever I played in front of him, I'd do anything for the guy. I'd never blocked shots in my life until I started playing with Eddie.

BRAD DALGARNO: I had one teammate on the Islanders — Joe Reekie — who was relentless in his verbal attacks. He would research shit to say about me. It was like high school, where the bully says stuff and the weak people laugh with him. I'd say, "Fuck you, shut up," but nothing changed. I'd go out for dinner with guys and they'd say, "Joe's an idiot, don't listen to him," but the next day, they'd be encouraging him all over again. Joe's sense of humour was always hurtful, until Steve Thomas showed up. Steve was the most inclusive guy I've ever met. He never feared that he'd be judged by sitting down beside me or anyone else who was being attacked. I was strengthened by the fact that Steve befriended me, and after that, Reekie's stuff bounced off whenever he tried it, which was less and less often because Stumpy brought us all together.

JOHN CHABOT: My first year in Montreal, I was perceived as competing for Pierre Mondou's job at centre, which was true in a way. But despite this, he stayed on the ice with me after practice and helped me work on my draw. It was total class on his part. Conversely, in Pittsburgh, if a younger player took an elder's spot, the old guy would give him shit and challenge him to a fight. But eventually Mario Lemieux took control, and that kind of garbage stopped.

STEVE LUDZIK: When I played with Moncton in the AHL, we ran into Adirondack during our run to the Calder Cup. Dennis Polonich was on their team and he was causing a lot of trouble. He was a chippy guy. Our captain, Bill Reilly, was one of the few black players in the league, and I still get shivers when I remember him standing up in the dressing room and saying, "I'm gonna grab that Polonich and I'm going to finish him off this series. And then we're gonna win the Cup." Their fight was like a John Wayne movie, and Reilly ended up KOing him. That was the turning point for us winning and coming together as a team.

EDDIE MIO: After playing in Birmingham and Indianapolis in the WHA, it was a great relief for me to be traded to Edmonton. Both Wayne [Gretzky] and I were very excited about coming over, and it was this kind of enthusiasm that infected the Oilers of the 1980s. The unity and togetherness of the dynasty started as early as 1978. We had guys like Paul Shmyr, Davey Hamilton, Claire Alexander, Ron Chipperfield: a lot of old pros, great guys. It didn't matter if you were married or not, we all met up after practice for lunch. We had a rule on the road that, once we landed, we'd have a team meeting. We didn't discuss strategy or anything; we'd just hang out together. When Kevin Lowe and Messier and Coff [Paul Coffey] joined the team as kids, this sense of camaraderie was instilled in them, and because Edmonton was such a small place, it forced us together. We were all so young and green. The first time we went to New York City, Gretz and Mess and everyone were just awed by the place. We were all so intimidated that we were afraid to leave the hotel.

HARVEY BENNETT, JR: These days, it's different in the dressing room. Hockey players are still great guys, but the camaraderie is not there. There's no bonding. In the Devils' dressing room, everybody's talking to their agents, stockbrokers — I guess if I had that much money, I'd do that too. I doubt very much that they still go out and have a few beers together. There's so much more skill now that fewer players have to rely on sheer character to get by, which was more the case when I played in the 1970s. Back then, there were a lot of hard-core, from-the-mines Canadians. Because they were professional hockey players, they had a great job, but as far as a Plan B went — well, there wasn't a Plan B. Very few guys went to college or finished high school, but they had tons and tons of character.

STEVE LUDZIK: A week before my son went off to the Windsor Spitfires' camp, he saw an article from 1980 about my junior days with Niagara Falls that said, WHO WILL BE THE OHL'S JUNIOR PLAYER OF THE YEAR? It was between me, Ernie Godden, and John Goodwin. My son said, "Dad, I know who you are, but who are Ernie Godden and John Goodwin?" I told him, "John Goodwin led the league in scoring that year, and Ernie Godden got eighty-five goals, but between the two of them, I don't think they played a game in the National Hockey League." I told him to think long and hard during camp about what he was doing, because you think you know where you're going and what's happening, but really, you know nothing.

ART BERGLUND: Back in the 1950s, it was hard to find a job in hockey. It was a closed shop and there was only a handful of opportunities. Because of this, more players just played for the sake of playing, because the future only stretched so far as your next game. In the 1940s and 1950s — certainly where I grew up, in Fort Frances [Manitoba] — hockey fans related more to the [amateur championship] Allan Cup than to the Stanley Cup. Our local team — the Fort Frances Canadians — beat the Stratford Indians in 1952, a year after losing to Owen Sound. The players had all come back from the war and had taken jobs in mills. They weren't about chasing dreams; they were about raising families and making a living, and the fans, community, and players were all one and the same. The atmosphere at the Memorial Arena used to get so electric that fire trucks would come to the playoff games in springtime and douse off the roof to cool the rink. Because there was no road heading east to Thunder Bay, the Canadians either went to Kenora or south to Minnesota. It was very limited. These days, if you can't find a place to play hockey, you've got to be pretty horseshit. The whole idea of what pro hockey is, is different. I always defined "pro" hockey as a guy who had an NHL contract. Nowadays, a guy can put on his Augusta, Georgia, team jacket and call himself a pro.

WALT MCKECHNIE: In today's NHL, guys spend time after practices with their personal trainer, broker, and agent. All you have to do is sign one million-dollar contract today and you're set. Someone once told me that Pierre Turgeon has saved $30 million already from his career. The whole scale is completely different now.

JOHN BROPHY: Guys used to take care of each other a lot more, whether it was in the dressing room or on the ice. If a guy needed money or was broke or was having problems, you helped him out. These days, everybody goes his own way. In the old days, if you saw a guy carrying a briefcase, you had to be careful of him. But now, most of the players have agents sitting on their lap, telling them how great they are.

EDDIE MIO: I don't see the same camaraderie in the game today. Players are too worried about how much the other player is making. In our day, contracts weren't disclosed, so you never knew who was making what. Because there was less money and less security back then, you had to play shift-to-shift, and because everybody was more or less in the same boat, it was easier to get on the same page as a team.

STEVE LARMER: The day I realized that hockey had changed was the day I could no longer get away with wearing my corduroy suit. I walked into the dressing room and everyone had on Armani, Hugo Boss. They looked great, but the clothes were hardly practical. You could burn or spill something on my suit and it would still look okay.

TIM ECCLESTONE: A lot of guys complain about modern players averaging out at $1.5 million a year. But the way I see it, I would have found some way of screwing up, no matter how much I made.

4 | THE ELEPHANT IS A ZAMBONI

The best arenas, like the most interesting people, are flawed and just wrong enough. Among the E! Cup's three rinks, St. Mike's echoes with the soft hum of history, DeLaSalle has beautiful Ivy League grounds and an old collegiate charm, but, to my mind, McCormick possesses the most character (and a little history: Muhammad Ali visited the adjoining rec centre before his second fight with George Chuvalo). This is owing to its pawed-over, skate-scraped life as a busy public rink. In an effort to combat the damage caused by weeknight skating hordes, the decision was made a few years ago to paint McCormick purple and gold. If you narrow your eyes, the main lobby looks like a corridor imagined by Douglas Adams, perhaps as an intergalactic pathway to some weird, ice-borne clan. I appreciate the colour of the rink because somewhere down the line, I know that either Billy or Paulie or one of the other rink attendants has been struck with a visual epiphany, dreaming of a great purple palace where slush-booted scrubs like myself would be dignified by the zazz and dash of this rich, fanciful hue.

To know Billy or Paulie is to know that these moments of Zen don't happen every day. Both have classic Zamboni-driver forms. Perhaps I'm being close-minded, but I've always believed that, in order to be trusted, these Andrettis of the ice rink should possess the figure of a tapir and almost always look older than they are. Billy, for his part, has the shuffle-step, slump-shouldered gait of an old-timer, even though he was only twenty-three at the time of the tourney. Back when I was playing four nights a week, he was the one constant in my social life, until, horror of horrors, he moved on, taking a job managing a local restaurant. Still, he was the one stranger with whom I shared some of the week's most important personal time, and because of this, I felt obliged to understand him beyond the arena.

This produced mixed results. Billy once confessed to our team that he'd had a strange dream in which he'd had sex with his girl-friend while riding an elephant. The meaning of the dream had been lost on him, and I must admit that it befuddled me too until I told Janet about it, who bolted upright in bed and shouted, "The elephant is a Zamboni!" as if she'd just cracked the Riddle of the Sands. I tried to hold back the mental image of my friend humping astride his sluggish ice truck, but at the next game, it was all I could do to avert my eyes as he wheeled his steam press around the oval, staring impassively at our team as we flattened our noses against the glass.

In the purple concourse, the rink's spongy beige tile gives way to a trophy case to the right, a lone pay phone to the left, and a fortress of junk-food machines ten feet wide that dispense cuspid-cracking gobstoppers and other hard, sugared candies — miniature bananas, pucks, and gumdrops — of indeterminate alchemy. Beyond that, a Plexiglas window reveals the rink, shining beneath a few memorial banners, a set of old speaker horns, and metal lamps throwing light on the unrippled lake of ice.

Past another set of purple doors, a rack of usually unbummed wooden bleachers stares out at the southwest corner of the rink. To its right is a darkened pro shop, which — the E! Cup notwith-standing — is used about as often as Peter Klima's left jab. That it is even called "Pro Shop" is ironic considering the calibre of players who frequent the rink. Still, even if Joe Sgro had been working the knife-buffer, I probably wouldn't patronize it, having developed an allegiance long ago to the skate-sharpening tech-niques of another master, a fellow named Fiorenzo, who runs Toronto Hockey Repair with his mom and brother.

On most days, McCormick has the stillness of a sanctuary, but for the E! Cup, the setting was akin to a hockey festival. Seeing the rink in full splendour was like coming across a stoner friend dressed in a suit and a tie. The games drew a great crowd of faces behind the cool glass; the bleachers rattled with fans blowing trumpets, shaking tambourines, and cheering; the pathway behind the stands was busy with skate-footed hockeyists making their way to and from the ice; and there was a constant turnover of teams settling into their chambers, unzipping their stuffed rucksacks, and talking non-stop until the officials told them to hit the ice. It made for a delicious energy as all of these hockey lives were swept together.

MIKE LAUGHTON: In Cherry Hill, New Jersey – home of the WHA's New York Golden Blades – the dressing room was so small, visiting teams had to change in the hotel next door. They'd walk across the street to the rink in full gear, in snowstorms or heat waves. Some teams tried changing in a Winnebago to avoid the humiliation, but it was really just as bad. I remember seeing Bobby Hull before practice sitting on the bench just shaking his head, because when you shot the puck at Cherry Hill, it would skip like a stone on a lake. It would rise off the ice, and if you could read the slope, you could make the puck do some pretty strange things.

HARRY HOWELL: I was the first coach of the Blades, and when I went to look at Cherry Hill, they asked me what I wanted to do about the size of the dressing rooms. Both of them were cramped and small. You couldn't fit a proper team into either one, so I told them: "Expand the home team's room. The visitors, just leave alone."

JOE DALEY: Cherry Hill was like one of those early tabletop hockey games with a big hump in the middle so that the ball bearing would roll back down. If a player hit centre ice at the right speed and shot, the puck took off like a rocketship.

DEAN PRENTICE: There was a practice rink at the top of Madison Square Gardens that was awful. It was too small and one end came in on an angle. There were aluminum boards, and if you scratched your skates, the trainer would have to go all the way down to the dressing room to sharpen them. It would take him twenty minutes.

EDDIE MIO: When I was with Erie, Pennsylvania, we played in a place called Mohawk Valley Arena in Utica. There was a stage behind the net where kids would do high-school plays. It wasn't a rink; it was a bombshelter.

SAM BETTIO: The Boston Garden had a train station underneath it. The rink itself was on the second floor, and the ice surface was suspended. In those days, steam engines would come roaring into the station and you could feel the ice rumble under your skates.

MIKE PELYK: When they built the WHA rink in Cincinnati, the boards ended up being three inches away from the ice. There was concrete all around the edges, but instead of fanning out the boards to meet the dimensions, they built a six-inch curve out from them. Every time you got hit, you were bent over backwards on top of the ledge. It was brutal. We once had a promotion where they put live turkeys on the ice for American Thanksgiving. They sent people out to get them, but the turkeys decided to fight back. They were scratching and biting and shitting all over the ice. Whoever got a turkey would have to drag it over to the end boards, where it would be bludgeoned, hacked up, and bagged. It was supposed to be festive, but it ended up looking like something out of a horror film.

GARRY UNGER: When I retired from Edmonton in 1983, I took a job as an international trade consultant. My first sale was an $80 million road construction job in the Solomon Islands, and since things were going so well, it was suggested that I help set up a company to get guys overseas playing hockey. The first person who called us was a fellow from Dundee, Scotland, who needed players. He and some others came over and watched my senior rec team play from ten to midnight in Edmonton. I told them who to watch as possible draftees, and, when I asked after the game who they liked, they said, "Well, what are you doing?" They offered me a player-coach position. My wife suggested that I ask for a crazy contract, just to see if they'd go for it, and they did. I played one year in Dundee, then moved to Peterborough, England, about eighty miles north of London, where they gave me a house for my family. It was strange being over there, but I had a good attitude. We were in the Second Division. I scored 238 points. I was averaging about eleven points a game, playing teams in Blackpool, which had a tiny Ice Capades rink. We played on a curling rink in Ayr, Scotland, with square corners. You could score from your own blue line. We played in Lee Valley, Bracknell, and Slough. We played the first pro game ever in Cardiff in a building that was the loudest arena I've ever been in. It was louder than the St. Louis Arena. In Glasgow, Scotland, we played in a huge rink that was built in the 1920s. It was like an Olympic-sized rink plus an NHL rink, just cavernous. After the second period, the Zamboni broke down and they couldn't get it off the ice, so we finished the game with the ice truck parked right on the blue line. If you played with your head down, you were in deep trouble, but hockey players will do anything just to play the game.

RICHARD HARRISON: When I walked into the lobby of the The Hotel in Abidjan in the Ivory Coast, the manager of the art gallery saw my pack, declared that he loved my country, and told me that he played hockey on the hotel rink. I asked him, "What

position?" He said, "Left wing." And I said, "Like Bobby Hull!"
Because Bobby's name was magic, the manager gave me the grin
of a man who knows that the other man knows his game. He
asked if I wanted to skate on the rink. It was still a week before
the end of harmattan – the dry season when the hot winds from
the Sahara turn the soil into dust. The rink was in a building
within a building to protect it from the heat. Even so, the ice was
still soft and off limits until "the hockey season" began. But he
said he'd make an exception. He could see how much it meant to
me. There were skates in the locker, but there was no stick, and no
puck. And the skates were figure skates. I talked to people at the
Canadian embassy; they loved the idea and lent me a stick and a
puck immediately. I walked through the streets of the city kicking
the butt of my hockey stick as I walked, the same way I've done all
my life. People stared at this strange object, then an old man yelled
out from the crowd, "I know!" He gestured for the stick and then
acted out the motion of a man skating, the puck shifting from
front to back of the blade, going "shush, shush" as if he knew the
language of the ice. We got everything together. I went around
the rink, which was soft and painted both for curling and hockey.
The parched red clay of Ghana at harmattan had crept in, and
turned the ice pink, like water frozen from a potter's wheel. I took
shots at the boards and savoured the familiar hollow boom. The
staff of the hotel took time off to watch me play. It was a beautiful moment. Only afterwards did it occur to me that, for one
hour, I was probably the only person on the continent on skates.

HARVEY BENNETT, JR: My brother Curt and I played hockey in
Japan. We played for Furukawa. There was another team –

Kokudo — that was owned by a hotelier who, at the time, was the richest man in the world. They had been sent to a hockey school in Vancouver, so they had more of a North American mentality. We were totally Japanese in a traditional sense; the elders talked and the young players listened. The first time we played against them, one of their players dislocated one of our players' shoulders after running at him. There had to be retribution, but Curt begged me not to do it. "No, Harv, no. Please, Harv, c'mon . . ." I went over to the penalty box and let myself in. The player looked up and in broken English said, "Hello! How are you?" I suckered him in spite of the pleasantries. I started beating him up in the penalty box and the fight dragged on to the ice. The other team — having learned the game in Canada — understood that this was a bench-clearing brawl situation, so they emptied the bench. Curt came to help out, but before we knew it, they were on us like flies. We were just getting hammered. I looked over and our team was sitting on the bench, watching with their mouths hanging open. The refs sorted things out and both teams were told to leave the ice. I'd only been with the team for a week, so they must have been thinking, What kind of a psychotic idiot did Curt bring in? My shirt was ripped, my shoulder pads were in disarray, and everyone was quite upset. Before the game could start again, I had to go up to the guy I'd beaten up, bow at centre ice, and apologize. I did it for Curt.

✦

When I found the 'Stars in the number 4 dressing room, the first thing I noticed was the camera. It was the size of a small rocket, sitting on a tripod at the end of the room and aimed at a row of thirtyish men stripping to their underwear. I wondered whether someone had been paid to shoot B-roll for a low-grade Hungarian sex film, but Steve pulled on his cup and told me, "Cheech is making a movie."

Moving to where Cheech was sitting, I asked him: "Steve says you're making a movie?"

"Gonna try. I've got all this film, so I figured . . . ," he said, getting up and moving to his camera.

"A movie about the Morningstars?"

"Well, it's about the Exclaim! Cup, but you could say that we're the lead characters," he said, pausing so my mind could dance excitedly at the thought.

"You can't do that!"

"Why not, buddy?" he asked, adjusting his tripod.

"Cause I'm writing a book!"

"A book about what?"

"About the Morningstars."

"You're writing a book about the Morningstars?"

"Well, the Exclaim! Cup too. But ya, the Morningstars."

"You think anyone would want to read a book about the Morningstars?"

"You think anyone would want to watch a film about the Morningstars? You think anyone would pay to look at that?" I offered, pointing at Andy, who was sitting in a corner taping his big toe.

"I don't know. See, I've got all this free film . . ." He examined his camera lens. "I wouldn't mind getting an interview with you later, if I could. You know, a few words of wisdom," he said, throwing me a cinematic bone.

"But with a film and a book, there'll be a glut of Morningstar stories on the market!" I told him.

"You think there's a market?"

Exasperated, I glanced over at my spot on the bench, where my notebook sat closed. It seemed so small compared to the hugeness of Cheech's rig.

"Really, Dave, a few quotes would be great," said Cheech.

"Well, maybe the book and the film could come out together," I conceded.

"Great idea! Hey, hand me that film canister, will ya?" he demanded.

During this exchange, I hadn't noticed that the voices of my teammates had risen to match the excitement of the day. Those who've never been part of a dressing room's klatch might suspect that, other than arguing over the respective merits of film and literature, players might use their time to probe philosophical concepts, take the temperature of the world's political climate, or muse on the general health of the planet. But instead, male athletes talk about their penises. Sometimes, we dwell on other matters too – like who is or isn't a big homo – but mostly, it's about my penis, your penis, the president of Swaziland's penis, and why the dirtiest player on the opposing team – who may or may not be a big homo – can't stop touching his penis or really wants to touch yours.

Dutch was the first to introduce this topic on game day. He told Brad that he was going to teach him how to trash talk in Dutch next year.

"How do you say 'dirty bitch' in Dutch?" Brad asked.

"I don't know, but my composition teacher called me a *lul* once. I think that means 'dick.'"

"And what about the word for 'tiny'? Cause it would help to have both."

"I'll try to find out," said Dutch.

"Hey, did I ever tell you what my favourite euphemism for my penis is?" offered Brad. "'My penis.'"

"That's wonderful news," I said, before trying to take the discussion to the real issue at hand: our opponent for the game, Sonic Unyon. "Those guys out there," I said, gesturing beyond the dressing-room door. "Their team hasn't changed that much."

"My penis changes depending on how much I'm stimulated," Brad remarked.

Of the 'Stars, Brad told the most stories in which his penis was a central character. Not that I'm a big homo or anything, but this made sense to me as Brad is easily the most beautiful of all the Morningstars (Al is beautiful too, provided you have a thing for Muppets who drink). On the second night of the Hootenany, he walked up to a young woman as things were closing down and told her, coolly, "You know, you should really come back to my place." A few hours later, he was bedding the young maiden in his King Street loft while the rest of us went back to Chris Topping's shed, where we listened to Al snarl like a pirate and passed around Chris's Indian Chief water pipe.

Brad holds the team record for using words like "booty" and "stoked" and, occasionally, "pimpin'." He is the only Morningstar who has a name for his stick ("the Howie"), which also happens to be the name of his shot (he likes to lace his enthusiasms with the word too, as in, "Did you see the Howie wire that Howie top

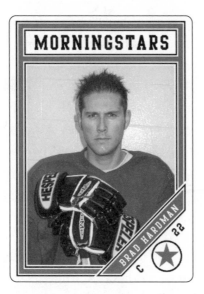

shelf!") Recently divorced, he'd been exploring his freedom over the previous year by travelling to exotic places. His last trip to Amsterdam provided a subject that he introduced while we prepared for the game: a sexual manoeuvre that he called the speedbag.

The only comforting part of the scene was in knowing that this kind of discussion happens on men's teams the world over. Still, there was something rather disturbing about standing in the dressing room with our yarballs hanging out, listening to Brad describe the pleasuring effect of the speedbag on women not moments before calling whomever we were playing "friggin' homo gaylords," that is when we weren't hugging or spanking each other after goals as if in the grip of romantic love.

Brad (whom I decided simply to call "Howie," completing the persona) and his Casanova ways hummed with a certain youthful verve that most of us had since abandoned for parenthood and responsible living, but his boasts were also cut with a measure of pathos. When I mentioned to Al that Howie's braggadocio seemed a little out of sorts, he said, "Ah, you like a bit of old-fashioned manly failure in there, don't you?" I had to confess that I did. Howie was my teammate and I loved him, but in many ways, his newfound hockeyness took me back to why I had despised the game as a teenager, and how sports – at least for kids who scored on their own net in gym class or couldn't tell the difference between Brian and Evelyn Glennie – can be as humiliating for some as it is anodyne for others.

Examined closely, hockey culture is as much about beer, sex, and violence as it is beauty, skill, and fearsome speed. All you have to do is spend a few hours watching *Hockey Night in Canada* with your four-year-old daughter to see the role that tits and suds play in our great national game, from bimbos necking in beer ads and the tight-shirted Leafs vixens on the ACC Jumbotron to a bunch of good guys going out for a few pops after the game; from the dearth of female sports journalists in a country insane for hockey to the occasional rec league goony bird throwing up in a salad bowl.

For better or worse, hockey's mythology is rife with illicit lore. A few books have already addressed this side of the culture. In *I've Got to Be Me*, Derek Sanderson wrote: "My habits [are] those of a bachelor who is not reluctant to combine sex with sport. I like a swinging chick who is . . . warm, wet and wild." (Rating the women of North America, the Turk added, "American women have completely blown it ever since they got the vote.") In *Thin Ice* by Larry Sloman – the most outrageous hockey book ever written – Donnie Murdoch told the author: "My first year, anytime I had a chance to get laid I would have taken the opportunity. Fat, skinny, ugly, good-looking, it didn't matter. All I was worried about was getting my rocks off." Teammate Mike McEwen concurred: "Quickies. Lots of quickies, heavy on the quickies."

I've told and retold the story about the French-Canadian puck star who used to employ a person for the sole purpose of trolling for women. One evening, this sex lieutenant approached a friend in a restaurant and told her: "Excuse me. Mr. X would like to fuck you." Egged on by her friends, she accepted, only to spend a frenetic five minutes doing the nasty in an elevator bound for the player's room.

In another instance, two best friends (let's call one of them B) on opposing NHL teams were skating against each other in a regular season game while their wives chatted in the stands. One wife asked the other how B was dealing with the crazed girlfriend with whom he'd fathered a child. Aghast, B's wife shrieked, "There's a child?" She stormed the players' dressing room and tried beating down the door, screaming B's name. The player came out and calmed her down, but, putting two and two together, he realized that it was his friend who'd spilled the beans. On the first shift of the next period, B went out and slashed at his erstwhile best friend, breaking his arm in two.

I once met a photographer who watched as two players adjudicated a best-breast contest during an All-Star weekend in the back of a hotel nightclub, grading the women by scrawling with a Sharpie over their stomachs and forming a line with the tens. Another friend told a story about sitting at a hockey game next to a woman who boasted about sleeping with a superstar player. When he asked her to prove it, she pulled out a Polaroid of the two of them doing the business. One of the more famous underground stories concerns two superstars challenging each other to a "craziest sex" contest, which was won after the more daring star produced a photo of himself in a hot tub with Martina Navratilova. That same victorious superstar also once slumped next to a friend at a table at a noted Western Canadian bar. Overcome by the chance of making small talk with one of his heroes, my friend grasped for words until the player, who was well into the spirits, grabbed his collar, pulled him close, and confessed, "I am a terrible alcoholic and an awful father," before a minder came and pulled the star away.

JEFF JACKSON: Bryan Fogarty was supposed to be the next Bobby Orr. He could do amazing things on the ice. I remember his zenith, which came during an early home game at the Colisée in the winter of '89. Bryan picked up the puck behind our net and headed up ice, and after a few feet, he'd reached a speed that most of us can only dream of. To Bryan, the first forechecker was no more than a bother. By the time he hit the red line, he'd beaten two more forwards and half of the guys on our bench were on their feet. He froze both defencemen, and just as quickly, he was back at full speed blowing around them before firing a bullet, top shelf. I remember thinking, Holy fuck. This kid is going to be a star.

I'd first met Bryan when he was thirteen years old. He was a gregarious kid, always smiling. He was the best friend of Brendan Roach, the oldest of two boys of the family I boarded with in my first year of Major Junior A hockey in Brantford [Ontario]. He

O-Pee-Chee/Hockey Hall of Fame

and Brendan had a mutual love of professional wrestling, and I got to see Bryan a lot that year. At the time, in 1982, he was a child star in the Brantford minor hockey system, the same minor program that produced Wayne Gretzky. In fact, the talk around Brantford at the time was that Bryan was more dominant at his age than Wayne had ever been. I was more than a little skeptical, particularly given that Bryan always seemed more interested in imitating Rick Flair's pile driver than pretending to score the Stanley Cup-winning goal. To me, this kid, who was always laughing and goofing around, didn't seem like the type of person who would go on to one day become a successful junior or professional hockey player.

During my second season in Brantford, I was placed with a different boarding family. But that didn't stop me from seeing Bryan and Brendan on a regular basis. I'd encounter them at high-school parties, wasted out of their minds at fourteen years old. It kind of scared me. After all, these two kids were like my little brothers and I found myself acting like the responsible big brother. I'd escort them out of these parties, admonish them for being drunk, and point them in the direction of their respective homes. In my naïveté, I actually thought that they'd listen to me. But the truth is, they almost never went home.

After finishing my junior career and beginning my professional hockey life, I never really thought about Bryan again. But one day in 1988, I picked up *The Hockey News*: Bryan was breaking all of Bobby Orr's junior records in Niagara Falls. There he was – "Fogie" – splashed across the pages and touted as the next great thing. But in the article, there were references to his drinking problems. I couldn't help but think back to those Brantford parties and wonder if I'd been witness to the germination of a lifelong struggle. I remember hoping that he would be able to straighten himself out.

The very next season, he was my Nordiques teammate in Quebec. By that time, I'd heard a dozen more stories about his drinking problems, but when I saw him at training camp, he looked and acted just like the kid I use to hang out with in the Roaches' basement in Brantford. There were flashes of brilliance on the ice, but he spent most of that first year playing air guitar. Everyone in Quebec had a soft spot for Bryan and we were all hopeful that he could leave his substance abuse troubles back in junior. But Bryan's behaviour told us that we were only kidding ourselves. Despite this, none of us seemed willing, or able, to do anything to help him. What made it worse was the realization that this wasn't how friends were supposed to treat friends in the real world. But we weren't living in the real world; we were part of the NHL, where you're constantly looking over your shoulder or across the dressing room, waiting for someone to steal your job. In pro hockey, it's a daily battle between looking out for your brothers-in-arms and looking out for yourself. The sad truth is that for the majority of pro players, self-preservation usually trumps the former.

Still, we worried about Bryan. Every one of my teammates wanted the best for him. We used to talk about it all the time. After a few seasons, we watched as he jumped from team to team, league to league, going south fast. And we hated it. We hated it because we all knew that Bryan had a good soul. We wanted him to succeed and be happy, not emotionally at war with himself and a bottle. We wanted him to conquer his anxiety and his fear of failure. We wanted to see him score the way he had that night in 1989. We wanted to see him laughing and smiling again.

When I picked up the newspaper in June 1999 and began reading about what had happened in Brantford, my heart sank. [Fogarty had been arrested and charged with break and enter and possession of a controlled substance after he and a friend jacked open the kitchen doors at the Tollgate Technological Skills Centre. Police found Bryan's friend naked in the kitchen with cooking oil spilled on the floor around him.] Then, less than three years later, Bryan was dead in a hotel room in Myrtle Beach, South Carolina. My first thought was that he'd died of an overdose or something, but the TV report said that he'd died of natural causes at thirty-two. At least Bryan hadn't gone like some flamed-out rock star. At the time, I didn't think about Bryan's struggle with booze.

I thought about him and the Roach boys, and the laughter that used to come up from the den.

Fogie's funeral was a few days later in his hometown. I didn't want to go, but I found myself driving down the highway to Brantford on a cold and rainy morning. I thought I'd at least see a few old NHL teammates and friends and we could grieve and commiserate over Bryan's death together. Maybe we could tell a few stories and share a laugh in honour of Fogie. But no other NHLer showed up. I sat near the front of the church and looked straight ahead. I can't recall the details of the service, but I remember that after his family and friends had eulogized him, they played one of Bryan's favourite Metallica songs, "Nothing Else Matters." For the first time, I really listened to the lyrics:

Never cared for what they say
Never cared for games they play
Never cared for what they do
Never cared for what they know
And I know

Then the tears came. Bryan had never really wanted to be a hockey player. It caused him too much pain. The only time he seemed truly at ease was when he was listening to Black Sabbath or Metallica. After the service, I saw some of Bryan's old friends. They told me that before his death, he'd been doing a lot better and was getting his post-hockey life together. I was happy to hear this. Although hockey is religion in Canada, the pressure and the expectations that come with playing this game at the highest level are not for everyone. I know that it wasn't for my friend.

5 | THE GHOST OF SAM LOPRESTI

After finishing his treatise on the speedbag, Howie got dressed with the rest of us. I spared a moment to tape my stick, then spared a second moment to swear at the tape. Hockey tape used to be something that protected your blade for days, months. But something bad has happened to hockey tape, and now it shreds and feathers well before its time. A few uncaring opportunists must have seized control of all hockey tape manufacturing world-wide for the purposes of evil. Sadly, the state of tape is a reflection of the hockey equipment industry as a whole, where standard gloves cost $80 a pair, wooden sticks snap after five games, $800 skates are made with eyelets that pop and heels that fray, hulking shoulder pads quickly wilt with sweat, and the plastic armour inside hockey pants slides off like the skin of a moulting lizard. Perhaps it's the old geezer in me, but hockey gear has never seemed so unreliable as it is now, all at ten times the cost.

After taping the stick I sat, stood, sat some more, then stood again to make sure everything felt right as the guys stuffed feet into skates, slid hands into varying vintages of armoured thumbs and fingers, inserted cold rubber plugs into yaps, pressed plastic to femur and tibia, snapped garter belts into soft stomach flesh, clacked sticks to the floor and across the benches, pulled sweaters over slumping physiques, and every now and then horked into a garbage pail. Once we were all armoured, we sat there quietly like Christmas pageant rejects before lifting ourselves off our cans twenty pounds heavier than when we'd walked into the rink. We shuffled out of the room past the gathering crowd – mindful of Cheech's cameraman, who skid-stepped backward like a member of the paparazzi – and leaned together against the bright arena glass waiting for the Zamboni's last turn. Mark was the first player through the door.

Following him, we hit the ice.

Whether I'm in a concert hall or a rink, I've always found the moments before the play easy. I'm at my best when neither a puck nor a set of rules is involved, skating with my hair swept back like Guy Lafleur in flight, spine bent in a Gretzkyian swoop, tongue and mouth agape *à la* Theo Fleury, eyebrows pointed with a mischief to match Esa Tikkanen's. Warming up is generally a fine time for any skater, with the new ice twinkling under the small ceiling lamps, water bottles standing proud and full on top of the boards, and the music inside the building – provided, for the E! Cup, by a fellow in a checkered blazer and fedora with a Casio keyboard across his lap – ringing around the curved glass. The whole landscape of the rink is distinct before the game. Apart from injury, there's no other occasion when players lie flat on the ice, stretching and warming up like prone acrobats trying to spell out the alphabet. And in no other circumstance does a scrub have the chance to shoot as freely as he does before the game, which, in this case, meant standing five feet in front of Mark and lobbing a puck into his padded belly without fear of being jumped by a guy banned for life from the Newmarket senior leagues.

After this routine, I made my way back to the bench. I thought the team looked pretty great in our sanguine jerseys and white stars – *statuesque* was the word that sprang to mind before my eyes fell on Al, his hair pushed sideways out of his helmet like a pair of Tribbles – seeming as composed as a figure in a Bruegel painting before the coming of leather fists, flying pucks, and slew-foots.

Our opposition was the Sonic Unyon Pond Hockey Squad, from Hamilton. As I've noted, the Unyons had an E! Cup history of heading down the QEW annually only to lose to the Morningstars. But this year's entry had walloped Long & McQuade in the opening game, and there were whispers, as there'd been with every previous Unyon team, that they'd shown up with a handful of college players, Junior B stars, or OHL prospects, depending on what conspiracy theorist was bending your ear. It was hard to tell from their warmup if this scuttlebutt was true, for their players seemed as scrubby as ours, hoisting the puck wide of the net and skidding to stop with the same unrefined style learned at Wednesday-night shinny and cottage goof skates.

Our game was refereed by a fellow known locally as "Steve, the Rock and Roll Ref." Steve was unlike other rec league zebras in that we knew his first name. Most were called either "Good Guy" or "Glasses" or "Weird Little Goatish Man" or "Stupid Jerk With the Moustache Who Won't Let You Talk to Him." Not that I need to give them more reasons to call penalties, but most of the tourney's justice-keepers were $25-a-game mugs whose skills were as sharp as the tongue of my hockey skate. In this sense, they performed on a level well matched with our own abilities.

Steve, however, was different. At the end of every season he threatened to retire, yet he was the first person to show up for duty in the fall, commanding games with fairness and accuracy. Steve took his refereeing seriously to the point that, off the ice, he affected a look of cool justice in wraparound sunglasses, grey goatee, and baseball cap, a smoke dangling from his top lip. Without his shades, he had the appearance of a man who'd slept beneath his truck, and his gravel-gargled voice was so rough and scratchy that he made Red Green sound like Norah Jones. Steve's dream was to host a "weird fishing show" on television, where "I take musicians like you into the woods and we learn about the environment and shit, catch some biggies too." When he first told me about it, I passed on what I knew about the kind of bodies that might finance this type of project. Later on during a game, he leaned over the boards as the play floated up ice and appeared poised to continue our discussion. Instead, he asked, "How'd your gig go in Hamilton last week? Any good poontang show up?"

I was startled by his use of the word *poontang*, which I'd remembered from Ted Nugent's early work. Steadying myself from this time warp, I broke the news to Steve — who may or may not have been trolling for an anecdote about topless maidens cavorting on a sea of backstage pillows – that we draw mostly science nerds to our shows.

Steve assured me as he skated away, "That's okay. They've got tits too."

When he returned a moment later, I stabbed at the kind of rejoinder I thought Steve might appreciate. "I guess it's like what a friend of mine once said, 'Never turn down sex with fat chicks.'"

"Whoaaaa," he replied, making a stop sign with his hand. "Let's not get carried away."

With the crowd settling into the stands, Steve the Rock and Roll Ref skated into the faceoff circle and Travolta-ed to both goalies, raising his hand over his head and tipping the puck in the direction of the opposing nets, first to Mark, and then to his Sonic Unyon opposite, who, from a distance, looked strong and square and shockingly white, a Detergent Box.

At Steve's prompting, the netminders showed that they were ready, shaking a helmet, lofting a glove. This moment – and the time preceding it – was as good as it would get for the netkeeps, whose studied coolness and quiet anger was, for now, unchallenged by gate-storming forwards. I tried to read the Detergent Box's character through his mild crease tics and the positioning of his pad-gloves, but there was very little to go on. He was uniformly white, except for the swollen black onion screened across the middle of his sweater, and I guessed that he would play as colourfully as he dressed. Secretly, I hoped that his style might belie his monochromatic appearance, for flamboyant goalies – those who yowl at their teammates, spank their stick on the ice, skate with the puck at ill-advised moments in the game, and pause before faceoffs to commune with the ghost of Sam LoPresti – are more likely to be terrible (they're occasionally brilliant too, but stoic goalies are more technically responsible and wall-like – the rec shooter's worst nightmare). One time, the Morningstars were matched against a team called Bruce's Bees, formed out of the Toronto Maple Leafs' club staff and captained by a theatrical goalie who was forever flipping up his mask, taking obnoxiously long draws from his bottle before spitting the water around his crease, and obsessively exercising whenever play moved down the ice. He was mouthy too, yapping at us whenever we skated within ten feet of him.

We met the Bees in a quarter-final of the Downtown Men's Hockey League and were tied 2-2 in the deciding game when we switched ends to start the third period. I was on the ice at the time, and as I crossed paths with the goalie at centre ice, I said, offhandedly, "Hey, man, I saw you in the parking lot before the game." He looked up to see if I had anything else to add, and, of course, I did: "You dress like a fag." The goalie went wild. He tried to spear me, but the refs rushed in. He threw his blocker at my chin, but missed. The goalie drew four minutes, we scored, and that was the end of the Bees.

Even though I wouldn't call Mark flamboyant – I would call him roly-poly, only not to his face – he certainly had more going for him in terms of style than the blanched Detergent Box. To start, Mark's mask was wild and beautiful, even though it gave us the same kind of on-ice advantage as Dutch's appreciation of Bulgarian reed players. Still, it stood out like a northern tribesman's headdress, as painted by my bandmate Martin Tielli in red and black acrylic that looked like something the shamanistic

Komi of northeastern Russia might have worn during a ritual. Above the eyeline was the image of a winterbird – a fierce, dart-eyed chickadee – and the grey sides of his mask were rivers of cascading fish. It easily trumped much of the van art favoured by contemporary pro goalies. I cared for Mark's mask not only because it guarded my teammate's head, but because I considered it an artistic treasure. I enjoyed upbraiding opposing crease-crashers for disrespecting its beauty, but these admonishments usually failed to get their goat. Instead they served to underline why the 'Stars were doomed from ever achieving rec league primacy: of all the possible motives for defending one's team, standing up for Impressionist Canadian art is pretty well near the bottom of the list.

So, with the Detergent Box to my left and the Winterbird to my right – his stick squared against his pads, catching hand raised high to protect the top corner of the net should a faceoff zinger come flying at him from the red dot (and really, with us, you never knew) – Steve drew the opposing centremen together, stilled the puck above the heart of the ice, and dropped it flat between their sticks. There was the sweet kickkockkickkock of wood on wood on rubber.

The game was on.

STEVE LUDZIK: My first game in the NHL was with the 'Hawks in Quebec City. During the game, I couldn't understand why the whole bench was standing up every time the Nordiques took a slapshot from the blue line. I finally asked Tom Lysiak why this was happening, and he said, "Because our goalie, Tony O

[Esposito], can't see the puck that far away." We lost 8-1 and I got our only goal. I intercepted a pass by Moose Dupont and beat Daniel Bouchard. After the game, Terry Ruskowski grabbed the puck for me, but he lost it a few days later. Larms and my girlfriend were listening to the game on a French station back in Moncton, and at one point, he turned to her and said, "I think Ludsy scored a goal, but I gotta be honest – I can't really understand what's going on here."

JOHN CHABOT: My first NHL game was the 1983–84 season opener in the Montreal Forum against the New York Islanders. I scored a goal to put us ahead 2-1. Mike Bossy tried to make a pass across the slot, but I knocked it down and scored on Billy Smith's short side. I thought I played pretty well, but because it was my first year in the league, I couldn't tell what the team was thinking. After the game, Serge Savard, who was GM at the time, was asked by reporters about what he was going to do about finding a centre for Guy Lafleur. "Guy Lafleur?" he replied. "Right now, it's more important that I find some decent wingers for John Chabot." It was something I'll never forget. The following game, I played well too, but we lost against Philadelphia. I sat out the next seventeen games in a row.

PAT HICKEY: My first point as a Ranger came at Madison Square Garden. We were playing Detroit, who'd picked up Eddie Giacomin on waivers, and the Rangers fans couldn't handle seeing him in another uniform. After I set up a goal to beat him, everybody booed.

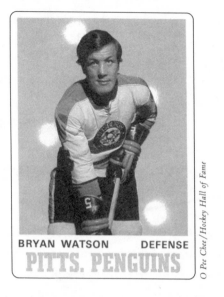

BRYAN WATSON   DEFENSE
PITTS. PENGUINS

O Pee Chee / Hockey Hall of Fame

RYAN WALTER: My first NHL game was with the Capitals against Chicago, at the Stadium. We were tied in the third period when our coach, Danny Belisle, tapped me on the shoulder and sent me out for a faceoff in our zone. He told me: "Go get it, kid." I skated into the circle, looked up, and there was Stan Mikita. I tied up his stick, and the puck just sat there. We eventually got it out of the zone and managed to tie the game. But the biggest wow, for me, actually happened before I'd hit the ice. It was during contract negotiations, when I was offered a $25,000 signing bonus. I went straight out and bought an aluminum canoe.

BUGSY WATSON: My first ever professional game was with Montreal against Toronto in Maple Leaf Gardens. I was so green that on the flight up after being called from Omaha, I left a tip for the stewardess after she brought my food. I had no idea what the hell was going on. On the way to Toronto, they lost my suitcase, so I had to wear Billy Hicke's skates, which just about killed me. That night, I hit Dave Keon, something that nobody from Montreal had been able to do. I knocked him flying, and it was a dirty hit, but the next day, in both cities, there was a picture on the front page of Keon coming off my hip straight into the boards.

AL MCDONOUGH: I can still remember my first rush in an NHL game. It was in the Spectrum in Philadelphia and I was playing with Los Angeles. The puck came to me out of our zone from a defenceman, and suddenly I was forced to make a play. I took the puck and got it up the ice, and I remember thinking, Well, that's kind of like what I always do. I got through the game, didn't get scored on, and felt pretty good. I scored in my next game and, because I was filling in for an injured player, there was a lot of talk that the Kings were going to engineer a trade so they could keep me up with the big team. But the trade never happened. I sat out a few games and was eventually sent down.

YVAN COURNOYER: I was nineteen when I got a call from GM Sam Pollock. The Junior Canadiens played their games on Sunday afternoon, so on Saturday night, he told me: "Tomorrow, you're going to Detroit." I was so excited that I didn't sleep at all. I played the game with Bobby Rousseau and Gilles Tremblay and we won 7-3. I scored the seventh goal. I was lucky that the game took place in Detroit, because the Olympia had very good ice. When Toe Blake touched me on the back to go out there for the first time, I thought to myself, I don't want to go. But I did and it was okay.

Still, what people don't realize is that even though it was hard to make the Montreal Canadiens, it was even harder to stay there.

FRANK MAHOVLICH: I can't remember playing my first NHL game, but the first hockey game I ever saw was in 1942 in the Northern Ontario mining leagues. My dad worked in a mine and his company team had three blacks on it: Herbie and Ozzie Carnegie, and a fellow by the name of Manny MacIntyre, from Windsor, Nova Scotia. When I saw them, I thought that if I ever played hockey, I'd be playing against lots of blacks. Of course, there hasn't been three blacks on one line since. Years later, my brother and I were going through the airport in Montreal when Pete – who was always joking around – grabbed the hat off one of the red cap porters and started running. The fellow chased us and was yelling, "I know you guys! You guys were just as bad when you were kids!" When we turned around, we saw that it was Manny MacIntyre.

LARRY PLAYFAIR: My favourite hockey team when I was growing up was the Boston Bruins, and my first game with the Sabres was in Boston. That afternoon, I was as nervous as could be. I was scared to death. I got to the rink, got dressed, took the pre-game skate, and felt okay. My very first shift was playing left defence with King Kong Korab against Peter McNab, Terry O'Reilly, and John Wensink. The puck got thrown in off the faceoff into my corner, and when I got it, I faked a pass up the wall to Craig Ramsey. I looked over my shoulder and saw Terry O'Reilly go for the fake. I went from the top of the faceoff circle to behind our net thinking to myself, Man, you just fooled Terry O'Reilly! As I came around the other side of the net considering what a great player I was, someone shut the lights off. John Wensink had come around on his off-wing and just smoked me. He hit me in the middle of my chest with his shoulder and they ended up carrying me off the ice on a stretcher. My first shift in the NHL lasted about eight seconds.

BOB LORIMER: I ruptured my spleen playing my first regular season game in the NHL with the Islanders. I went to check Craig Ramsey, but he put his stick out to protect himself, hitting me in the side. I remember skating back to the bench, thinking, Man, that kinda hurt. It happened in the second period, but I played the rest of the game. After the game, I had a bit of a stomach ache, so I told the trainer about it, but he said, "Ah, you're probably just nervous from your first game." The team went out for beers — the beer didn't taste very good and I knew something was wrong right away. I went back to my hotel room, and about two hours later, I phoned the trainer and told him that my stomach ache was getting worse. He said it was probably still nerves and that I should get myself some Maalox. I went down to the front desk, but all they had were TUMS. The pain got worse, and at around 3 a.m., I talked to the trainer and he said, "Well, there's really nothing I can do for you." He told me to drive myself to the hospital. So I got in my car, and as I was walking through the doors of the emergency room, I collapsed and passed out. I was bleeding to death. The doctors performed emergency surgery and probably saved my life.

6 | HOSERS' PROMENADE

Because the E! Cup was such a bright light on the CanRock hockey player's social calendar, we always had more than enough players to fill our tournament roster. This was a good thing, considering that Schmiddy — another 'Star regular — had passed on the tournament, and T had suffered a rib injury in our first game versus Capsule. T was forever breaking ribs. Or straining his neck, twisting an ankle, pulling a groin. There were few shifts when T wasn't doubled over, skating to the bench or tipping his head back in pinch-faced agony. There were even fewer shifts when he wasn't out there minutes later, ringing a shot off the post or smoothly riding out an attacker into the corner.

Once, T found himself on the wrong end of a Jim Cuddy spear. As T tells the story, the singer stood above him and asked whether the point of his stickblade could work in a pinch should he require an emergency tracheotomy. T replied, less eloquently,

The Morningstar
known as T.

"Fuck off, fuck," and rose to his feet, before striding in heavy drama to the bench. The confrontation so upset the young defenceman that, upon leaving the rink, he threw his equipment and stick into a Dumpster, which he later retrieved after bolting upright in the middle of the night, realizing what he'd done.

   T was working for the Barenaked Ladies when we first met in the hallways of Maple Leaf Gardens. He was also there the night the Rheos first sang the anthem at the Gardens — an occasion he orchestrated as our band's publicist — as well as the time we were bounced from the bill a few hours before the game. Though we were properly awed for our debut, by our third performance we'd become so blasé about singing the anthem that, while sound-checking, we goofed around with the team's microphone, bouncing it off our skulls to produce an eerie *boammmm* that rang around the walls of the old rink. In one of the worst instances of bad timing in our band's history, Steve Stavro, the Leafs owner, was wandering the building with friends, and he witnessed the whole thing. Appalled by our disrespect and embarrassed by our behaviour, he ordered Leafs publicist Bob Stellick to find us – we'd gone for dinner at a local café – and fire us. When Stellick broke the news to T over the phone, we thought it was a joke. T said that we could still go to the game if we wanted, and so we did, sitting in the golds as chanteuse Madonna Tosi – sensing that it could be her big break into the anthem-singing racket – delivered a rafter-peeling rendition of "Star-Spangled Banner" and "O Canada," her arms thrashing as if Mr. Zeigfield himself was watching from the bunker.

T was also with me the night that I experienced a hockey epiphany on a throbbing dance floor in New York City. The moment came just after the Rheostatics had finished our set at the Bottom Line, opening for Blue Rodeo, of all people. Even though there were more chairs than fans – really, you could have burst through the door waving George Steinbrenner's head on a pike and not bloodied anyone for the emptiness of the club – our show went pretty well. Still, the gig left us melancholy, but the evening got better once we arrived at a Manhattan apartment belonging to one of T's friends, a record company executive who treated us to a cupboard full of dope and little white pills – ecstasy, the love drug of the day. After gulping down a few tablets, we were shepherded in our down jackets, Kodiaks, and toques to the Sound Factory, New York's most happening (and hardest to get into) dance club. We were searched at the door by a dude who looked like Danny Tartabull in his Yankees warmup jacket, then led down a long hallway hung with black-and-white photos of men in varying stages of male love. I found myself standing in the coat check in front of a couple with their tongues down each other's throats. This was as far from pickled-egg night at the Monarch tavern in Toronto as possible. We must have looked terribly awry to the chronically hip Manhattan clubgoers. I wondered whether our appearance was just wrong enough to be considered avant garde ("Kodiaks matched with a pair of blue jeans? Those fellows walk the knife edge!"), and part of me expected to open the next issue of *Details* to discover that Hoser's Promenade was being pegged as the look for next fall. Then we sat on bleachers at the edge of the dance floor while men in chaps and women in bras tramped through our snow-boot slush, which quickly melted into little pools of water, refracting the club's strobes and pinwheels into swords of white light.

Then, the love drug took hold. Not that I felt a sudden pull for the cowboy-booted fellow with the hairy bum, but the E had its effect. I felt a great surge of love, it turned out, for hockey. Within that darkened room, squirming with half-dressed bodies, my mind reeled back to McCormick. Suddenly, I saw hockey for the subculture that it was – tribal, fetishistic, Canadian – a ritual that had been cloaked against much of the outside world, sort of like mumming or falconry. If the crowd at the Sound Factory had been drawn to the club (as I had) by the promise of something wild and strange and secret, what would they have made of the men and women back home who struggle through blizzards in search of an even colder place, where they huddle together in rank enclaves that smell of cabbage, only to remove their clothes in favour of sweat-heavy armour, which they layer across their bodies until, one by one, they hit the ice looking like Yeti hunters. Viewed through the prism of New York's underground, I saw how weird this ritual is, and how tame the Sound Factory's subterranean theatre was, coming as it did from the pages of a self-conscious style magazine. The E urged me, "David, make love to your source" (or something equally embarrassing) and as I contemplated the exoticism of my country's game, I wrapped my arms around the woollen shoulders of my friends and whispered epithets about home into their ears. Had one of those spike-necked fellows prowling the room asked me to check out his chainmail, I probably wouldn't have heard him. I was too busy leaning against T and effusing, "Man, Bob Rouse is one beautiful defenceman."

"Boy, are you ever high," he said, sliding away.

But it was true.

I was stoned in love with hockey.

T is my main connection to the world of industrial rock and roll, as for the past few years he's held down a job as publicist for a handful of big record companies. Along with Dave Bookman and me, T helped to organize the first ever Rockers Play the Classics charity hockey game. We did this in concert with the Harris Institute for the Arts (a local music college), which recruited a pair of mainstream Canadian rockers, Andy Curran and Carl Dixon, to help out. As it turned out, we got along worse than Bob Clarke and Bonnie Lindros. During our first get-together to decide which bands would or wouldn't play for the Rockers (the "Classics" were NHL alumni), these two former members of

Coney Hatch lobbed Gowan, Helix, and the Killer Dwarves; we shot back with Sloan, Lowest of the Low, the Bourbon Tabernacle Choir. Our list probably sounded as lame to them as theirs did to us, but when Carl asked, "These bands . . . they're actually, like, gigging bands?" I wanted to do to his head what an ape would do to a hairy coconut. Instead, I declared, "These bands are playing in the game. Or we're not."

We reached the weakest of compromises: a unified team. The slags would send out their line, we'd send out ours. Gowan, it turned out, was easily the best player on the ice. Whenever he had the puck — which was always — Tyler Stewart of the Barenaked Ladies warned the old-timers, "Watch out for that guy, *he's a straaange animal!*" The Classics won 24-22, and while I got to play against Paul Henderson, Mike Palmateer, and other heroes from my childhood, what I remember most was my turn with the boys from the mainstream.

The following year's game was much better. The slags decided to hold their own game in Hamilton, and we held ours. This time we invited whomever we wanted and there was a much better feeling in the Varsity Arena dressing room. At one point during the game, I took the puck in the corner and rushed up the ice, gathering a great head of steam. As I approached the centre line, former Bruins' defenceman Dick Redmond came toward me, but I blew past him. I realize that Dick Redmond will never be mentioned in the same breath as Wes Walz or Sami Kapanen when it comes to the skating wizards of our time, but still, I was overwhelmed that I'd outmanoeuvred a real live ex-NHLer. Even though I lost the puck while approaching the goal, the giddy sensation lasted for weeks, until I was given a tape of the event as a keepsake. I immediately forwarded to my rush, at which point it was revealed that Redmond hadn't tried to stop me at all. Slowing down the tape, I saw that he just couldn't bring himself to get in the way of such a determined scamp. He'd simply glided toward me, reached out with his stick and waved it in my blazing path. I bashed clean through, racing hellbent and head down to the open lane.

We didn't know it at the time, but the Rockers events were E! Cup prototypes, if less well run and with far fewer serious musical types. Over the past few years, the star quality of the tournament has increased, with names like Sam Roberts, the Sadies, and the Constantines being drafted into the hockeyrock ranks. I'd been warned by Gord Downie that Sam Roberts was "probably really good. He's very competitive, so I'd be a little worried." And when I watched Sam's team – the Jokers – play in a must-win round-robin game during the '02 Cup, I was impressed with the way Roberts skated. He had quick ankles, a studied stick-to-puck technique, and moved in a low crouch, his chin pointed forward in the classic form of a pro. Worse, he had a perpetual playoff beard that gave him the look of a warrior who'd just finished one gut-grinding series and welcomed another. But Roberts was also half the size of Rob Blake's shinpad, and while I'm no Lurch Chara, I knew that if I got him in my sights, I might be able to cream him along the boards.

The Jokers played us extremely tough. They seemed struck with a "Must beat the Morningstars at all costs!" drive, and the game was a crazy, three-period war. We were ahead by a goal late in the game when two things happened. First, Tyler Stewart found himself in the slot with a clear shot on goal. He raised his

Tyler Stewart (vocals) *and Chris Murphy* (drums) *help rock the rink.*

stick to shoot, but fanned on the puck while swinging through. He vaulted off his skates like an astronaut hurtling through inner space before landing on the full weight of his brains.

With forty seconds to go, we lined up for a faceoff. The arena band – featuring Chris Murphy of Sloan and the twins from White Cowbell Oklahoma – played the opening of "Won't Get Fooled Again." While I'm loath to suggest that the standard twenty-second arena sound clip is anything but a sporting event's vibe polluter, this was one of the few instances where a snippet of loud rock actually made sense, especially considering the nature of the game's skaters. Usually, musical programming in pro rinks is a case of *sonic interruptus* – a White Lion chorus bumped against a Shania Twain verse bumped against the intro of "Bad" by U2 – resulting in one long annoying Frankensong. But at this moment, A-E-D never sounded better.

After Tyler's pratfall, a series of wild scrambles followed an important faceoff in our end. Each time we tried clearing the disc, it was blocked by a Joker defenceman, who put the puck on net. The Jokers' last shot of the game came heavy and hard from the point, and it hit me square in the stomach. It was punted away by my belly, but instead of rebounding down the ice, it sat there in the cold nothing of our zone. Both teams lunged after it. I made an attempt to join the fray until I realized that my leg was being held from behind. Looking down, I saw the face of Sam Roberts.

It was then that I was presented with a serious moral and ethical dilemma: if I pushed off with the leg that Mr. Roberts had in his grasp, I risked bringing my blade down over the young howler's face, throat, and chin. Then again, if I merely submitted, there was a chance the Jokers would turn back, collect the puck, and try for one last shot on goal. Both you and I know what I did. Giving Sam the "Sorry, man, but I hope this doesn't either kill you, destroy your face, sabotage your career, or clip your vocal chords before their time" look of a person for whom succeeding in the E! Cup was pathologically important, I pushed off. Sam moved his glove to blunt my swiping scissor as I thwacked at the puck, which sliced over the blue line as time fell to zero on the big red clock.

The story of CanRock remained forever bland.

JIM SCHOENFELD: Joe Crozier was the coach in my rookie year. Before an eleven-day road trip out to the West Coast, Joe told me to bring my guitar. We were fighting for the playoffs and he

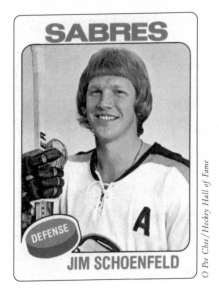

© Pee Chee / Hockey Hall of Fame

wanted to keep the guys loose. I remember sitting in the airport, playing "Taxi" by Harry Chapin. The guys loved that song. Pretty soon, they were all gathered around the guitar, singing. Joe had an eye for things that weren't the norm, and he figured that having some monkey bringing his guitar on the road would help the team play better. And it did. A while later, an interviewer in Buffalo asked me if I had any hobbies and I told him that I played guitar. A local disc jockey, Danny Nebrith, read the story and said, "How'd you like to go into a recording studio and make an album?" When you're a kid, everything seems like fun, so I went down, demoed some stuff — you didn't really need a great voice if you were a Buffalo Sabre in the 1970s — and later on, we brought in some studio musicians and did the record. I wasn't the only one: Jim Lorentz did a record; Rick Dudley did one too. We were a young, exciting, wild team, and these albums were a natural extension of that. On the jacket of the record, someone wrote that it was a goal of mine to make an album and appear on *The Tonight Show*, but that wasn't true. I was twenty years old, and it was fun. Thankfully, nobody owns turntables any more.

FRED STANFIELD: Schoney was the biggest Beatles fan I've ever seen in my life. He knew every Beatles song written. He and Jimmy Lorentz would bring their guitars up to the room and we'd have a few beers and sing. Big Bert [Gilbert Perrault] was another entertainer. He'd been singing his entire life, and when he'd break out his Elvis, people were just in awe. They were floored by this guy, by how good he was.

AL MCDONOUGH: My son Gabe's a musician. We've had a lot of bands stay with us, and when Gabe's on the road, he'll stay with them. They're very supportive of each other. I remember him talking to another band, saying, "Your CD's great; you guys are gonna be huge!" and thinking how different it is from sports, hockey in particular, where kids are always saying to each other: "You suck. Our team's gonna kick your ass." The way it is in music is the way it should be. You shouldn't degrade each other. You should show support to someone who's in the same boat.

GARY GREEN: When I was coaching Washington, a lot of celebrities would drop by: Sinatra, Bruce Springsteen. When Springsteen showed up, I let him and Clarence Clemons into the dressing room. I went to my office for a while, and when I came back Bruce had dressed Clemons up in Mike Palmateer's mask, pads, and goalie gear.

JEFF JACKSON: Al Iafrate was nuts about music. From the second he showed up, you could tell that he was a different dude. Russ Courtnall, Al, and I lived together in the Westbury Hotel in Toronto. Before going to the game, we'd meet in one of our rooms and Al would play this tape by Morris Day and the Time really loud on his boom box. Then we'd walk over to the Gardens. Al was always quite paranoid about losing his hair. He'd come into the dressing room, sit down, take off his ball cap, and immediately throw on his helmet. Then he'd get dressed with his helmet on. Other days, he'd actually wear his helmet in the shower. No one paid attention because it was just Al.

JOHN BROPHY: Al was so self-conscious about his baldness that whenever he took off his helmet for the anthem, he bent down and hid behind Alan Bester, who was a few feet shorter than him. One time, he jumped up along the boards in a sitting position after getting checked and ran into the spot where the boards met the glass. He fell to the ice hard and his helmet flew off. He was hurt, but he had enough energy left to reach out and put the helmet back on his head before he passed out.

FRANK MAHOVLICH: I was introduced to music as a kid in Northern Ontario. I was in an orchestra in which I played a string instrument very similar to the Russian balalaika — a tamburica — which is Croatian in origin. Duquesne University in Pittsburgh had a tamburica orchestra that used to come to Toronto a lot, but the guys in Schumacher were just as good. My dad had an awful time trying to get me to take lessons — I always wanted to be out between the snowbanks playing hockey — but I was glad that I

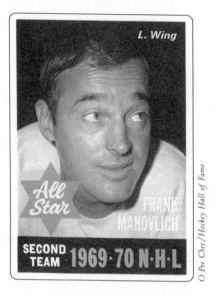

L. Wing

All Star

FRANK MAHOVLICH

SECOND TEAM 1969·70 N·H·L

O Pee Chee / Hockey Hall of Fame

did. It was a very special period in my life. As for art, I was introduced to that while in school. There was a contest for the best painting and I won, but because I was into sports, I didn't really follow it up. I got back into painting once I'd made the NHL, and when Robert McMichael (of the famous Kleinberg gallery) contacted me about patronizing his gallery, I became friends with some of the Group of Seven painters. A.Y. Jackson would come to the house and A.J. Casson spent two weeks every year for ten years at our cottage, painting and hanging around. He'd leave us with a painting each time. We had a lot in common because he had great knowledge and interest in a part of Northern Ontario, near where I was born in Schumacher. When he talked about the Group of Seven going on their famous camping trips, I was familiar with what they'd gone through in the wilderness.

YURI BLINOV: Valeri Kharlamov was a deep, soulful person. He loved to sing and play the guitar. His mother was Spanish, and there was always lots of music in his house. It was Valeri's idea to go record shopping in Toronto in 1972. We'd been given $150 spending money during our time in Canada, so we had to invent ways to bring things back. Valeri decided to trade a Soviet banner for records, so we went down to this big store in Toronto, Sam the Record Man, and got to pick out three LPs each. I chose Tom Jones, because he was my favourite. I got to see him perform once in New York, at Madison Square Garden. At the end of the show, there was a riot. Everybody was jumping on stage, so I did too. The day before, the Red Army had played against Team U.S.A. on the ice, and the next evening I was standing up there with Tom Jones, going crazy in front of all these people.

TODD HARTJE: In sports, as in life, music is a universal language. One night during my season playing with Sokol Kiev in Russia, we were having a bit of a blowout at the *basa* – which is what we called our residence with the team. The coaches and managers had all gone home and the players who were left behind invited some of their lady friends over. They had to climb through the window of my room to get in. A party started to happen, and the guys wanted some music, so they said, "Benatar! Benatar! Pat Benatar!" Until this point, I'd felt like a fish out of water and was finding it difficult to establish my place within the social rank of the team, but once I put that tape on, things got better. When the song ended, they took the tape out and rewound it using a finger or a pencil; it wasn't until later that I realized they were saving batteries. The whole scene brought me right back to Harvard, to dancing at a party with my friends. The Russian dance moves were a bit different and the refreshments were vodka and salty fish, but it was one of those moments that took our friendship to another level. We were all just a bunch of buddies sharing a good time, grooving to Pat Benatar in the middle of the Russian nowhere.

BRAD DALGARNO: When I was with the Islanders, my stall was right next to the stereo. There was a lot of inconsistency in the music, and it was killing me. So I went home and made mixed tapes, thinking them through in terms of rhythm and flow, to get some energy going in the room. Darius Kasparaitis loved these tapes, and because he'd come from Lithuania, everything was new and exciting. It didn't matter if it was Lionel Richie or Frank Sinatra or Beck: it was all new. One day, he got so excited that he ran into the dressing room, waving a CD. He was shouting, "You've got to hear this music! It's so amazing!" We were all excited because Darius was excited. He fussed with the machine for a while and finally got it working. When he pressed play, the music started and it was "Have You Seen the Love Tonight" by Elton John from *The Lion King* soundtrack. It was so not a dressing-room song, and we told him this in simple terms. He couldn't figure out why we thought it was such a piece of crap. He kept harping, "But it's so good! Listen. It's fantastic!" I think he was crushed that we couldn't get behind it.

JOHN HALLIGAN: Tiny Tim — who was born Herbert Khaury in Washington Heights — was a huge fan of the Toronto Maple Leafs. He was a regular whenever the Leafs visited Madison Square Garden in the 1960s. His dishevelled appearance, falsetto voice, unkempt hair, and shopping bags crammed full of God-knows-what tended to disrupt fans in the side prome-nade, flush against the dasher boards. After he arrived at a game, a lot of people got up and moved elsewhere.

RICHARD HARRISON: The first time I met Bobby Hull, I was asked to present him with a poem I'd written. At the reception, Bobby already had a little crowd around him when we were intro-duced. I handed him the poem and he pocketed it right away, looked me in the eye, and said, in that gravelly laugh of his, "Poet, eh? All I know about poetry is Robert Service: 'The Shooting of Dan McGrew.'" And right there he began: "A bunch of the boys were whooping it up in the Malamute saloon." He stretched out his arm with his fingers that had been busted and healed so many times he couldn't flatten them. He spread them as wide as he could to describe the length of the bar that ran from where we stood out the door and into the hotel corridor. He continued: "The kid that handles the music-box was hitting a jag-time tune . . ." He paused. "You know this?" Sure, I nodded, and he went on, drawing out the syllables. He dropped lower into the gravel: "Back of the bar, in a solo game, sat Dangerous Dan McGrew." It was a wonderful moment. Bobby Hull – whose shot could knock a man off his skates and back into his own goal – reciting something immortal from my chosen art form, admitting that he didn't belong in my world as a creator but that something from that world had become part of him.

JAMES DUPLACEY: I'd heard stories that Bobby Hull would sign for any fan that asked him, but I'd never seen it for myself until the 1993 All-Star weekend in Montreal. Following the game, I took a private coach to the evening's gala. My buddy Will, who has made every Styrofoam target used in every All-Star Game skill-shooting competition in every league in every ice hockey rink in every part of the ice hockey world, was with me. Will is different; he's still a fan. So, when he spied Bobby Hull sitting on this bus, he asked the Golden One to sign one of his targets. The Jet, like Moses, took the tablet in his hands, glanced once, chuckled twice, then stood up and addressed his congregation, "This looks like Debra's eyes when she wakes up in the morning." Bobby signed the target. He signed it with the methodical deliberateness of an artist creating a masterpiece. He refused to make a single stroke with his pen unless the bus was stopped at a red light or stalled in traffic. It took us thirty minutes to get to our destination and it took Bobby thirty minutes to sign the stranger's autograph.

ERIC ZWEIG: Frank Fredrickson was the captain of the Winnipeg Falcons, Canada's first gold-medal-winning Olympic hockey team in 1920. He spoke more like a retired university professor than a retired hockey player. This may or may not have had something to do with the fact that, while teaching hockey at Princeton in the 1930s, he walked to work every day with his neighbour, and fellow violinist, Albert Einstein. Winnipeg newspapers said during his heyday with the Falcons: "If Frank Fredrickson ever decided to embrace the concert platform as a means of livelihood, it is quite on the boards that he would win out." On the night that Lester Patrick signed him to a professional hockey contract, Frank was performing in the grand ballroom of Winnipeg's Fort Garry Hotel, where he was playing violin in a five-piece orchestra. When his troop ship was torpedoed in the First World War, Frank recalled that he "began thinking about what was important to me and went back to my bunk to get my violin." He had his violin with him again on another ocean voyage two years later, when the Winnipeg Falcons were en route to Antwerp for the Olympics. On board the RMS *Melita*, Frank played the piano in the lounge, and during the trip, the Falcons organized concerts on board that involved Frank and his best friend, Konnie Johannesson, performing a duet on their violins. Falcons' treasurer Bill Fridfinnson wrote that after dinner, "Konnie and Frank took their violins to play for the third-class passengers who are not allowed upstairs." This was typical behaviour for the Falcons, who earned as much praise for their sportsmanship in Antwerp as they did for winning the gold medal.

FRANK MAHOVLICH: Art and music have always complemented hockey. Painting allowed me to focus and relax, to get my mind off of things instead of dwelling on them. To be too into something sometimes isn't healthy; you need a diversion. To be able to play an instrument or paint is a great getaway from the pressures of a game. I think that the player gets the same feeling skating down the wing as the artist does filling his canvas.

PAT HICKEY: As a child of the 1960s, I had to find my own path to freedom, which, in my case, meant getting out of Brantford. Some people did it by playing the piano or the guitar; others did it on hockey skates. Rock and roll proved to young people

PAT HICKEY • L.WING

O Pee Chee / Hockey Hall of Fame

that you could see the world and have fun doing it. I studied the words to "Sgt. Pepper's Lonely Hearts Club Band" to see what was in there and what I could learn from it. One of my English teachers spent a month teaching us the inside and outside of "For What It's Worth" by Buffalo Springfield, and by the time I made pro, I was following Neil Young and Jackson Browne and the way they sang about politics, love, divorce, everything. When I was drafted by New York, I used the city to extend this sense of discovery because so much was happening there every hour of the day. I went to galleries, saw plays, concerts, a bit of everything. I remember going to see *Man of La Mancha* on a Wednesday matinee after the morning skate and thinking, "Man, these singers, actors, dancers, musicians are working it. They're prepared, they're into it." Three hours later, I got to stand in front of seventeen thousand people and do my thing. The way I viewed it, the rink was my stage and the fans were my audience.

The following year, I was eating in a restaurant when a fellow came up and asked if I'd like to join his table, where Margaux and Muriel Hemingway were sitting. Of course, I accepted, and during dinner, I invited them to come and see me play. They were all giddy and excited about it. The next night, I remember going out for warm-up and skating hard across the rink – I always liked to hit the ice fast – and seeing the two of them sitting right across from me. That night, I scored two goals and two assists, and realized that maybe having someone famous in the crowd was what I needed to give me that extra boost. Billy Joel was the person I brought in the most. I'd sneak him into the corporate box. His song "Sleeping with the TV On" is about his relationship with me and Mike McEwen and the Rangers. One time, he asked me what a hockey player's routine was, and I told him, "Our job is to go back to the hotel room, get off our feet, lie down, and fall asleep with the TV on." I'd never thought of hockey as poetry before, but all you have to do is see it from the other side to know that it is.

7 | THE PINCH OF THE NINJA

Even though I've played thousands of hours of hockey over the last ten years, it's a new experience every time I take to the ice. It's not like being a ballplayer shuffling to your station at first base, or a basketball centre planted under the rim. In hockey, a game's beginnings take the skater along a different path every time, an entirely new hieroglyph carved into the ice. Sometimes, the randomness of the sport makes it difficult to find one's space over the course of a game, let alone its opening minutes, so it wasn't until I'd collected the puck behind our net, squared myself up the ice, and trusted my passing eye enough to thread the Timbit along a northern seam toward Tom Paterson that I actually settled into the game, pushing out a wave rather than spinning in a whirlpool of action.

The puck hit in the middle of Tom's stickblade. Unlike most modern excaliburs, this blade lay relatively straight and true; it

hadn't been warped, bent, or wheedled into one of the many vari-
ations on the concave scoop. It was more like the straight angle
recently favoured by Doug Gilmour, and, before that, by every
player who preceded Bobby Hull. Hull's scandalous banana blade
was the pop-cult cousin of the banana seat, *The Banana Splits* TV
show, the film *Bananas* by Woody Allen, the Velvet Underground's
banana album, and artifacts of the late 1960s, early 1970s, when
the phallic fruit was a catch-all for bigger and better. While
Hull's wonky curve — pictures suggest that it was more like a
Jai-Alai *cesta* than a stickblade — was met with outrage by hockey
purists, goalies were the ones who suffered more than any
old-timer or journalist whose aesthetic sensibility had been
challenged. Andy Bathgate once told me that he used to soak his
stickblade in a bucket, then bend it into the crook of the washroom door for just the right angle of weird. The first time he
used the hook, he fired a few heaters at Johnny Bower, who threw
down his gloves and asked Bathgate if he was trying to kill him.
Knowing a good thing when he saw it, Andy headed back into
the dressing room, where he gathered more sticks and found an
even bigger bucket.

What the straight stick possesses that the banana blade doesn't
is one of hockey's small aural delights: the *stapp* of the puck
hitting the blade's square panel of wood. Because of the banana
blade's curve, the sound of the puck hitting it is muffled — admit-
tedly, what happens once the disc leaves the stick is actually more
important than what it sounds like when it gets there — but the
straight blade has a tone all its own, like a hammer on plywood,
a Czar's handclap, a high-school textbook raised above one's head
and dropped to the floor. It's a satisfying sound.

My pass to Tom was a sure-handed, whippy-wristed horizontal, neither as dunderheaded (and reasonably safe) as the board-bank, nor as cunning and skilled as those quick, pro passes that cross the ice as cleanly as a fishing line hitting the water. Passing the puck is one of the things I'm pretty good at, but this hasn't always been the case. I once littered the rink with cupcakes before learning when and when not to throw the puck up the ice. Cupcaking is one of the many ways to describe what happens when a player sends the puck — usually up the heart of the rink — without noticing an opposition player hiding on the periphery. It's too easy for the puck-carrier to be tantalized by so much impossibly open ice. Like a swimmer at the edge of a dock pausing to enjoy the still beauty of the lake, there's a certain satisfaction in seeing a teammate floating against a naked canvas of ice. Since hockey is such a mad rush of flurrying pucks and rising elbows, it's only natural that players want to savour this moment.

But cupcaking can be among the hockey player's most vivid and humiliating moments. One's misfortune is heightened because everyone else on the ice or in the stands sees the accident coming before the puck-carrier does, having a wider perspective on the play. It's like a film audience knowing there's a dagger-wielding fiend lurking in the bushes while a nymphet and her boyfriend test their tonsils in the front seat of a car. Cupcaking is a broad, dramatic death because of the time it takes to execute the missed play, a time of gathering misery in which the player goes from hero to goat in the bright harrowing spotlight of the ice.

During the tournament, Jeff Marek, the young Toronto radio host who played for the actors' team, Sergeant Rock, suffered this cruel fate after dishing a pastry to one of the Jokers, who skated in with the puck and tied the game 2-2, in the dying seconds, no less. For Marek, it seemed like it happened fast, but anyone who was in the rink at the time saw him take a stride with the puck, raise his head to gather in the illusory openness of the rink, comfort the disc on his blade, and wire it, unknowingly, to his opponent: a tragedy in four acts. After the game, he was inconsolable. When I went to tell him not to be ashamed, that most of us do it at least once or twice a year, he said, as if quoting something Shakespeare might have written about the game, "When I woke up this morning, the day held such promise. But now, there is none."

The heart-of-the-ice, telegraphed Timbit is one of hockey's horrible blunders, but the game provides more than a few ways of making a player want to melt into the ice faster than the Wicked Witch of the West. A recent all-star gaffe came while Sweden played the unrated Belarussian team during the Salt Lake Olympics in 2002. In the final period of their elimination game, a theretofore unregarded forward fired a slapshot from inside the red line at Tommy Salo, Sweden's former gold-medal-winning goalie and tenured Edmonton Oiler. Salo, who, along with his Tre Kronor mates, had been the early sensation – having hammered Canada 5-1 in the opening game – buckled like an old man protecting himself from a snowball, throwing his hands over his head in an effort to deflect it from his face, forgetting, it seemed, that there were three inches of reinforced plastic between the spiralling rubber and his chattering teeth. The puck became entangled in the goalie's glove, then climbed like a pet mouse out of the webbing and down the leather gauntlet until it fell and bounced through the crease into the net. As the B'Russians hugged, Salo calmly swept his stick side-to-side in the crease, but inside, he must have been dying. He'd played the puck as if someone had thrown him a poison dart. After the game, the stricken netkeep was at a loss to explain what had happened – nor did his teammates have an answer for why the B'Russians had dominated them, either – and, from that moment forward, Salo seemed to lose his competitive power. After he was traded to Colorado in 2004, he announced that he was thinking of retiring to Sweden, where, the morning after the national team's defeat, the major Stockholm paper ran a single word on their front page – "FÖRRÄDERI" (TREASON) – with mug shots of all their Olympic hockey players below the banner.

PERRY BEREZIN: The Flames were very confident going into Game 7 against Edmonton in 1986. Mike Vernon was standing on his head and Bob "Badger" Johnson had prepared us so well to defend against Gretzky that we knew every little detail of the Oilers' attack. With about nine minutes left in the third period, I was in the latter part of my shift when I got the puck near our bench. I stepped over the red line, dumped it, and turned to change. Before I could find a seat and with my back to the play, I heard a lull in the crowd and a handful of guys on our bench going, "Ya!" I asked what had happened and someone told me that I'd scored to break the tie. I asked, "How?" and everyone said, "I dunno." Steve Smith had put the puck in his own net. We won the game, and Smith's goal was the difference, but there wasn't a lot of celebrating on our bench. If it had been a real goal, we would have gone wild, but it was anti-climactic. Of course, I felt terrible for Steve. We all did. Just as I was about to be interviewed after the game, one of the older players grabbed me and said, "Don't you feel sorry for him or anyone else on that team." Despite the fact that he'd lost the series for his team, Steve Smith was tough and he bounced back. He hit me with everything he had in every game afterwards, as if it been my fault that he'd bounced the puck I'd dumped off Grant Fuhr's leg into the net.

JOHN CHABOT: I scored on my own net a couple of times, but my biggest gaffe was when I tried to jump over the boards onto the ice for a change on the fly. I hit my feet on the stick of the player standing beside me, fell flat on my face, while the player I was supposed to be checking went down the ice and scored. It was on *Hockey Night in Canada*, so everyone got to see it.

JEFF JACKSON: My most embarrassing moment was in 1987 when I was playing for the Rangers. I think it was Game 5 of the first round of the playoffs versus Philadelphia. We were down by a goal with a minute to go and I was on the ice (I was hot offensively at the time). The puck bounced out of their zone and Brian Propp took off on breakaway. Our net was empty and Propp was about to score and for some strange reason, I threw my stick, making it an automatic goal. What was embarrassing about it was that I'd always considered guys who threw their sticks in that situation to be complete knobs and there I was doing it. As I watched my stick fly through the air, I wanted to go hide in the dressing room, but it wasn't any better in there. Phil Esposito, our coach, agreed that it was an idiotic move. He tore a strip off of me in front of the guys as soon as the team got back in the dressing room. He said that was something a twelve-year-old in minor hockey might try. I felt about an inch high, and it was most embarrassing because I agreed with him.

PERRY BEREZIN: I was once caught from behind by Terry Ruskowski with an open net at the end of a game. He hooked me as I shot the puck and it ended up going twenty-five feet wide with fifty seconds to play. It almost cost us the game because Pittsburgh took it down to our end and nearly scored. Usually, I don't mind getting caught from behind, but not from an old fart like Terry Ruskowski.

IGOR KRAVCHUK: I pinched on Team Canada's winning goal against Russia in 1987, the famous Gretzky-Lemieux goal. I was on the ice with Igor Stelnov — my defence partner — and when I looked up, Mike Keenan was sending out the big line. I wouldn't say it was a mistake that Tikhonov put us out there — after all, we'd played pretty well in the tournament — but Kasatonov-Fetisov were the top unit, not us. When the puck came up the boards, I moved in to stop it, but it was chipped past me. Racing up the ice, I saw Hawerchuk hook our forward and bring him down, creating Lemieux-Gretzky's famous two on one. I watched as the linesman brought the whistle to his mouth, stiffened his arm to make the penalty, and then, all of a sudden, dropped his arm to his side.

KARL-ERIC REIF: Most folks won't remember Larry Mickey because he was a third-line forward who had a very short cup of coffee with six or seven different NHL clubs before Buffalo got him from the pre-evil Flyers. He was a flinty-eyed guy with wispy, tousled blond hair, who, when he played along the boards, was a flurry of elbows and knees. He wasn't a penalty-minute guy, just an animated grinder. He came to the Sabres early in 1971, their second year, but hardly played until the next year, when he had his best campaign, scoring fifteen goals. One game, the Sabres were up by a goal or two – it was either late in the second or midway through the third – and somehow Mickey got the puck at centre with only one Flyer defenceman to beat. He had a full head of steam, and as he crossed the Philly blue line, he tried stickhandling around the Flyer rearguard, who put his stick between Mickey's legs, reached out, and grabbed him. As Mickey raced past, the Flyer spun him completely around and dropped him to the ice, but without slowing him at all. Somehow, Mickey kept sliding on the seat of his pants toward the Philadelphia net like a little kid on one of those snow-saucer things, slowly revolving, and looking around for the puck with this vaguely disoriented expression, but still sliding endlessly toward the goal. The goalie stood his ground, but Mickey slid into his pads, bowled him over, and both players wound up inside the net. Mickey and the goalie clambered out of the net to find the puck lying in the mesh. He'd landed on it after getting dumped at the blue line, and had ridden the puck all the way for a goal.

After two or three shifts, Hamilton's ringers announced themselves. They emerged like behemoths out of a forest of elves, skating powerfully and with grace, shooting the puck on a dime, and their quick dancers' feet allowed them to make tight turns and stop hard on both sides. One of the fellows – an Asian player who wore a red helmet and skated powerfully – was strong at both ends of the ice, and until I lined up against him for a faceoff, I couldn't tell whether he was a forward or defenceman. I nicknamed him the Red Chevron because checking him was like checking a flying anchor. The two other players wore sparkling earrings and had dyed hair – one was blond, the other had gold streaks in his brown locks – and they were easily the class of their team. Every time they got the puck, they accelerated to top speed in seconds flat, their chins pointed forward and arms fully extended. I called the blond one Chad and the dark-haired one Brad, because they were much younger and more likely to surf than me.

It was Brad – the taller of the superstars, with shoulders the breadth of a Great Lake's shoreline – who proved that he was to be feared beyond others after he nearly scored on a rush from his blue line. Unfortunately, I had a front-row view of this trans-gression. While advancing the puck, he observed our generally wonky defensive positioning and decided that my positioning was wonkier than the rest. After slicing through the middle of the ice and gaining the zone, he immediately came at me. Barrelling forward, he drew me wide before cutting in with as little effort as it takes to push back a turnstile. I tried to measure his velocity, but ended up spinning hopelessly and was left sniffing the ice. I'm sure it amused the rink's young fans, but I felt mildly sick as I lay flat on the ice. I could see the Winterbird hop out to meet this bladed Goliath, who zoomed in on goal and tried putting the puck into the top of the net. But he couldn't pull the trigger, at least not this time. The puck kissed Mark's arm and flew out of play.

We changed lines. The departing Morningstars looked dazed and worried while our new skaters nodded to each other with mock confidence. Surprisingly, the new line – Cheech, Andy Ford, and Steve Stanley – won the puck and managed to push it back toward the Unyon end of the ice. This was owing, in large part, to the way Cheech occasionally controlled the game, working the puck in a manner that reflected his namesake. Small and dynamic – nearly half the size of his camera – one of his favourite gambits was to carry the disc along the blue line, cleverly stickhandling between the defending forwards until he was almost perpendicular to the goal. It was always an impressive show of puck control – in a deep, bong-haul kind of way – and while this time it neither got us any closer to the Detergent Box nor nearer to Mark, at least we possessed the puck, that is until the Red Chevron decided he'd seen enough and stripped Cheech of the Joe Louis.

The Chevron fired the puck from the red line into Mark's pads before heading off the ice. Andy won another draw, and for a while, I thought that our defence – Dutch, Tom Goodwin, the Chizzler, Craig Barnes, and I – were doing a pretty good job of offering the Unyon a veneer of resistance. But no sooner had I breathed a sigh of relief at the thought of not being totally humiliated in front of the biggest crowd ever to amass at our home rink when the scoreboard got busy, counting two goals for Hamilton, and none for us. Chad struck first, then the Red Chevron, with some help from Brad, doubled the score:

2-0 Unyon.

First, Brad, he with the dark, gold-flecked hair, streaked down left wing and blasted a shot, using Chad – the blond-maned ace –

as a decoy, in which yours truly played the role of the suckered duck. When Brad wound up to shoot, Tom Goodwin, skating on right defence to my left, moved to block the puck, but the rubber barged through his legs like an outlaw through saloon doors, eating enough of a deflection to find the far corner of the net. The puck punched an emphatic bulge in the twine. Chad skated over and pulled Brad into his arms before skating with him to the bench, where the rest of the Unyons stood and cheered. Not a minute later – exactly the time it had taken for Tom and I to rest, then return for our next shift – the Red Chevron came down the same side, handled the puck around the net, spun into the slot, and promptly fired at Mark, who was screened by a blob of Morningstar red.

I hadn't felt particularly responsible for Brad's goal, but my contribution to the Red Chevron's more than made up for my lack of creative misfortune on the first goal. I was caught making a terrible pinch, a play that has forever been the albatross of my rec league career.

Moments before the Red Chevron's rush, the puck had bounced in my direction at the left point. I raced in and collected it, sensing that Cheech, the stoned waterbug, and Steve, who skated with the combined passion of the 1989 Flames, would be in position for support were I to lose control of the puck. Had the 'Stars been leading by seventeen goals, I probably wouldn't have risked pinching, but having just been scored on, my feet and heart went out for a quick coffee, kicked around a few ideas, and decided, over a zesty orange cruller, to maintain pressure in the Unyon zone, forgetting, for a few fatal seconds, that games are won and lost over sixty minutes, not twenty seconds.

Pinching is a rare sensation for defencemen in that it provides an opportunity for the rearguard to travel to where they hardly ever go: deep in the offensive zone. It's like discovering in your own home a whole other room with big windows and fresh air and the sunshine of hope. It's a dizzying sensation for any defenceman to see the goalie just a few feet to your right or left, especially when, for most of the game, the net appears as far away as a lobster trap bobbing on the ocean. Different players live in the corners too – namely, the other team's defencemen – and if there's a reason why I've concentrated on the Unyons' forwards in this book rather than their rearguards, it's because I spent a lot more time, and in greater proximity, trying to contain and occasionally facewash centremen and wingers than with those who defend the other end of the ice.

As I wheeled into the corner, I imagined the other team shuddering, "My God, has that defenceman lost his mind? He's crazy enough to do anything, boys!" I figured that the presence of a big unwieldy d-man who might not be responsible for his actions would unglue the Unyon back staff. I cut hastily toward the net and was immediately poke-checked by one of their defenceman. My Turnbullian wander meant that I'd abandoned my blue-line post, and as the player rang the puck around the boards, I saw that nobody was covering the point. Well, not nobody. The Red Chevron was in perfect position to accept the pass.

My glorious burst of offensive freedom turned into a cold glide down a strange alleyway. Looking up the ice, I saw Tom Goodwin and his sideburns – they were apparent from almost anywhere on the rink – spin into a backwards skating crouch, having been left to thwart the Red Chevron and his streaking teammates on his lonesome. Scrambling to get back into the play, I fancied taking a shortcut in front of the Unyon net, pausing to look the Detergent Box in the eye and telling him in a raspy Ninja whisper that he was powerless against the aura of the Morningstar. But before I could, one of the Unyon defenceman — a nerdish, usually agreeable fellow in glasses named Tim, who runs Sonic Unyon records — hooked my arm with the crook of his stickblade. So instead of taunting the Detergent Box and getting a good look at the man behind the wirework, I had no choice but to slash the offending indie music executive in kind, adding a few seconds to my return home.

Once I got back, I did my best to chase, contain, box in, take outside, nip, and hack the talented Chevron, but I ended up following him around the zone until, alas, I was perfectly positioned between the puck and the net, at which point he put the shot through me. The disc rose over the shoulders of the rest of the 'Stars, who'd amassed in front of the net, and Mark could only swipe at it as if batting away a mosquito.

You didn't have to be Harry Neale to see we were screwed.

8 | HEY, NEDVED!

These sudden offensive strikes by the Unyon's ringers had a sobering affect on our team morale. Instead of our usual mid-play penis jokes and pirate yarls, the Morningstars suddenly fell silent. Our spirits hung lower than Georges Vezina's GAA. My teammates' eyes showed one part fear, another part worry, another part defeat, so it wasn't a minute too soon that I allowed myself to get punched in the head.

Being the victim of a clubbing isn't the kind of heroic sporting moment cited by generation upon generation of hockey experts, but it was the best I could do at the time. It wasn't as if the team had called a timeout, rallied around our phantom coach, and demanded that we overcome adversity in the name of the fair Morningstar, but, privately, we knew what we had to do.

Johnny, Dutch, and I – to name three – understood that it was time to start winning a few battles. As we were being so badly

MORNINGSTARS

PAUL STEENHUISEN

The Morningstar known as Dutch.

outplayed, we decided to attack the Unyon with words and the occasional shoulder-high jab. We hoped that this combination of elbows and nouns would help us somehow blunt the Unyon's scoring fury until we could find our touch around the net, or at least figure out where in the frig the net was.

Despite having spent a large part of his life hunched over a piano, Dutch is a master of the hockey taunt. In the 2001 Downtown Men's Hockey League playoffs, he exclusively spoke Latin. I once heard him tell an opposing player before a faceoff, "Listen, man, I'm really sorry for what I'm about to do to you." To small players, he jibed, "I'd kick your ass, but sorry, I can't punch that low." He told Sam Roberts, "I feel this game is passing you by," and he once informed an offending forward, "Listen, I'd get Johnny to fight you, but right now he's beating the shit out of a guy on our own bench." Whenever I sought verbal advice from Dutch, he told me that guys who tuck their sweaters into their pants "hate all of that gay stuff," and that comparing players to Czech skaters like "Nedved and Reichel" can be pretty effective too.

Johnny was big on calling people "corncob" and "Jesus" and pointing the portly and ill-behaved in the direction of the snack bar, tactics he must have learned on the frozen ponds of Saskatoon, his hometown. A few months after the tourney, I was asked to define the term *hoser* for a group of Russians, and Johnny leapt to mind. This isn't to say that the hoser quotient of my fellow teammates didn't make it a touch choice. Andy Ford, for instance, once invested his life savings in the purchase of a Thunder Car brandished with Doug Gilmour's sweater number, which he drove competitively every summer weekend at Peterborough Speedway. (Hoser.) As a boy, Tom Goodwin once fell asleep to the sound of his grandpa's hockey buddy – Doug Harvey – doing the dishes in his parents' kitchen. (Hoser.) T, in his capacity as music publicist, had to tell Ron MacLean and Don Cherry that Shania Twain would not appear on *Coach's Corner*, moments before the duo went on air and described him as "some guy in a beaver hat." (Hoser infamy.) Dutch boasted that, before league games in Paris, France, he'd try to throw opposing goalies off their game by speaking to them in Canadian English (total hoser move), and Howie once confessed that he'd chosen sweater number twenty-two in honour of Wiarton Willie (hoser critter), who is the most famous rodent to come from Brad's hometown. (Very hoser-ish, if a little gay.) I admit to screening the final minute-fifty of Game 8 of the 1972 Canada-Russia Series at a nightclub in Omsk, Siberia, oblivious that I was surrounded by sad and teary-eyed fans, watching their fabled team lose while yours truly cheered Cournoyer, Espo, and Henderson for the five millionth time. (Hoser abroad.)

Johnny once told me a story about growing up in Saskatoon that convinced me that he was King Hoser among the Morningstars. As a bored prairie teenager living in a make-your-own-fun kind of town, Johnny and his friends used to wreck shopping carts. "First, we'd get somebody's car," he recalled. "The driver would pull up next to a shopping cart and whoever was sitting on the passenger side would reach through the window and grab a cart and hold on. The driver would then accelerate to about forty to forty-five miles an hour. The passenger would hold the cart until the driver swerved or hit the brakes, at which point he'd let go of the speeding cart. We smashed them into the sides of shopping malls, Dumpsters, telephone poles, whatever. We thought it was hilarious. The cart would be jumping and shaking like the Apollo on re-entry. We'd find one on the side of the road and send it whizzing into whatever target we could find. Sparks would fly as it took off. If it hit the curb straight on, it would sometimes go straight up and somersault into the air. It was absolutely beautiful."

Johnny plays hockey as if every other player were a shopping cart. He is a relentless moving force. Unlike Dutch or I, he grates on the opposition because he is an offensive dynamo, as well as being quick-witted and mildly psychotic. He is Goony Good instead of Goony Bad. Over the years, I've found that it's a lot easier dealing with a goon who couldn't hit a Great Lake with a gob of gum, rather than with someone who gets in your face before he gets into your net. The Goony Bads are always a little pathetic, while you secretly wish that the Goony Goods played for your team, even after they've given you a facewash, scored twice, and called your mummy a very bad name. Johnny skates at the opposition like an anvil – barging into the goalie's crease, throwing his shoulder at a defenceman, digging his stickblade under a lazy forward's arm to steal the puck. After a few seasons of this, he became the most despised Morningstar, a mantle I was more than willing to pass on.

Whenever they were on the ice, Johnny and Dutch derided every Unyon equally, but the magnet of their attention – and mine – was Walter, a marauding former 'Star. Besides Brad, Chad, and the Chev (and potentially, the Detergent Box), there were two other Unyons that mattered: a huge, pasta-fed, goateed winger who was as big as two Hakan Loobs pressed together, whom I nicknamed Ponytail (for he also had one of those), and Walter. We figured that getting Walter to lose his temper was as good a place as any to start our comeback. Walter had been ousted from the 'Stars after spitting at an opponent, but had caught on with another team – and another after that – with whom he'd committed similar offences. At first, I was surprised to see Walter skate with the Unyon until I realized that he'd been recruited by team organizers for the very purpose of getting us off our game, without their realizing that it *was* our game. With a dumptruck's haunch, huge arms, bulbous helmet, and thick-lensed sporting glasses, Walter was an imposing figure on the ice. I both relished and feared playing against him.

Whenever we shared the ice, Dutch, Johnny, and I gave Walter a tickle: pricking the back of his leg, shouldering him while passing by, lightly swatting his head from behind. Sadly, this brought no reaction. If Walter skated by our bench, Dutch and I would scream epithets about the size of his caboose or slowness of his stride, but there was no reaction. Once, he stood directly on the blue line, and — feeling no less of a lout myself — I reminded him about the time he'd spat blood and how he'd been kicked off two teams and why no other team — except the loathsome exception — wanted to play hockey with him. I was still shouting as he corralled the puck and sent it across to Chad, who rung a shot off the crossbar, very nearly killing our E! Cup experience there and then. Later, while lining up on their blue line for a faceoff, I sugared my venom, patting Walter on the top of the helmet while he was sitting down and saying, "Hey, I didn't mean what I said back there."

"Don't touch me on the bench," he replied, staring straight ahead.

Walter never cracked, but we gained in other areas. Brad and Chad, riding high on their achievements, saw what we were trying to do and, feeling the mantle of leadership, tried to take matters into their own hands. Part of the art of confrontation is getting your opponent to rise to the bait, and while you risk motivating the player to new heights through anger and retribution, I took Brad and Chad to be players who liked the idea of chivalry, but weren't really prepared for what they'd have to go through. Because they were ringers — and because the Unyon hadn't had the personal history or years playing together that the 'Stars had — their leadership, I sensed, was largely cosmetic.

Brad and I found ourselves battling for the puck in the corner. I'll never be applauded for my sidewinding rushing patterns or perfect wristshot or skating dexterity, but I'm indefatigable when it comes to protecting and winning a puck in the defensive corner. I'm able to work my legs and position my body and hack and scrape and dig with my stick so that the puck either dies or leaves the zone safely. When Brad came at me after I'd reeled in the puck to Mark's left, he saw it as an opportunity both to win the puck for his team and to teach the mouthy defenceman a lesson.

I enjoyed the confrontation. I treasured it. Brad and I pushed, fought, and shouldered each other. I rammed my breastbone into his chin as he brought his elbow to my ear. I dug my stick against the back of his leg and he cracked his shaft over my forearm. I rolled him face-first into the boards, but he spun in my arms, twisting and wrenching them to my sides. I pushed my helmet into his clavicle and he tried forcing my head to his waist while I watched the puck hop and bobble between our skates. As he pushed down on my neck, I made one last surge, throwing his shoulders against the glass. Looking at him nose to nose, I smiled. Unable to comprehend such happiness, he hardened his brow, reared back with his fist, and slugged me on the button. My head stopped boinging long enough to see the Bradster float to the penalty box.

BUGSY WATSON: Gordie Howe was the dirtiest player I've ever seen. Huge and great too, but dirty. Once, in practice, I bumped into him, and he went ass over tea kettle into the corner. I thought, Holy shit, am I in trouble, so I went over and apologized. But Gordie, with his face all cut up and bleeding, said to me, "Listen, don't you dare be sorry. I'm so pissed off at the guys on this goddamned team who leave me alone all the time. The reason you got me is because I let my guard down, and I did that because I don't have anything to worry about here in practice." I figured that he was going to kill me, but, essentially, he was asking for more.

MIKE PELYK: Hockey is a tough game and no one was tougher than Gordie Howe. He once gave me a two-hander across the face. He didn't even get a penalty for it. He fractured my jaw, took five of my teeth, and I almost lost my lip. I was cut from one side of my face to the other and there was blood everywhere. A big chunk was hanging off where the lip was supposed to be, like an Ubangi warrior. I was on the operating table for three hours and I wore a football helmet for about a month after. It wasn't even me he was trying to get, it was Rick Ley, who'd knocked him down from behind. I just happened to be standing there.

TIM ECCLESTONE: I came from Scotty Bowman's militaristic style in St. Louis to Detroit, where they had a big television in the middle of the dressing room. Needless to say, there was never a TV in Scotty's room. Mickey Redmond and I were amazed at how different a Gordie Howe room was. One time, the buzzer went to signal the start of the game. Mickey and I were shouting, "C'mon guys! Let's go get 'em!" but Gordie and Alex Delvecchio, who were watching golf, told us, "Hold on, boys. Let's see if this guy makes this putt." After the game, I'd be cut over one eye and Mickey would be all bruised and worn out, and I'd look over at

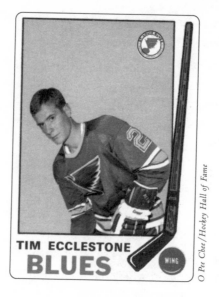

TIM ECCLESTONE
BLUES   WING

O Pee Chee / Hockey Hall of Fame

Gordie and Alex and there'd be only a few beads of sweat on them. We'd have won the game, and they'd have scored two goals and got a couple of assists. They were just so much better than anybody else.

DEAN PRENTICE: I got hit in the corner by Gordie with his elbows. He said, "Rookie, get out of here or you'll lose your teeth." But I'd already had my teeth knocked out, so I had no problem with him. Gordie was so strong. He'd hold you off with one arm. The Rocket had the legs and upper body, but so did Gordie. On the ice, he was so aggressive, but off the ice, he was just the sweetest man, soft-spoken and gentle. He never didn't sign an autograph. All he wanted was a kid to be polite.

GARRY UNGER: When I first got to Detroit with Gordie Howe, I told myself that I didn't want this game to make me not normal. I wanted to be able to sit down with a bunch of people and not have them think I was above them just because I was blessed with talent to put me in the limelight. I purposefully worked in the off-season at the lumber yard to keep myself level. Gordie was like that, 100 per cent. I never saw him turn down an autograph. There are people whom you really want to meet that end up being jerks when you meet them. But not Gordie. When I first met him, I had an idea of where he was on the pedestal, but he was above that. People were always thrilled to meet him, but what they took away was what a genuinely beautiful guy he was.

RON MURPHY: We were in Madison Square one night when Bobby Crystal, who played for the Rangers, got trapped in the corner and was getting the hell beaten out of him. There was a whole mob around there, so I went in to help out. Apparently, I took on Geoffrion in the melee, but I don't remember doing it. After the dust settled and everyone had been cleared away, I was standing at centre ice thinking about god knows what when Boom Boom came up and hit me with a two-hander across the head. He caught me with the heel of the stick in the upper part of my jawbone. I passed out, and when I woke up, the fans were howling. I went after Geoffrion, but he was already skating off the ice.

MIKE PELYK: I once slid in front of a Dennis Hull slapshot. I had it timed perfectly until he decided to do a little two-step, at which point the puck headed straight for my head. It was a glancing blow and the puck deflected fifty rows into the stands. I got up, and my head was sore, but not too sore. When I got to the bench, I said to Joe Sgro, our trainer, "Geez, it's a good thing that puck didn't ding me dead-on," and he said, "Mike, you've got about a four-inch divot out of your head." I couldn't even feel it because my head was so numb.

HARRY HOWELL: Once, I ripped up my knee on the ice. I didn't know the extent of the damage, but I knew that it was bad. When I came off the ice, I told the trainer that it wasn't right. He told me I'd be fine, then he sat me in the shower with my leg extended, and set the shower to its coldest possible temperature. He was convinced that the cold water would be enough to repair the ligaments, which had been shredded.

RON MURPHY: In my day, teams hired veterinarians to work on you. One time, a blade came down underneath the tongue of my skate and tore out a hunk of skin and opened up a wound about the size of a silver dollar. I went down to the dressing room in Chicago to see the doctor. He was related to our owners, the Wirtzes, which was never a good sign. He hunted around for about a half an hour trying to find material to stitch me up. The next day, I went for dinner at Mikita's house and my foot started hammering. Bobby Hull was there, and he said, "C'mon, Murph, we're going to the hospital." It turned out that I had a staph infection. The doctor at the rink had grabbed whatever was lying around and thrown it on the wound before stitching it closed.

JOHN BROPHY: One night in Johnstown, Larry Regan butt-ended me in the side of the face. There was no doctor around, and so nobody ended up looking at it. I spent the whole night lying on my face in the hotel room throwing up and with my head hurting like murder. I didn't know it at the time, but it was a major, major concussion.

MIKE LAUGHTON: Montreal was the only team in pro hockey that had a medical staff. When I played for the New York Golden Blades in the WHA, I once went all the way across New York to go to the doctor, only to find that he'd prepared the brace for the wrong knee. When I complained, he brought me into a room and showed me all his certificates, but it didn't make up for the fact that he'd got the wrong knee.

BOB LORIMER: In the minors, one of our guys got cut above the eye. They stitched him up and he finished the game. Later that night, he went to bed but he couldn't close his eye: they'd sewn his eyelid open.

JOHN HALLIGAN: Frank Paice was the Rangers' trainer for thirty-one years. No one in the team's seventy-eight-year history worked more years at the same job. In fact, he's the only trainer in NHL history to have his own hockey card [TOPPS, 1962–63]. One of Frank's favourite ploys was to downplay injuries. "Tape an Aspirin to it," he'd tell a player, and more often than not, the guy would be out there for the next shift. He was once asked by a reporter how he decided whether to use ice or heat to treat an injury, Frank replied in all honesty, "I try one, if that doesn't work, I try the other."

MARK NAPIER: My worst injury happened when I was playing for Montreal in Minnesota. I went to hit Dan Mandridge of the North Stars behind the net. As I hit him, his skate came up and went between my shinpad and skate on the left side of the leg, just above the ankle. Steve Shutt was in front of the net yelling for the pass, but when I went to push off, there was nothing. It felt like my skateblade had broken. I made my way over to the bench and told the trainer that I'd broken my skate, but when he went to look at the blade, he saw blood pouring out of my boot. He took me into the doctors' office and he [the doctor] started fishing around in my foot – it was some of the worst pain I've ever experienced – to see if I'd severed the tendon that runs up the side of your leg. It was three-quarters severed, an inch-deep gash. They stitched up the inside and outside – thirty stitches in total – and I was out of the lineup for a while.

SAM BETTIO: I was pitchforked in the mouth with a stick during a game in Providence, Rhode Island. My opponent knocked seven teeth off the top, six on the bottom, and one on the other side of my mouth. Two teeth were still connected to a piece of my jawbone. It was a complete disaster: 125 stitches in all. I was so swollen that I was a solid balloon from my nose to my ear. You couldn't look at me, and on the flight home they put me at the back of the plane. When my landlady saw me a few days later, she threw up.

FRED STANFIELD: I played with a fractured ankle for the entire 1974 series. I froze it every game by plunging it in a pail of ice water. Back then, if you had a pulled groin, they'd wrap it tight. You couldn't play as well, but they knew you'd heal. Other times, you'd get cut for twenty stitches and be right back in the game. I took twenty in the chin from a slapshot when I was with Buffalo. My whole jersey was covered in blood. I was number 17, but they didn't have another jersey, so I had to wear number 19.

DEAN PRENTICE: We wore no protection back when I was playing. I'd used caps in my shoulder pads that were sewn onto my suspenders, nothing else. Our skates were made of kangaroo leather; I once took twenty-two stitches in my foot after Louie Fontinato's skate went through mine. Another time, I fell over Fleming Mackell and the ulna bone popped out of my wrist and came down into my hand. The doctor gave me a Band-Aid and an Aspirin. I also got hit with the puck in junior; it broke my nose and a bunch of teeth. Alfie Pike, our coach, ran out onto the ice and said, "I'll fix that!" He grabbed my nose and straightened it out, on the ice.

LARRY PLAYFAIR: It felt good to play hurt. Being injured gave you more of a reason not to mess up, because you didn't want to use it as an excuse. And because I was a marginal player, I had to keep playing through the injuries. I had to worry about who might step in and play in my place.

TIM ECCLESTONE: The scariest thing I ever saw on the ice happened during an exhibition game in Ottawa when St. Louis took on the Bruins. Wayne Maki was in his first training camp with the Blues. Back in those days, Teddy Green was pretty tough in front of the net, and you had to watch yourself because he'd spear you or do anything to get the advantage. Maki was aware of this, so when he found himself staring Teddy down in the crease, he took the offence, knowing that he was going to get speared, and brought his stick right on top of Green's head and split him open. The benches cleared, an ambulance was driven in. They got Teddy to hospital and they actually gave him the last rites. As we know, Teddy got out alive, but we had to go back into Boston to play later in the year. Scotty [Bowman] didn't dress him the first time – Maki had three bodyguards sitting with him in the stands – but, the second time, when Scotty read out the lines, most of the forwards were thinking, Whatever you do, don't put me with Maki. We played the game and that was that, but there were some harrowing moments. I guess the irony is that Maki died a young man, of a brain aneurysm, no less.

DEAN PRENTICE: Once when I was killing a penalty, I got tripped on a breakaway by Stan Mikita. I went flying past the net into the boards. I hit my back and head. While I was lying there, Bobby Hull came up and said, "You're not going to let another one of these dummies take your penalty shot, are you?" I told him, "No way." I got up, deked the goalie the opposite way, and scored. I sat back on the bench and cooled off, but I couldn't move. They got a stretcher and took me out. I'd broken my back and spent half a year in a body cast, right over my buttocks.

GARRY UNGER: When I was eleven years old and spotting someone on a box-horse, I was kicked in the face. It broke my nose, but I had a game that night. My dad said, "Well, I guess you can't play the game," but I told him, "Does my nose affect my skating?" That was my attitude all along. Besides, I have a sister who is five years younger than me who had polio. Because of her, I saw what it meant to love life even though you're confined to a wheelchair. I give her a lot of credit for my iron-man streak [662 consecutive games] because it was hard feeling sorry for myself about getting a whack on the shoulder or knee when I knew that she could never get out of her chair. It was a great motivating factor. I also had a high pain tolerance. I never took any drugs, never got frozen, and if the doctor said I could play, I played. There were times when I couldn't walk, but I could skate. I'd take my shift, they'd put the heat pack on me, then I'd go out again.

The reason the streak was important to me was because of my mother and sister. I didn't really care about it; I just wanted to play every game, as any player would. When I left St. Louis for Atlanta, the streak continued, but there was some uneasiness on the team, and our coach, Al MacNeil, was forced to deal with a lot of talented players fighting for time on the power play, penalty kill, and so on. The previous year, I'd been assigned as Team Canada's checking centre against the Russians and the big Czech forwards, so I went to Al and suggested that he solve the problem by putting me on the checking line. But I think he took what I said the wrong way, as if I'd do anything to keep my consecutive games streak alive.

Right around that time, we had a road trip out west and I separated my shoulder during a scuffle in the corner in Winnipeg.

Our doctor looked at my shoulder and, because our farm team was in Birmingham, Alabama, and couldn't get anybody up for the next game in Edmonton, they just taped it and I played. We weren't playing again until Saturday night in Toronto, then we were getting a week off. I thought that if I could get through the Toronto game, I'd be okay. I knew about applying heat and cold and moving the blood around because of what I'd learned from Tommy Woodcock, our trainer.

By Saturday, I was feeling a lot better, and in the afternoon in Toronto, I worked out at the Y instead of lying down before the game; again, Al seemed to take it the wrong way. We lost the game and Al got angrier. During our week off, he told me that I had to practise, that I couldn't just get treatment for the shoulder. So I practised. Next, we had a home-and-home series versus St. Louis, of all teams. One day, Al wanted me to stay late after practice and show him that I could take a slapshot, which I did. Then he told me to go see the doctor, who gave me the green light. I played and we lost again, in Atlanta. Al's mood became more and more severe. We went to St. Louis for the back end of the home-and-home, and I felt as if I'd finally battled through the injury. But by the end of the first period, my skates hadn't touched the ice. The second period was the same. Cliff Fletcher came up to me and said, "Hey, I thought your arm was better." I said, "Yup. I'm fine." With about five minutes left in the game, the players started realizing that my streak was in jeopardy, so they began to offer me shifts. I told them, "All he's going to do is bench me the next game. We've got enough turmoil going on now, let's just play." With thirty seconds left to go – we were winning 7-2 – the puck came flying to where I was sitting. I stood up so that I wouldn't get hit, but Al thought I was getting ready to jump on to the ice. He spent the rest of the game with his hand on my jersey, making sure I didn't go over the boards. The crowd was yelling and screaming, and then it was over. I haven't talked to Al about it since. We've had conversations, but I've never asked him, and he's never brought it up. For the record, I didn't miss another shift the rest of the year.

9 | BURTON AND ME

Hockey is, by nature, a "reactive" game, which is to say that a large part of the game is about luck. The world's nightly sports-desks replay and replay any hiccuping baseball that results in a freakish game-winning run. In football, there's the occasional fingertip folly, and in soccer, the game's spinning fruit deflecting off an oddly shaped cranium can produce something unexpected. But in hockey, more accidents result in goals than in any other sport. How many times have we seen a point shot, for instance, winged into the net by a skate, shinpad, or shaft of a stick? How many pucks have caromed off the inside of a goalie's pad, the back of a defenceman's leg, or Stu Grimson's face? Maple Leafs fans, in particular, will remember the time that Mike Foligno scored a late-season goal with his butkus. The puck behaves like a pinball, wildly angling off whatever it last struck. While today's skaters are much better puck jockeys than in the days of yore, every elite scorer is forced to admit a handful of times each year: "Geez, the puck just bounced my way."

This element of happenstance has made the game easier for scrubs like me in that it gives us both an excuse — "Man, the puck took a crazy bounce!" — and a good-natured way of accepting a compliment — "Hey, I just threw it up the boards and good things happened." Pure luck intervened more than a few times in our game versus the Unyon, and it was near the end of the first period that the puck's whimsical path robbed the opposition of a chance to pad their lead, which had swollen to 3-0 after they scored while I was changing pens.

The crazy bounces started to happen after the Unyon returned to full strength following our impotent power play. After the penalty lapsed, I found myself being chased in our end by one of the Unyon forwards (it had become sickeningly apparent that many of their average players were now performing above their heads after witnessing the glory of Brad and Chad) and, in an attempt to end the chase, I threw the puck up the boards. You've probably heard the term, "The boards are your friend," a phrase concocted, no doubt, by someone who's never been checked face-first from behind into the scratchy plywood. The disc whipped high around the rink, where, I figured, Howie or Johnny would be waiting at the blue line. Instead, as I admired the dot's progress through the air like a bird watcher tracking the flight of the red-necked grebe, it was Ponytail whom the plywood rewarded. I'd already established an on-ice relationship with Ponytail, and when we weren't trying to get each other to sniff our gloves, we were conscious of where each other was on the ice. His eyes widened upon seeing the puck, and fearful that he might

knock it down and fire a shot on net, I took off toward him. But the puck dipped at the last moment and bounced off his knee, clicked against another player's skate, hopped past a few sticks, and jitterbugged safely over the blue line.

It was at this point that Al picked up the puck. There are three things one notices when Al becomes part of the play: his nose, his hair, and his feet. Al's nose is as long and crooked as a baroque door handle, his hair is a lawless, tangled frightwig, and his skating style is a slash-footed technique that's more like running than skating, as if he'd rather kick the puck than push it. This loose, ragged style, however, plays to the forces of fate and accident, and while it has resulted in two cracked collarbones after he went flying into the end boards, I think of Al as the Morningstars' secret weapon. Firing him into the zone is like attacking with an alien sporting missile, something no opposing player has ever seen.

Al gathered the puck, sized up the players standing in his path, bit his lip in a moment of deep concentration, then raced into the fray. Playing to the game's bounces, the puck never stayed too long on Al's stick. It jumped and rolled while his combatants tried clubbing it like men with shovels after a rattlesnake. Gaining, then regaining control of the puck, he moved it from stick to skate to stick until he found himself a few feet from the Detergent Box, poised for a shot. From the bench, we rose to take in what appeared to be a glorious opportunity to get the 'Stars back into the game. But one last lunge from the Red Chevron — who apparently had "tireless backchecking" on his résumé — tied up Al's wrists, handcuffing him so that the Unyon netkeep could sprawl easily over the puck. As the linesman collected the puck out of the Detergent Box's catching basket and tamped it in his palm while the next set of forwards gathered, we drew a small morsel of confidence from Al's bust over the Unyon's blue line. It wasn't much, but it was something.

Whenever I'm playing hockey, my mind absorbs the scene in a flurry of small moments. Naturally, I remember the sky-tickling highs and sagging lows of a season, but often the game comes as a series of single images or moments lined up like flash cards to create the overall impression of what a game was like, and how I felt playing it.

Many of these images come from the crowd, of faces flickering behind the glass. Whenever we set up for a draw, I looked to the stands for a reassuring nod or sympathetic eye, even at the risk of coming across Cheech's eager cameraman, or a rival player for whom watching the 'Stars lose would be a total delight. I noticed three silver and blue tom-toms being carried through the concourse, a row of young girls in long scarves eating ketchup chips, one baby with what appeared to be a yellow mohawk, and three Dan Clowes characters glaring at the ice. The crowd was relatively young – relative to my age, that is – and almost everyone had a pierced tongue or a myriad of tattoos. These decorations reflected a trend that I first noticed in hockey dressing rooms *circa* 2004: men (other than the old-timey Morningstars) who took off their shirts to reveal Japanese dragons and tigers, Celtic crosses, the face of Rob Zombie, or PEARL JAM ROOLS inked across their chests. It was an odd blurring of club culture and rink life, and while I wondered what Tiger Williams would have thought (he once told T before sharpening his skates at a charity game: "Want me to sharpen that earring for you too, faggot?"), it was simply another way that Tom Goodwin and the E! Cup folks were busting down the walls of hockey traditionalism. They were making it safe for kids to like P.J. Harvey and P.J. Stock, the old 97s and the Ottawa '67s.

One image that kept popping up again and again from the crowd was the face of Burton Cummings. You couldn't miss Burton, or rather his silk-screened facsimile. There's something about that *Love Boat* moustache and those chipmunk eyes that are completely his own, and while I wasn't exactly reassured to find him staring back at me from the stands, I wasn't threatened either. At both McCormick and DeLaSalle, Burton's gaze followed fans and players like a heavy cologne, his moonish image lording over the ice on four-foot-diameter discs taped around the

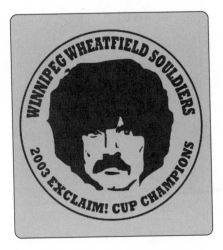

rink by the Winnipeg Wheatfield Souldiers, who'd also slapped Burton's mug on their team jackets, shirts, buttons, pucks, postcards, and the front of their jerseys. He was their club's totem, and to skate against sixteen Burtons — as the tier two teams had — was to be challenged by the spiritual icon of piano-driven, fuzzywuzzylovincupexplosion CanRock, a daunting task for even the hardiest, prairie-loathing squad.

The Souldiers love of their hometown was devout to the point that, each year, they held a pre-tournament ceremony honouring the career of Dale Hawerchuk. One of the players wore the jersey number of Morris Lukowich, while another had been Jimmy Mann's paper boy as a youth. The Souldiers' worship of Winnipeg and all things Burton was such that, even though their musical hero had, for many, become a kind of William Shatner of the keyboard, there was no irony in their carrying his image on their chests and backs. They did, however, have to occasionally explain that it wasn't Ron Jeremy on their sweaters.

I've always played the middle when it comes to assessing the work of the Guess Who's frontman, but I partly blame the moustache for this mixed opinion. I first encountered Burton while on tour with the Rheos in the early 1990s. We were killing time in the Saskatoon airport's cafeteria, waiting for our flight, when he and his road manager walked in and sat down at a booth at the opposite end of the room. The manager – young and ponytailed – drew a PowerBook from his briefcase and started typing. Burton yawned and reclined against the booth, all quick-darting eyes, thick eyebrows, and broad, shaggy moustache. From a distance, he appeared to have the smug, self-satisfied look of a man daring the world to call him a dickwad.

At first, we were thrilled to be in the same room as a bona fide CanRock Hall of Famer, but it wasn't long before the moustache got the best of us and the lovincupexplosion jokes started. As I've mentioned before, there's a natural rivalry between musicians – especially in a place with as few bands as Canada – so we fought back the real fear and nervousness of being in his presence by trying to take him down a notch. We giggled over the memory of being at one studio, where the engineers had stapled all of Burton's solo LPs on a wall, including his notorious album inserts, one of which featured Burton running through an English garden astride a young woman with a paper bag on her head.

When our flight was announced we crossed the floor, eyes downcast, guitars slung over our shoulders, and slipped behind Burton, leaving the cafeteria and forgoing a brush with the 'stache. I walked beside my bandmate, Martin, who sighed, "Ahhhh, fame."

"Whaddya mean, 'Ahhhh, fame?'" I demanded.

"Well, the poor guy's probably sitting there thinking, Man, that band walked right past me and didn't even say hello," he said, shaking his head.

It was the first time I'd thought of the Burton behind his moustache. Instead of imagining him as a pompous, self-absorbed star, I saw him as flawed, sad, vulnerable. And now he was sitting with his road manager having been ignored by a young (well, younger) band who refused to give him his due as the first Canadian musician to reach number one on the *Billboard* charts, among countless other laurels.

"We're going back," I told Martin, turning both of us around.

We walked over to his table, and I said, "Hey, Burton, we just wanted to introduce ourselves. We're Dave and Martin from the Rheostatics."

"The Rheostatics!" he exclaimed, when the most we'd expected was that he'd nod his head, throw out his hand, and give us that 30 per cent "How ya doin', man" rock-star treatment. Instead, the Manitoban's eyes widened as he sunk deeper in his chair.

"Man, I was just telling MacLean and MacLean the other day about *Whale Music* [our third LP]. I was telling him — and I'll tell you guys now: that's one of the greatest albums ever made. It's right up there with *Sgt. Pepper*," he enthused, jabbing a finger into the air.

We were left wordless, not knowing what to say. It was one of the most gratifying moments of my life, the kind of event where you just want to stand still so that nothing changes.

"Are you guys touring?" he asked, breaking the silence.

I mumbled that we were.

"Me, I just got back from opening a casino in Prince Albert," he said, to which we continued nodding. "Not the greatest gig in the world, but hey, it's working for me!" he told us, winking and firing out that forefinger again.

DAN DIAMOND: For a while, Winnipeg was a hockey freeport. It was a place away from the pressures of a major hockey centre, where the game could load up on other values. Because Hockey Canada and Father David Bauer had set up shop there, fans were tuned to how the Russians, Czechs, and Swedes were playing, so when the WHA came, the "World" in World Hockey Association was very meaningful to us Winnipeggers. It was a spoken compact with the fans, that the WHA would bring a world style and all that represented to the hockey fan.

ANDERS HEDBERG: The Vancouver Canucks called me in 1971 — they had just entered the league — and asked if I'd be interested in playing in the NHL. The thought had never even crossed my mind, but my answer was firm: I still had to finish school. Truthfully, I really wasn't that interested. Being the first Swede in the NHL was probably something better suited to an older player, anyway. But, staying at the university indirectly led me to the Winnipeg Jets because one of the professors had done an exchange between Canada and Sweden. His name was Jerry Wilson, the father of Carey Wilson, who went on to play in the NHL. We'd done research projects together at school, and because he was the doctor for the Winnipeg Jets, he introduced me to the thought of Winnipeg, how they wanted to bring Europeans to their game. At the time, I was listed by Toronto, but in the end, because Lars-Erik [Sjoberg] and Ulf [Nilsson] were going to Winnipeg, I decided to go there, even though Toronto was offering me a bit more money.

JOE DALEY: Because of Dr. Jerry Wilson, the Jets travelled and held training camps in Sweden, Finland, and Czechoslovakia. We played in Moscow in the Izvestia Cup, in 1977. We went to Japan and played the Russians in exhibition games before coming home, where we were the only club team to beat Russia's national team. Because we had Swedes and Finns on our team – as well as Bobby Hull – we were recognized and accepted as a hockey force around the world. In Sweden, especially, they were grateful that we brought Anders, Ulf, and Lars-Erik back home, giving local fans a chance to watch first-hand them compete with their adopted club.

ANDERS HEDBERG: There was a bench-clearing brawl in my first game with the Jets. We didn't have these things in Sweden, so Ulf [Nilsson] and I had no idea what was going on. When I looked into the crowd to find my wife, she was sitting next to Ulf's wife, and they were laughing.

EDDIE MIO: The Anders-Ulfie-Bobby Hull line was almost impossible to defend against. Whenever they passed the puck to Hull in the offensive zone, you were dead. Bobby Hull could always unload his big shot – which was hard enough to stop – but it was worse when he'd pass the puck back to either Anders and Ulf. You'd be so far out of position, and they almost never missed.

JOE DALEY: When Hull-Nilsson-Hedberg would hit the blue line swirling, the defencemen had no idea who to take. They put on a show, and were way ahead of their time. At first, a lot of GMs and other teams thought we were going to get mangled because of our European factor, but once we proved we could do it, everyone was lining up.

ANDERS HEDBERG: The line might not have clicked if they'd thrown out a couple of Canadian guys with Bobby Hull. They would have been intimidated by Bobby's personality and history, especially in a new league with top billing. Some of their freedom would have been taken away because of the pressures of playing with this superstar. We knew about Bobby, but not in the same way. For me it was like, "Geez, this guy's a pretty good left winger," and I think Bobby embraced this. I think he liked that we didn't pause to show too much respect; we just played. It also forced him to bust his ass to make it work. Bobby read the game beautifully, and Ulf was simply an Einstein on the ice.

DAN DIAMOND: Everybody remembers Hull-Hedberg-Nilsson, but before that, the Golden Jet played with Christian Bordeleau and Normie Beaudin, and they also had a very fluid style. They'd swoop and swoop and never slam the brakes on. It was a perfect style and the Swedes fit right in.

BARTLEY KIVES: If you want to understand why Winnipeggers have such an unusually strong regional identity – and continue to fetishize the Jets long after their demise – you need to understand the geographic isolation that forces this town to look inward.

The nearest big city is Minneapolis-St. Paul, an eight-hour drive to the south. Calgary, the nearest large Canadian city, is thirteen hours away. Toronto is twenty-six. As a result, Winnipeggers form better loose relationships than residents of other, similar-sized centres, such as Hamilton or Quebec City. That's why everyone knew someone who'd shovelled Bobby Hull's walk or dated Keith Tkachuk or berated Dave "Stone Hands" Neufeld in the middle of the Safeway checkout line.

MIKE SMITH: Glen Sather told anyone who'd listen that he'd based the Oilers' play around the Jets of the 1970s. That statement is interesting by itself, but what makes it ironic is that while fans showed up en masse to watch the Oilers play, only ten thousand fans ever really supported the Jets. We were ahead of the curve in terms of using European stars, but most Winnipeggers didn't want Europeans – they wanted Canadian sluggers, the third-liners. Winnipeg is a royalist city, unhappy with itself because Canada left it behind. It's extremely provincial and insular. The Ukrainian population of Winnipeg is clearly second class. You'd think it would be wide open to Europeans because of its roots, but that wasn't the case.

DAN DIAMOND: At one point in the 1980s, the Jets had eleven Russians on their team, a Russian assistant coach, a Russian pub-licist, and a Sovietophile for a general manager: Mike Smith.

MIKE SMITH: People actually resented the European players in Winnipeg. It should have been different because of the legacy of the national program, but the conservative nature of the city turned on the Jets. They wanted Western Canadian players. In the WHA, there was more of an acceptance, but when the Jets got to the NHL, it was different. The NHL has a history of being discriminatory, and so when the Jets got to the NHL, certain people discriminated. The fans used to yell at the Russian players: "You fuckin' commies, go back to Russia. Get out of our country, you assholes!" I don't have a lot of good memories about Winnipeg and how they treated the Europeans. As soon as I left, they had a pogrom and got rid of the cultural aspect of the game. They brought in Western Canadian players and staff. They could have been at the forefront of the globalization of hockey, but they turned their backs on something they'd started. For that, Winnipeg should be ashamed of itself.

TODD HARTJE: I was a Jet in the 1980s and I have nothing but positive things to say about Mike Smith. He was good to me and he gave me the opportunity to be the first North American to play pro hockey in Russia. He had the confidence that I could go over there and be a positive force, ultimately forging relationships that the Jets could build on later. It was also a grand social experiment. Mike has his master's in Russian history, so he wanted to see how a kid from the farm would take to the Russian sporting climate. It's probably too strong a term, but I think that Mike wanted to have his hand in the great cultural revolution in Russia, perhaps even a little more than developing me as a player for them.

MIKE SMITH: When I was the assistant GM to John Ferguson in Winnipeg, I was one of only two assistant GMs who had the authority to draft whoever we wanted. Most GMs wanted to run the draft, even though it's the assistants who know what's out there, what's available. The other assistant was Marshall Johnston in New Jersey. In my mind, Teemu Selanne was the best player in the draft – it wasn't even close – but because we were drafting tenth, I didn't think we had a chance. But GMs like Tony Esposito of Pittsburgh told his assistant, Ken Schinkel: "If you draft Selanne fourth, I'm going to fire you." They picked Darren Shannon, thank you very much. But that's the way it was in the NHL. Nobody had the guts to draft Europeans, even though many of them were the best players out there. The press didn't understand either. On another occasion, when it came time to make our ninth pick, I wanted to take a Russian goalie, but our head scout said, "Look at these [writers]. They're hanging over the boards yelling at you." He was right, people like Ed Willes were hollering, "Take a Canadian, Smith! Take a North American fercryingoutloud!" I told him, "They're going to yell at me no matter who I take."

CHUCK MOLGAT: Teemu Selanne was the best thing that ever happened to professional hockey in Winnipeg. He used to play street hockey with his neighbours' kids in River Heights, and on a regular basis too. He was a lonely superstar from Finland and these kids were his pals. They'd call on him and ask him to come out and play, and he would. I don't think that could've happened anywhere else but in Winnipeg. In the press box of the arena, there was a big roast beef spread before each game that was supposed to cost $20 or something, but they never sent us a bill. Still, as great as that experience was, it just made it that much harder to take when the team finally up and left for good.

BARTLEY KIVES: As a kid, I was a big fan of all the players who came from unusual places. Paul MacLean, who used to score thirty goals a year by just standing in front of the net, was born in France. Don Spring, a solid defenceman with the one of the weakest shots in NHL history, was born in Venezuela. Brian Mullen learned to play hockey on roller skates in Hell's Kitchen, New York. These men were heroes to this Polish-Belarussian-Romanian-Moldovan-Turkish-Israeli-Canadian Jew who grew up in a Slavic-dominated part of Winnipeg, where there were no kids with last names like Jones or Smith. One of the highlights of my teens happened when I was thirteen and Morris Lukowich visited my Pop Warner football team, the Maples Vikings. Standing in the concrete bunker of the Nev Elwick Community Centre, he told us to eat pasta instead of steak on the night before games. He seemed smaller in stature than an NHL all-star should be, but he still exuded an aura of greatness.

DAN DIAMOND: Generally, Winnipeggers craved a winning team. It could be made up of Canadians, Russians, Martians, or Scottish terriers, it wouldn't matter. The Jets had the misfortune of being stuck in a division behind the Oilers and Flames. It's a small town by NHL standards, without a big expense-account cohort, but it supported its team with all its heart. If they'd won five Cups between 1984 and 1990, as the Oilers did, the team would still be there. As for the media, they were nowhere near the Jets table at the draft. No one pays attention to the 204th selection. Igor Kuperman suggested they take Nik Khabibulin because he had performed well in Euro junior tournaments. Igor's role was widely reported after the Bulin Wall did well in the NHL. Also there are more than a few Winnipeggers — my family included — who endured a pogrom or two in the old country. Rebuilding the Jets around Keith Tkachuk, Craig Janney, Alex Zhamnov, and Teppo Numminen hardly qualifies as an atrocity.

10 | THE STARS ARE COMING DOWN

In 2001, the 'Stars reached the Cup final versus Capsule Music – a Toronto music store run by guitarist/goalie Peter Kesper. I took a circuitous route to the championship. For me, the event started six hundred kilometres to the east, in Montreal, where I'd been invited to read at the Blue Metropolis literary festival. My plan was to read on Thursday and Friday, then fly home to Toronto for the weekend games. My heart was divided between the booze-and-books circuit, and thinking about my friends back home cracking helmets with teams trying to unseat us as Cup champions. It wasn't long after I'd arrived in the City of Lights, however, that I forgot about the ice, for Janet, Cecilia, and I stepped into the hotel elevator and standing there was Norman Mailer.

He was a smallish gargoyle of a man with an old appleface and a rich sprig of white hair. I drew in a long breath and asked him with the verbal weight of a young person addressing one of his heroes: "Are you looking forward to the events of this evening?" (Mailer was to be fêted by festival organizers for his literary achievements). Instead of answering, Mailer trained his eyes on our daughter asleep in her stroller and said, "You know, I'd forgotten what a trial it is to travel with young children." I responded, dumb-wittedly, "Yes sir, uh, yes, it really is, sir . . ." It didn't matter. Running into one of the continent's great literary lions in my first five minutes at the festival blunted whatever concerns I'd had about how the 'Stars were getting on in my absence. It also promised that my time in Montreal would be well spent.

Through some scheduling quirk, I was booked on the first day to read alongside Margaret Drabble, her husband, Michael Holroyd, and Linda Spalding as part of an event that appeared to have a "What to do about Bidini? Might as well just put him in here" theme. Drabble had just published *The Peppered Moth*, Holroyd was promoting his acclaimed biography of George Bernard Shaw, and Spalding had come out with a historical novel co-written with her daughter. My two books, by contrast, concerned the ravages of Canadian rock and playing hockey in, among other places, the Transylvanian interior. I was as nervous as a roach in a boot factory. The long room was filled with about three hundred people, mostly middle-aged women in print dresses, broad hats, and scarves, Drabbleians all. While every author likes to think that his work has a certain universal appeal, I'd pretty much handicapped the crowd as one that had never heard of Jerry Korab, nor listened to Fludd. Rifling through my two books laid flat across my lap, I had no idea what to read before stepping up to the table mic.

Linda Spalding went first, and she chose a rather serious and poetic chapter, a Conradian bit about the darkness of travel. Having written very little that would be considered either serious or poetic, I knew that my reading, next up, would stand out even more. I reached for *On a Cold Road* and decided on a passage about a band who bombs while playing to a savage, resentful crowd.

I read about the Ramones.

There was little reaction to the piece at first. But as the tale evolved, I heard the occasional squeal of delight, a laugh that punched the silence, a few hiccups of sudden joy. Remarkably, as the story unfolded about how the Ramones were pelted with food, batteries, and garbage after being booked to play at a summer hard-rock festival in Toronto, I could feel the crowd become drawn in, and by the time the piece was done, there were belly laughs and wild applause. Being accepted into the Rock and Roll Hall of Fame must have been quite an achievement for the Ramones, but having their tale win over a room full of literary ladies was no small feat either.

Ms. Drabble, to whom I'd earlier confessed my apprehension about the bill, was as chuffed as anyone in the room. While reading my piece — she and I were seated next to each other — I could see her head bob in approval, and after my last word, I stole a glance. A broad smile had spread across her face. Before starting into her bit — the opening chapter of her novel — she told the crowd: "This story takes place in the slow past, long before the Ramones." There was more laughter. I felt like a million and a half bucks.

The next day, our family jetted home to Toronto. Janet and Cecilia hopped in one cab, I hailed another, and, sliding across the back seat of the car, I told the driver that I had only twenty minutes to get to my game. He got me there in eighteen, and I was on the ice for the opening shift. Riding a literary high, I played like a devil, firing the puck at the net, hitting forwards by rote, stealing and winning the puck in battle. I carried this through to the semifinal the next day, when we defeated Sonic Unyon, who'd enlisted two members of the Plymouth Whalers in an attempt to break the Morningstar jinx. We were booked later in the afternoon to defend our title against either Capsule Music or Boom, the team that had been formed for the express purpose of feeding us our lunch.

Before the game, my teammates and I gathered at a falafel joint just off Yonge Street and tried not to vomit (from nerves; the food was terrific). After killing an hour talking about strategy and who was or wasn't a big homo, we shuffled toward DeLaSalle arena, the fear and anxiety gathering in our hearts and stomachs. Then, on Farnham Road, I saw Michael Enright.

In sports as in life, athletes look for signs to tell them whether a game will play itself out as it should. There was a time when I bowed to the forces of superstition, and while I still believe that sport is rich with magic, I think that the rest of it is a lot of hooey. I came to this conclusion during an earlier E! Cup, when a member of the Songbird Millionaires gave me one of Phil Esposito's sticks from his training camp days with the Bruins. I brought the stick with me during our Downtown Men's Hockey League run of 1998, and it seemed to work its magic for two good weeks, until we reached the final.

The 'Stars were matched against a lawyers team called Life: The Nightclub. They were a grim, goateed unit, who played effective, if unsmiling, hockey. We defeated them in the first game, lost the second, and going into the rubber match, I was convinced that my Espo lumber would provide the difference. I was almost right. We scored twice in the last minute to tie the game at 3, but neither team could find the net in overtime. The match was eventually decided by a shootout, where we were edged by a single goal, whose scorer passed by our heart-stricken bench, grabbed his protective cup, and told us: "Now you guys can all suck my cock." From that day forward, my Espo talisman has hung on my wall, drained of whatever minor powers it once possessed.

Mark Robinson, our goalie, is a terrible one for taking these symbols to heart, and I believe his attention to karmic details heightened my awareness of such things after swearing off the hoodoo. Mark claims that once, on his way to a 'Stars playoff game, he heard a traffic reporter say, "Things are moving well on Morningstar Drive," only to correct himself: "What I mean to say is, 'Morningside Drive.'" On another occasion, he'd celebrated his son's birthday by filling his room with red star balloons. Waking Rudy on the morning of the important game, the little boy pointed at the balloons and said, "Dad, the stars are coming down." Mark remembers feeling a shiver of doom, but had a change of heart after realizing that it could have been much worse. "Rudy could have said, 'The Stars are falling,' but he didn't," reasoned the goalie. "'Stars are coming down' is actually kind of cool. It's like, 'Man, we're coming down to beat you.'" In the end, Mark's interpretation rang true. We won the game and Rudy was spared having to watch his father savage his balloons with a hat pin.

What was curious about seeing Michael Enright wasn't so much that I'd come across a famous CBC Radio personality in the flesh, but that he was wearing a baseball cap with a red star in the middle: a morningstar. I ran into Enright's wife, Karen Levine, on an outdoor hotel terrace while following my Italian baseball team during a playoff series in Palermo, Sicily. After introducing ourselves – and expressing astonishment that two Torontonians had crossed paths in such a faraway port – to be certain his cap hadn't been a product of my imagination, I asked her flat-out: "Your husband. He has a hat with a star on it, right?" She told me it hung in the hallway.

Confident that Enright's star had appeared for a reason, we continued to the gates of the old college, where we made our way across the parking lot to find one of the Boom players – a local deejay, Brother Bill – shlupping his gear into the trunk of his car. When he saw us, he held out his hands and shook his head.

"What happened, man?" I asked.

"Kesper. He was incredible. What could we do?"

At the rink, the stands were abuzz with the story of how Peter Kesper had stoned the tournament's favoured team, thereby eliminating the single greatest stumbling block in the 'Stars pathway to victory. Onlookers described how Kesper had used every part of his body and equipment – the cherrytop of his helmet, the gauntlet of his catching mitt, the pulp of his thigh, the inside of his arm and side of his stomach – to win the game. He'd made fifty stops and many near-impossible saves, pinwheeling his arms and legs to keep the puck from poking the twine. The victory was doubly sweet for Kesper and his teammates because, just months earlier, the butterfly goalie had braved chemotherapy to combat the cancer that doctors had found in his stomach and elsewhere. By all accounts,

Peter had performed like a phoenix, beating back the shadows while playing a game he must have wondered whether he'd ever play again.

In the end, we defeated Capsule Music 4-1. Kesper stoned us in the first half, but the effort was too much, too soon after the last game for the tired goalie. He left to a standing O in the middle of the second period. Later in the evening, Tom Goodwin asked me to present Kesper with a trophy at the Paddock. I swore a lot during my speech to keep myself from crying. I finished by saying, "This fuckin trophy goes to a fucking guy for whom 'heart' is too small a word."

With the world karmically in order, I slept a sweet, boozy sleep, only to awake the next morning to the sound of my answering machine clucking in the kitchen downstairs. It was the voice of Dave Clark, the old Rheostatics drummer. I hadn't spoken to Dave in six years, despite have been best friends for the better part of our lives. Sleepwalking down the hallway, I half-listened to what he was saying, and then it hit home:

Joey Ramone was dead.

Too late to pick up his call, I grabbed the newspaper from the front door, and there it was: JOEY RAMONE: DEAD AT 49. My first reaction was, "Man, the Ramones finally made the front page of the *Toronto Star*." Over the next few days, there were testimonials in the *Globe and Mail*, the *Rolling Stone*, and most British broadsheets, saying how Joey and his band had changed the course of rock and roll. Having documented the Ramones impact on my life in other books — how seeing them perform in 1979 changed my dreams; how they taught me to stand up for what I believed in, to energize that which had long been burning inside me — I was asked to talk about them on the radio — the CBC — a half-hour later. I told announcer Brent Bambury most of the story that you've just read. I told him that the events of the previous three or four days had been a crazy cocktail of beauty, pathos, retribution, home, art, and death, not forgetting to remind listeners that in rock and roll and hockey there is life, even when the 'Stars are coming down.

BRAD DALGARNO: I had no idea what it was going to be like when I got to the NHL. When I joined the Islanders, certain people had the notion that I was going to be Clark Gillies, Bob Nystrom, and Butch Goring all rolled into one. But I wasn't a great fighter, and once I became aware that that was how they envisioned my role, I got stressed out and developed ulcers. The team's expectations were completely unreasonable. I wanted to play hard-checking hockey, but I didn't see myself as a fighter, and the friction between what they wanted and what I wanted paralyzed me. I got hung up on it. There were two ways I could have responded to this — roll up and become a possum devoid of emotion, or attack the situation and become the bear. But I'd never been the bear before. I'd only ever played devoid of emotion.

One night against Detroit in Long Island, I took a boarding penalty. It wasn't a particularly dirty hit; at least I didn't think it was. But from the minute I sat down in the penalty box, Joey Kocur kept his eyes on me. Even though his team was on the power play, he wouldn't go deeper than the blue line in either end.

He basically skated between the two blue lines. He looked at me and said, "You're fucking dead" over and over again. I was sitting in the box thinking, Shit, okay, this is going to be interesting. I was getting more tense by the second, until I considered that he couldn't fight me unless I fought him. I decided I was just not going to encourage it. I came out of the box convinced of this plan, but because coach Al Arbour wanted to prove a point — and because Detroit's coach wanted my head — I kept being put out against Kocur. I tried to avoid the situation, skating away, skating away. Finally, it got to the point where the linesman dropping the puck looked at me and said, "Are you going to get this over with?" The fans wanted it, the coaches and refs wanted it. Everyone wanted it except me.

We fought that shift. I was punching him and having what was a fantastic fight for me. After a while, we tied each other up, and in any other situation, it would have been over. Instead, the refs said, "Keep 'er going, boys." In the time it took for them to say that — ten seconds — he worked his arm free and cracked me once on the temple. I wasn't even cut, but it broke three bones in my face: the orbit and both cheekbones. I just collapsed. It felt like an egg had broken in my face. I got off the ice, but because there wasn't any blood, nobody thought much of it. I got thrown in the back of the team doctor's car, who dropped me off at the worst equipped, but most convenient hospital for him on his way home. Inside, I had to fend for myself. The only person even tangentially connected to the team with whom I spoke over the next few days was Tammy Gilbert, Greg Gilbert's wife, who knew my girlfriend at the time. From that point on, the team didn't acknowledge me. They facilitated some doctors' appointments, but that was it. It took two surgeons to repair my face.

My season was over. I came back in the fall with a visor. I was in a worse condition mentally than I'd been prior to the incident with Kocur. I wasn't confident and I struggled at camp, but all I heard on the road was, "When are you going to take off the visor?" My agent told me that the team had told him that I probably wouldn't play unless I took it off. I told them that it just wasn't possible. I started to wonder what I was doing there, what I was doing with my life – all of those big questions that you end up asking yourself. I was eventually put on a list bound for the minors, but first they wanted to meet with me. There were two folding chairs in the middle of the dressing room, like a scene out of a movie. Bill Torrey sat in one, I sat in the other. Bill said, "Brad, you're a first-round pick and you're struggling. We have to talk." I said, "Bill, we certainly do." He told me to speak first, so I said, "I think I'm going home. I can't do this any more." Thirty seconds later every coach and scout in the Islanders organization was standing behind Bill Torrey. Gerry Ehman, the team's big grumpy head scout, made out like his son was leaving home or something. He was exhibiting a passion for me I'd never seen before. I left the meeting having told them that my decision had been made. No one thought it was the right decision. I had to pass by the rest of the guys in the hallway and there was a mix of shock and jealousy on their faces because most of them couldn't have done what I'd done. I walked across the Nassau Coliseum parking lot and I couldn't feel the ground beneath my feet. I was on a high. I'd taken control of my life. It was the first real hard decision that hadn't been made by somebody else.

Away from the game, I discovered something about myself that a lot of young players never realize: that everything you do is externally motivated. Everything in hockey is about getting that pat on the back. Everything is immediate: Did I have a good or bad shift? You're like a dog, unable to judge yourself without acknowledgement from others. I couldn't look at myself and know whether I was floating, or whether I'd had a good game. But all of this changed during my year off. I started a business. I remember sitting in a temporary office in my mother-in-law's basement when I realized that no one was there to give me my plan for the day. If I didn't take responsibility for myself, nothing was going to happen. After long days in the basement, I'd come up for dinner and no one said, "Good job today, Brad! Way to go out there!" Silly as it sounds, I realized what motivation was, and how to find satisfaction internally in what you did.

One evening, after I'd taken an exam for a design course at Sheridan College, I went down to the Gardens and bought a scalped ticket for a Toronto-Islanders game. I caught the last period. That's when I thought, If only I had played the game as the person I am now, what a difference it would have made to my career. Confidently, I went down to the dressing room and said hello to the guys. Bill Torrey saw me, didn't make a fuss, then called my agent the next day. When I came home that night, my wife said, "There's nobody telling you that you can't go back. There's nothing stopping you."

Returning to the team was like starting a new career. My first day back at training camp, I lost four teeth and had my jaw broken. It was done on purpose. I've always had a problem with the first day of camp because they throw guys out to scrimmage and no one's loose. Bad shit happens. I could hear talk from the other dressing room saying that I was a quitter, and that some kid had to teach me a lesson. Ironically, the guy who was the voice of reason in the dressing room – Dean Chynoweth, who was telling the other players to cool down and worry about their own performance – ended up being the guy who turned his stick into my face. My bottom palate was pushed back so far into my mouth that my gums were folded up and whatever teeth were left were pointing back down my throat. To this day, Dean feels sick about it. In some weird way, he did it so that someone else wouldn't, but what happened wasn't about him, it was about me. The way that I dealt with it was completely different from how I'd confronted the Kocur incident. I picked up all of my teeth off the ice, brought them to the dentist who wired them into my mouth, put on a face guard, and said, "Screw it, I'm going to play." My reaction to the injury when it happened was completely new and different. As soon as I got hit, I thought, "Fuck it, I'm getting up. I'm going to stand here and pick up every one of my teeth in front of everybody." It became the focal point of my comeback. I was a new Brad, and I made the team. Things were going quite well until the *National* – a daily sports newspaper in America – put me on the cover as a poster boy for the anti-fighting movement. Al called me straight into his office. He had the paper spread out on his desk. And that's when he shipped me to the minors. But I fought back. When I got called up, it was for good.

11 | THE UNHOWIE

Hockey is the snottiest of all sports. I couldn't help but take note of this after clearing my plugs for the umpteenth time in the middle period. Everybody sweats in all sports, but since hockey is played in the cold, all of that mucus gives way to a chorus of *argccckacks* and *snnngggrggggsss* unheard on any other sporting bench this side of Everest base camp. Hockey players spit and hork as much as they curse, often in a kind of two-beat combination — "Fuck! Agggccack!" — that sounds like an old, swearing car. Spitting is also an effective means of communication. For instance, expectorating fiercely at the floor means that one is disgusted with one's play; gobbing lightly and repeatedly over the boards shows that one is satisfied; and taking a long slug of water before spewing it out in a messy mouth fountain indicates one's sudden focus and determination to lead one's team to victory.

A few minutes after the start of the second period — and despite the fact that we all sounded as if we'd suddenly developed pleurisy — the Morningstars stopped spitting long enough to find the net. I wish I could find a less cynical term to describe getting on the scoresheet, but considering the sluggish nature of our play, it is appropriate. "Finding the net" is the kind of phrase a broadcaster uses to describe the underwhelming nature of a goal. It suggests that a team couldn't have located the opposition's posts and crossbar were its players equipped with field glasses, and, on this afternoon, that might well have been true.

Predictably, it was the Chizzler who got us on the board. The Chizzler (Paul Chisholm) is like Joe Sakic or Brian Leetch in that from his friendly, sympathetic face, you couldn't possibly imagine that he possessed enough growling mettle to survive in such a fierce, brutal game. Unlike Sakic or Leetch, however, the Chizz drove an old, bumper-stickered car, worked a day job, ate doughnuts, listened to garage rock, played rhythm guitar in his friend's band, and was as unlike a hockey star as Ilya Kovalchuk is like one. We've all come across guys in the dressing room in great shape wearing the most expensive skates with the coolest helmet who, once they're loosed on the ice, move with the speed of a patio flagstone. Instead, it's those potbellied, past-thirty guys in peewee shoulder pads who catch you by surprise (there are also those who don't catch you by surprise). The Chizzler was our team's dominant player, having won the tournament MVP trophy in 2001.

Because the Chizzler had such a mellow deportment, opponents often held back for a second — usually a second too long — before his strong, hard stride carried him to the net. Raised in

Mimico, where he starred in hockey and lacrosse, the Chizzler made passes that snapped and shots that rocketed. He also had the uncanny ability to ride out players along the boards like a flat palm pressed to clay. Because of these tools, he was our default leader in almost every game. While trailing 3-1 in the deciding game of our '02 DMHL championship versus Life: The Nightclub, I'd moaned aloud about there being very little time to mount a comeback, at which the Chizzler, stepping on to the ice for a shift, turned back, took off his glove, pointed a finger, and told me: "We're *not* going to lose." Then he skated into the offensive zone and scored. We tied it a moment later to send the game into overtime, but lost in a shootout to the goateed lawyer who asked if we'd fellate him.

But you get my point.

Against Hamilton, the Chizzler, who was partnered with Dutch, caught the Unyon Bradless and Chadless as he took the puck on a lateral pass and slipped through the opposition like a noodle through oil. He kept his head up and skated forward, weaving around the Unyon players as he surged toward the net. The end-to-end rush is a lost art form in trap-era hockey, and to see it executed first-hand at any level is to relive the game of the late 1960s, early 1970s, when pretty much every player was encouraged to fly solo. The end-to-end rush is the equivalent of a running back breaking a tackle, a hitter stretching a double into a triple, or a fast-break bursting up the heart of the court. It's about speed and swiftness and *gathering a head of steam*, the linguistic opposite to many of pro hockey's current catch phrases: *containing the rush* or *defensive shell* or *kitty bar the door*. When the Chizzler gathered his head of steam, he was nearly unstoppable.

He passed through the Unyon until he found himself to the left of the Detergent Box, but instead of dragging the goalie wide or cutting in farther, he fired a quick shot that hit the netkeep on the shoulder. As the puck flopped onto the rink's netting and out of play, the Chizzler's reaction was typically dispassionate. He glided in mild disappointment around the net, freed his fingers, regripped the shaft of his stick, gave a nod to himself, then surreptitiously looked over his shoulder at the very point in the top of the net that he'd misconfigured by a matter of degrees. And on the next play, he scored.

3-1 Unyon.

Despite cutting the Unyon's lead, we couldn't follow the Chizzler's marker with any momentum. It's not like we didn't push hard. Steve Stanley found himself with the puck on his backhand at the side of the Unyon net, with the Detergent Box looking the other way. He leaned into the disc with heroic determination, but the puck flew straight up from the ice, over the crossbar, and into the netting behind the goal. Minutes later, Dutch wristed the puck from the blue line, but it was deadened by five players on its way to the Detergent Box, who collected it with the nonchalance of an elderly woman removing a gum wrapper from her front walk. Following the disappointment of these shifts, we stared at the nothingness of the rink's ceiling struts long enough to let either Brad or Chad walk in and ding the puck off the post, or force Mark into a cartilage-bending save behind his airheaded defenders. Our only solace over this sequence of plays was that, as the middle period wore down, the Unyon probably could have seized the game right there and ground our hearts into pulp, but, for some reason, they did not.

After announcing to the bench, "It's Howie time!" – or something equally absurd – Howie leapt off the wood and tried slugging the 'Stars back into the game on his lonesome. But his efforts only drummed home the inadequacy of the red and white's attack. Charging down the right wing like the second coming of Bobby Schmautz, the oversexed winger showed Howie, faked Howie, and then unHowied what should have been a sure-fire Howie. He managed to unload a sort of combination wristshot/slapshot – a slashshot – that tumbled end over end into the Box's glove. Howie came around the net red-faced and skated to the bench. He brought his stick to his eyes and frowned at the blade.

"That was weird," said Howie, sitting down.

"Don't you mean 'That was lame'?" said Cheech.

"Ya, that's what I meant," said Howie, correcting himself.

"Maybe it's because we haven't talked enough like pirates on the bench . . . ," said Al.

"You want me to *darrrggghhh* a little?" I asked. "Take some of the pressure off you?"

". . . or the firefighters calender. We should be talking more about the firefighters calender."

"I was thinking that we'd need more gay guys on the team if we did a calendar, on account of their posing skills," said Howie.

"I always thought you were gay," said Cheech.

"Brad's bi," said Al.

"Bi's not gay," I reminded him.

"Sounds like a chapter title," said Steve.

"If we went gay, it would bring a whole other kind of goal celebration to the team," said Al.

"Speaking of gay, where's T?" asked Chris.

"Injured," said Andy. "I think I saw his wheelchair parked outside."

"Hey: what's the hardest part of sitting out Morningstar games? Telling your parents you're gay," said Howie. "No: what's the hardest part of T sitting out Morningstar games? Telling his parents he's gay."

"At least he gets to park in the handicapped zone," I said.

"Ya," confirmed Howie, finishing his thought. "Totally gay."

Once we'd established T was either injured or gay or both, I hopped over the boards to find the Bradster swooshing down the wing. While Howie's wonky Howie defined the nature of our play, Brad's moves were the very picture of folly and confidence. His rush came as the second period was winding down and with the earringed forward sensing that he might catch me with a case of late-period ennui. He was almost right. After a faceoff outside their blue line, Chad won the draw, kicked it over to Brad, and bore down on me. There wasn't three feet between us when he showed me his hotshot move. I can't say that I expected him to do what he did — he could have chosen any number of moves from his tacklebox of talents — but from the second he flinched his wrists, I *knew* what he was going to do.

I probably have the Russians to thank for my familiarity with the play. If the North American game hadn't become impregnated with the flavours of Eastern Europe and Scandinavia, I doubt that I would have recognized his move. It would have struck me the way it probably struck those Canadian players who competed against the Soviets in the 1960s – free, wild, weird, and dangerous; bebop to listeners raised on big bands and orchestras. But because the European influence is such that they now captain our teams, win Conn Smythe trophies, and pitch cars and clothes on local television and radio stations, Brad's dipsy-doodle – which had once been the sole domain of the tapdancing Russians – was now as typical of the twenty-first-century game as goatees and obstruction.

As he drove toward me, the Bradster shortened his gap from four feet to three, then two, then one, then peeled off his move in the blink of an eye. For a second, he was so close to me that I could see the excited hiking of his brow as he pushed the puck to his rear skate, blew past my shoulder like a thoroughbred on the rail, and waited for me to fish for the disc before kicking it forward to his stick.

But fish I did not. Instead, I closed my legs and pushed the Bradster a little nearer to the boards. I could hear him *nrrrgghhh* through his mouth-plug as my shoulder caught him in the chest – one of the dangers of executing such an open move is that you leave yourself vulnerable to certain axe-grinding rear guards – and the puck landed on my stick, not his. He yelled, "Shit!" as he looked behind him. Pausing a moment to feel satisfied with my endgame, I panicked upon remembering that I possessed the puck, at which point I immediately did what any good defence-man would not have done: I threw it down the ice as if it were a rat with scabies, then turned to watch the clock count safely down to zero.

DAN DIAMOND: When the Russians played Team Canada in Winnipeg in the 1960s, they introduced swirling speed, the five-man unit, outstanding foot skills, and great strength on the puck; things that were later revealed to greater Canada in 1972. Anatoli Firsov, who was the precursor to Kharlamov, played in Winnipeg, and so did Viktor "the Bear" Konovalenko, who has the same resonance for me as Johnny Bower. Ragulin and Starshinov came over too, using heavy hardwood sticks and antiquated skates. I recently saw a Russian hockey manual from 1953, and the move where you dump the puck into your skates and kick it to your stick while moving past or through a player is in there. It was a move taught in 1953, even though they'd only been playing since 1948. Because of what we'd seen, Winnipeggers knew that the NHLers wouldn't win in a walk in 1972. That was the perception in the rest of the country, but we knew how fast and dynamic they were.

IGOR KUPERMAN: In Russia, we were instructed in school that the United States was our enemy and that Canada was our friend, because they were suppressed by the United States. I'd always dreamed of Canada, but there were never any documentaries on television about it — only films showing the troubled side of the United States. So when I saw the Montreal Forum on TV for the first time in 1972 — the music, the crest on the ice, the people — this glimpse of Canadian life was so special. North American sports fans had seen the Russians play in the Olympics and on tours of Canada, but we never saw the NHL. Not once. Nowhere. Never. Not even a clip. It was all new to us that night in Montreal. And winning made the evening more memorable.

The next day in the paper – after our 7-3 victory – the headline was: THE MYTH IS DESTROYED! Because of that first victory, a lot of Russians don't consider the series as being lost. On paper, they lost, but in reality, Russia proved that it could skate with – and defeat – the best.

YVAN COURNOYER: The 1972 Summit Series was a lot of pressure. It was a great unknown playing the Soviets, and more than a little frightening. I remember telling Frank Mahovlich outside the Hotel Champlain before leaving for Game 1: "Frank, I'm really afraid of this game. I don't know what to expect." Frank didn't say too much; he never did. I guess that's why he's in Ottawa now.

VLADIMIR MOZGOVOY: When they asked coach Anatoli Tarasov how he thought the Russians would do against the Canadians, he took his time and then answered, "I think the series will be tied 4-4."

ANDERS HEDBERG: All of Europe was equal in talent throughout the late 1960s and 1970s. It wasn't until our players started to come to the NHL that the Russians dominated European hockey. So when the Russians proved themselves in the NHL in 1972, it gave us hope and confidence too. The mystique of pro hockey was taken away, and like the Russians, we understood how truly competitive Sweden was with the best in the world. The term *superstar* was devalued and the NHL was no longer unreachable. They were great players, but they weren't as superior as everyone had thought.

SETH MARTIN: Russians are as passionate about the game as anyone. They love to talk hockey. While playing for the national team, I got to know Sologubov, the great defenceman. Solly had fought in the Second World War and was wounded three times. The doctors told him that he'd never skate again, but he was a mainstay of the Russian team for years afterwards. He was a great guy. He could speak just enough English to get by. One time, I was rooming with Harold Jones in Lausanne, Switzerland, site of the 1960 World Championships. After beating the Russians in the final, we all went back to the hotel. I had a bad shoulder, and Jonesy was aching; everybody on the team was hurt. Jonesy had a bath, then it was my turn, but as I was soaking in the tub, there was a knock on the door. It was Solly. He had a bottle of Russian vodka and three glasses. He came in and shouted through the bathroom door, "Martin! Out! Out! Out! We drink!" He filled three eight-ounce glasses and Solly swished his back like a pro. Jonesy looked at me, shrugged his shoulders, and said, "Well, okay, let's go." We shot it back and, holy Moses, it was awful. But we got through it.

IGOR KUPERMAN: People in North America don't know it, but Russian hockey crowds are nuts. They're as committed as any fans in the world. It was impossible to get tickets for games in 1972 at Luzhniki Sports Palace because of the demand. You'd stand in line for hours, sometimes in the middle of the night. They also had special booths in the city, but if you wanted to go to a game, you had to buy two or four more tickets for concerts, sometimes with unknown artists. They made it very difficult for the rabble to get in; the Summit Series was considered to be for high-ranking officials only, who were ordered not to cheer. But because of the importance of the series, my mother told my dad to go out and try to buy tickets from scalpers, but he said that they were too expensive, ten rubles. My mom said it didn't matter, that it was worth it. My dad went back and reported that, mysteriously, the price had gone up to twenty-five rubles. She told him, "Buy them for twenty-five!" but the next day, it had gone up to a hundred rubles. They made it impossible for the real fan to attend.

LOU VAIRO: Before 1972, there was Anatoli Tarasov. I consider Tarasov to be the greatest coach that ever existed on the face of the earth in any sport, the King of Kings. The Russians won more medals with other coaches, but Tarasov was the man. I first saw one of his teams play on a black-and-white television set on a Sunday at my grandmother's house. It might have been the 1950s, I'm not sure. Afterwards, I wrote him a letter and he wrote me back. He invited me to Moscow, and I went over there. It was the beginning of our friendship. At the end of his life, USA Hockey honoured him in Boston and we had an artist paint a magnificent portrait of him. He told us that we couldn't possibly imagine how much he appreciated it, but offered two caveats. First, he asked why we couldn't have painted him as a younger man, and second, he wondered how much the painting cost? I told him: "You're not young, you're an old man!" As for the cost of the commission, I confessed that it would have been a question I'd have asked, as well.

Tarasov changed the game. What we're seeing in the NHL today is the product of his genius: attacking hockey, off-ice training methods, the assembly-line method of practising. Mikhailov and Petrov — to name two great Russian stars — were castoffs from other clubs that he turned into superstars. He made many average players into very good players; turned very good players into stars; and took stars and made them into superstars. He did this in mass, generation after generation. He showed us the importance of changing lanes, of using the whole ice, of men in motion. He used to say, "The least important man on the ice is the man with the puck." He talked in a particular way, saying things like, "The four players other than the puck carrier have a devout responsibility and absolute obligation not only to get open, but to do so by changing speeds and positions." He pioneered the idea of calling for the puck without yelling, of letting another player know your whereabouts by placing the blade of your stick on the ice in a convenient manner. He was an innovator in the way we train goalies — as athletes rather than a sedentary last line of defence. The way defencemen are active today has a lot to do with Tarasov. For a time, he wouldn't let his Central Red Army defencemen to go D to D. He'd fine them if they did. He once asked me, "What is the most important responsibility of the defenceman?" I answered, "To defend one's zone and net, of course," but I knew the minute I said it that I was wrong. He put his left hand up and smacked me across the chest, nearly knocking me over: "*Nyet!*" He instructed, "The defenceman is expected to defend, but it's not his most important job. It's his most necessary duty, but not the most important. His responsibility is to strip the attacker of the puck and, in no more than two steps, make a hidden, accurate lead pass up the ice to a teammate before joining in the attack." And that is modern hockey.

GARY GREEN: When I was twenty-one, I started the first ever International Hockey Coach's Symposium out of Belleville, Ontario. Boris Kulagin – Russia's national team coach – wrote me out of the blue and asked if he could attend. Prior to coming, he'd been in the hospital for three weeks. Nobody in Canada believed that a twenty-one-year-old kid was having Boris Kulagin as his guest at his hockey symposium. I'd already gone around to people like Fred Shero, Bob Pulford, Roger Neilson, Tommy Woodchuck, and Father David Bauer, and had convinced them to come to the symposium. I ended up with 150 coaches, from Lou Lamoriello to Steve Dryden. I told people that Kulagin was coming, but nobody believed me. I couldn't get any help bringing him to Belleville; all I had was a Telex that told me what time his Aeroflot flight was due to arrive in Montreal. I tried to get the government to help, but they wouldn't believe me. The Russian embassy said, "No, no, no, the national team coach is very sick. He is not coming." They went over the Aeroflot passenger list and he wasn't even listed. So I rented a small plane, went to Dorval airport in Montreal, hopped in a car that took me to where, I hoped, Kulagin was landing, and waited. Sure enough, he arrived as planned. I grabbed him, his gym bag, and his interpreter and hopped in the car to take us back to my plane. Just before getting on board, the interpreter said, "Mr. Kulagin wants to know if you have life insurance to ride this plane." I put him on anyway.

It was eight o'clock at night, a beautiful evening, and you could see that Kulagin was mesmerized. The interpreter kept saying, "Mr. Kulagin, he loves this." He'd never been on a small plane before, let alone one swooping over eastern Ontario. He must have felt free as a bird up there. Then, all of a sudden our pilot was radioed with instructions to divert our flight to Trenton Military Air Force Base. The authorities wanted Kulagin. When we arrived, dignitaries were waiting with a huge presentation; the MPP, the mayor of Belleville, the red carpet was all laid out. They had a special car, everything. The buzz was incredible, whereas twenty-four hours earlier, they'd treated me like I was insane. The dignitaries asked if I'd go with them to a reception, but I told them I couldn't stay; I had a symposium to prepare. Later on in the middle of the night, I got a phone call from the Belleville police. They said, "Mr. Green, are you responsible for the Russian national team coach?" I said that I was. "Uh, can you come and get him?" they asked. I told them that it was impossible: Mr. Kulagin was staying at the Four Seasons. But it turned out that he'd got up and decided to go for a walk by himself. It being a Sunday in Belleville, no one was on the streets at that hour, so they thought he was some sort of deranged rummy. All he could say was, "Gary Green! Gary Green! Gary Green!"

LOU VAIRO: In 1979, I'd arranged with Tarasov to come to the United States on a tour of eighteen cities to do a dry land training seminar. Everything in those days was done in clandestine meetings at junior world championships and things like that. We'd be very careful. We always found a person who could translate for us who wasn't from an official body of the state. Tarasov was all set, thrilled to come. I made all of the arrangements in all eighteen cities, all of the brochures were set up and ready to go. We invited the Canadian coaches to attend, NHL coaches too. But two weeks before the World Championships in Moscow in 1979, we received a Telex from Russia stating that Tarasov was gravely ill and not able to attend. We called over, and someone told us that it would take one week before our call could be placed to him. Someone from the federation said that they were very sorry about Tarasov. I told him on the phone that I didn't believe him. He said, "Are you calling me a liar?" My comment was, "If the shoe fits, wear it," but the translator didn't know how to phrase it.

We ended up going to the World Championships in Moscow to see for ourselves and, of course, the first day there, the first person I ran into was Tarasov. Gravely ill, he was stuffing his face with little sandwiches and drowning them in vodka. He hugged me and told me, "Stop wasting your time with the federation, go to President Brezhnev. The federation hates me and wants to punish me." We called a meeting with Vladimir Sitch [*sic*] – he was later gunned down – who was the minister of sport, while the head of the fed was Viacheslav Koloskov. He was a terrific scientist and physiologist, but I didn't trust him. I said, "We've got people coming, brochures. . . . How could you cancel like this?" They continued, "He's very sick." I said, "I just saw him eat three hundred sandwiches!" They didn't like the tone of my voice. I was asked to leave the room. I said to my friends in the U.S. delegation, "If you have any balls, tell these Soviets they'll never play any team ever again in the United States unless they let Tarasov come." I slammed the old wood panel door. I was called in ten minutes later, thinking that I was about to be fired. The Russians said, "We'll let you take Tarasov, but he's not our greatest coach: Arcati Chernechev is. You must take both of them." We agreed. I dragged Tarasov around America for a month, from west to east. We made eight grand, and I snaked Tarasov an extra two grand, cash.

SETH MARTIN: I got to know Tarasov very well. I used to try to go to the Russian practices and see what they were doing, because it was always something new and fresh and innovative. I was supposed to play against Tarasov one time in Spokane, but I got suspended for ten games because of a stick-swinging incident. When I walked into the old Coliseum in Spokane to watch the game, Tarasov saw me and shouted at the top of his lungs, "Martin! You hooligan!" Then he came over and gave me one those bone-crushing bear hugs.

ALEXANDER GUSEV: Tarasov used to gather the wives together. He'd talk to them about us and suggest how they might help get the husbands mentally prepared for a big tournament or game.

IGOR KUPERMAN: The two teams that made the Russian players' blood boil were Canada and the Czechs. With Canada, it was a battle of styles; with the Czechs, it was a battle of political will. Those games between the former Czechoslovakia and Russia weren't pretty, especially after 1968. There was a lot of spitting, mostly by the Czechs. They hated when the Russians called them Czechs too, because some of them were Slovaks. The games were very political; the fans in Prague had a slogan: You give us tanks, we give you goals. In 1975 at the Izvestia tournament, the Russians played three games in Prague, and three at home; they lost all three away games: 9-2, 6-2, and 4-2, which was unheard of in the era of those great Soviet teams. Tretiak was replaced during the series. In the last game, there was a huge fight where Alexander Gusev broke the jaw of Marian Stastny. After that, the entire Soviet team was summoned to the Kremlin, where they were admonished for their behaviour and told that fighting would not be accepted, no matter the circumstances.

ANDERS HEDBERG: Four years after the Russians invaded Czechoslovakia, the two national teams met in the 1972 World Championships in Prague. It was an incredibly sensitive period. Sweden was scheduled to play afterwards, and we were told to be in the dressing room two hours before our game, but I could not leave the stands. It was impossible. There were fifteen thousand people packed into the rink; you couldn't get another person into the standing-room section, which was overflowing with bodies. Games between these teams were exhibitions of heroism, hatred, and viciousness, and because they feared a riot, much of the crowd had been hand-picked by the authorities. But when it really came down to it, even these hand-picked fans — many of them party members — couldn't resist the excitement of beating the Russians. It was political and it was personal. The opponents knew each other very well because they'd played against each other many times. The Czech players had played both as free citizens and as citizens living in an occupied country. They played as if trying to prove that they would not lie down, that they would survive in spite of it all. It was as if they were saying, "You can point a cannon at me, but at this time, I can do anything I want." The Czechs ended up winning, and Jaroslav Holik was the most visible person in the middle of this guerilla warfare. He blocked shots fearlessly, without regard for his well-being. He threw himself around the ice trying to show, as a

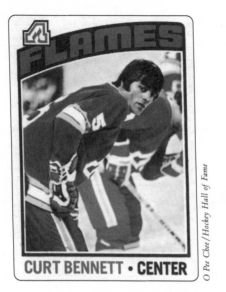

CURT BENNETT • CENTER

O Pee Chee / Hockey Hall of Fame

people, how the Czechs would not be dominated. And then, midway through the game, he brought his hockey stick to his eye like a rifle, and aimed it at the Russian bench.

CURT BENNETT: I played with Shadrin and Liapkin — two former Soviet stars — during my years in Japan. They were a little older, but they could still play. Because I spoke Russian, the coaches put us together a lot, and after a while, we got into these protracted philosophical discussions about hockey. Once, I told them, "It's like what Punch Imlach said, 'Hockey is war!'" They were outraged. They talked about the slashing, hacking, and hitting and how unnecessary it was. Then, one game we were playing against a touring Czech team, and, of course, Liapkin hit everything that moved, because nothing gets a Russian going like a game against the Czechs. He was a wild man out there. After the second period, I said to him, "Liapkin, hockey is not war!" He laughed. I'd caught him.

MIKE SMITH: One of the phony biases is that Russians aren't tough hockey players. But they're second only to Canada in toughness. They're hard people, poor people. The players come from more or less the same experience in terms of the lack of material comforts, and in almost every case, they've risen above it.

LOU VAIRO: In 1975, the Canadian school of hockey was about resisting change. I was the first one in North American to run Soviet-style drills, to change the way people thought about how you were supposed to run a team. I was called a Communist, hideous names. The Canadian scouts were really mad at me because I discouraged fighting. Tarasov's comments to me were, "Lou, you Canadians (he always called me 'Canadian'), do you think we Soviets have no courage? Even though we don't believe that fighting has a place in sports, we have all kinds of courage. We lost over twenty million in the war. Did your capitalist books not tell you about the great seige of Leningrad?" It really changed my attitude. I've listened to Cherry, Melrose, and Chelios, and I still think fighting should be kept to a minimum. Tarasov used to say, "The Canadian pros play a kind of hockey that borders on cruelty. It's not just toughness and courage; it's cruelty. It should only be tolerated on the battlefield. And hockey is not a battlefield."

ART BERGLUND: The Russians that I remember best from 1972 were Anisin, Lebedev, Bodunov. They were called "the Line from the Mine" because they'd all grown up together in hardscrabble Russia, the same way that Clarke and Leach had come up through small-town Canada.

FRED STANFIELD: When the Sabres got the chance to play the Soviet Wings in the Memorial Auditorium, we beat them 12-6. It was the best game Jerry "King Kong" Korab played in his entire life. Punch Imlach had videos of the Russians for us to watch, which was very rare for the time. He wanted to beat that team so badly, it was like a Stanley Cup game for us. We knew their system well, so we just outchecked them and got in their face. We knew what was going to happen before it happened. Then we started scoring like crazy.

LOU VAIRO: After Fred Shero saw the U.S. national team play the Soviets during a friendly match in 1972, he declared openly that the Russians put on "the greatest exhibition of hockey I've ever seen." Fred later told me in private that Flyers owner Ed Snider went ballistic on him and chewed him out. He told him never to say anything like that in public ever again.

MIKE SMITH: It's always been easier for the Russians to play hockey in the United States than in Canada. American markets accepted them where Canadians did not. The Russian Five that Scotty Bowman put together was seen as a positive in Detroit, whereas it was a negative in Winnipeg. These days, you've got to be a real numbskull to think that the only way to succeed in hockey is to be Canadian. Canada's view that it's "our game" is so antiquated. Because it's no longer "their" game, a whole world of international and American minor pro jobs that weren't there before are available to Canadians.

ART BERGLUND: I scouted for thirteen years, discovered and drafted lots of Europeans. But no matter how many quality players I found, NHL GMs would tell me: "You can only have one of them on your team." Canada gave the world a great game, but other people can play it. To this day, there are folks in hockey who don't believe that.

MIKE SMITH: I remember talking about Brian Mullen, who was American, and people would say, "Well, he just hasn't paid his dues." I told them, "What does it matter whether they ride the buses in junior or college? A long bus ride is a long bus ride." But that was the perception: unless you'd cut your teeth coming up through the Canadian system, you weren't half the player that a Canadian was.

LOU VAIRO: In 1975, there were two or three Americans in the NHL. I remember meeting a bunch of GMs when I worked at the American Hockey Association. We needed funding. Canadian junior hockey was getting millions, and since we were putting a coaching program together, we requested some help. I won't name the GM, but he said that we didn't have much to offer because there were so few Americans in the league. He kept parroting: "Where are the players? You have no players." I told him that, in ten years, there'll be a hundred, but you have to give them a chance. Like a clock, I waited those ten years, then, in 1988, I sent a note to that GM: "There are 106 Americans playing in the NHL today, thank you very much."

GARY GREEN: Canada-Russia was always intense, but Russia-America had its own dynamic. We were supposed to play the Russians when I was coaching the Capitals, but with the escalation of the war in Afghanistan, and the Americans' reaction to it, they wanted to back out. They were holed up in their hotel rooms; people had called in bomb threats. There was major security around them. They had a phone installed on my bench, and told me that if that phone rang during the game, I was to get my team off the ice right away. During the national anthem, I looked up and there were SWAT teams with snipers positioned in the upper rafters. The Capitals fans booed the Russian anthem all the way through. If we hadn't tied the game – using a system that Scotty Bowman helped me develop – there would have been hell to pay. Who knows what would have happened.

IGOR KRAVCHUK: We toured North America in some very intense times and every game was important. As most people know, playing for Victor Tikhonov in the 1980s was no picnic, and he wanted total success in every shift of every game. We'd get up at eight in the morning, have a team meeting, run for three kilometres, exercise, and then have breakfast. Then we'd practise on the ice, once in the afternoon, and again in the evening: two practices a day. It was the same routine every day, even on the road. I wanted to go to a movie, but couldn't, not when Tikhonov would call surprise team meetings. If he called a meeting and you weren't there, you were in trouble, so you stayed in and did nothing. Even when you were playing in your hometown, you couldn't go out and visit friends. I know that some players, like Alex Mogilny, got fed up and defected. I think the turning point for him came when Tikhonov punched him in the stomach on the bench. I didn't see it, but I did see him kick players behind the bench to try to motivate them.

LOU VAIRO: Tikhonov controlled every aspect of his players' lives. I used to get into arguments with Kulagin all the time. I'd say, "You guys are 50 per cent coaches. I'd like to see you coach if you had players who could tell you to screw off. I'd like to see Krutov hop on alternating feet with weights over his head three times a day all summer long if he had a convertible, a hot chick, and a pocketful of cash. I'd like to see you treat an NHL player like a dog, take away his car and apartment, let him see his wife one day a week. I'd like to see you do that and win. Then I'd call you a great coach."

IGOR MUKHIN: Viktor Tikhonov and his teams represented the last great era in modern Russian hockey. It's changed so much since then. There's more recruitment going on in modern Russian hockey than ever before and it's no longer a game of the masses. The transition of hockey into an elite sport has had a bad impact on the game overall because unless a player can show he has the skills at an early age, he's not encouraged to keep improving. Hockey schools are expensive now and they prohibit most kids from getting proper coaching.

IGOR KRAVCHUK: Teams take kids when they're five and six years old, and it's wrong. A little boy has to have a childhood. He has to be able to spend time in his neighbourhood, kick around a ball, play in the sand with his toys.

ALEXANDER RAGULIN: I only started skating when I was thirteen years old. Today at that age they would have already thrown me out. In our time, the greatest mass of boys came from the streets, and we weren't streamed into the elite program until we were fifteen. These days, some kids are five or six years old. In the old days, the poorer people were the basis of Russian hockey, but now, the ones who excel have parents with big cars, money for uniforms, sticks. It used to be a game of the people. We'd play from morning to evening in the yards, but today, all of that empty space is stuffed with cars and garages. There's no room for the ice to bloom, where games can start in an instant.

LOU VAIRO: Tikhonov made a statement at the end of the '04 World Championship: "The players made too many mistakes." It was an old, hard-line Communist ploy. When Igor Larionov recommended that Larry Robinson should become the new national team's head coach, the Russians were horrified, but from a North American's point of view, it makes so much sense. There are no coaches in Russia any more, but until Putin and Fetisov can put Larionov in power, there'll be very little change. The guys who run the federation are old-time hard-line Communists who would love nothing more than to go back to the old days and imprison their people.

12 | TOE BLAKE IN HEELS

One of the charms of tournament hockey is being able to immerse yourself fully in the sport, boiling in its details over a short period of time. Before the E! Cup, I decided that in order to have a well-rounded sporting experience, it was important to observe the game from every bent, so when I wasn't playing for the Morningstars or following the NHL playoffs with the obsession of an astronomist witnessing the birth of a star, I found myself coaching the Gas Station Islanders. While I'd like to report that I came to the tier-three Islanders after its captain begged me to guide his rudderless ship into the black waters of competition, the truth is, it was me who did the begging. Formed by ex-Rheos drummer and Toronto Island resident Don Kerr and by Dale Morningstar — who gave the 'Stars their name after he'd backstopped us in our first season — the Islanders gave me the chance to observe hockey above its usual sightlines. I would be exploring the peculiarities of a sporting role that is regarded by players either with pure contempt or total reverence.

The first thing that perplexed me about coaching was how I was supposed to behave after walking into a dressing room that I'd entered as a player two or three times a week for the past fifteen years. Not being required to strap moist plastic to my limbs or tape my scythe, I had no sense of belonging. I paced the floor for a few minutes until Jack Larmet, one of the Islanders' corner-stones, did something far more coachingly than anything I'd done so far when he patted an empty patch of bench beside him and ordered, "Dave, come. Sit here." After pausing a moment to decide if this would be appropriate for someone to whom the team would have to surrender their ego, pride, and self-worth, I parked my caboose and let my fedora fall into my hands.

"Hey, coach," said Dale, dragging goalie gear from his old bag like a bushman pulling bones off a carcass.

"Ya, it's great to have you," said Jack.

"You ever done anything like this before, coach?" asked George Collins, the Islanders' senior centreman.

At this point, I had to decide exactly what kind of coach I wanted to be. Were I cut from the Mike Keenan/Pat Burns/Scotty Bowman mould of paint-peeling fear and authoritarian rage, I might have lunged at Jack, clasped my hands to his neck, and shouted, "Great, is it? You wanna see how friggin' great it's gonna be?" Were I somewhere in between – maybe Ron Wilson, Pat Quinn, John Tortorella – I might have risen slowly, and, affecting a tall, imposing posture, approached George Collins and asked him, "Have you ever dealt with anything like this before?" Were I Ken Hitchcock, I might have walked out of the room and sent one of my assistants in to tell the boys just how pissed off I was, or were I King Clancy or Chief Armstrong — which was probably a lot closer to the truth — I might have told Dale that he looked about as comfortable as Yanni in a barber's chair, and suggested that he relax, because, "Hell, boys, it's only hockey!" Instead, I put my hat back on my head and clapped twice.

"Guys," I told them, encouragingly, "Today we're gonna take care of business!"

RON MURPHY: Sometimes our old coach with the Rangers — grumpy Phil Watson — would come in after a loss and sit in the doorway between the dressing room and the shower. When you tried to walk past him, he'd block you off and stare you straight in the face. Once, I stood there waiting for something to happen when, all of a sudden, he started bawling his eyes out like a baby.

MIKE PELYK: Leafs coach Red Kelly did whatever he wanted to do. He had the habit of not telling the players who he wanted on the ice whenever we pulled the goalie. Instead, he'd yell, "Who's going? Who's going?" and, inevitably, two guys would jump over the boards. Red caught hell for this, but he always stood up to management and Harold Ballard. Whenever Harold would come down and tell him, "Whatever you do, don't play this guy," you knew that that guy would be starting the game. Red was a players' coach. One time in Oakland, we were down to three defencemen — me, Borje Salming, and Ian Turnbull — and he was having a helluva time trying to keep it together. During the game, some guy came out of the stands and started banging on a drum right behind the bench. He was yelling at Red and driving him crazy until the coach decided to go after him. Red climbed into the crowd and chased the guy, who ran and started falling over everybody in the stands. We won the game and the guys were ecstatic. The next night we were playing in Los Angeles, where Red had also coached. We were losing 3-2 with about six minutes left when another guy came out of the stands and started yelling at him. Once again, he bolted off the bench and ran into stands, chasing the fan all the way into the Forum Club. He came back to the bench just as I got the puck, whacked at it from about ten feet out, and scored. Two minutes later, Turnbull won the game on a slapshot. We thought, "Oh no, we're going to keep winning, and Red's going to get himself killed."

DEAN PRENTICE: During a series versus St. Louis, the fans were on us something bad, so Red went out and bought earmuffs for the players. He made us wear them out on the ice to start the game.

JOHN CHABOT: When I played for Halifax in the Hab system in the AHL, we weren't allowed to lose to either Moncton, who were Toronto's farm team, or Fredericton, who were Quebec's. One night we went into Fredericton and played well, but we blew it at the end and lost 3-2. Our coach, John Brophy, was livid after the game. He had a $10,000 Rolex that he placed on the floor and smashed into smithereens. He took off his jacket and tore it to shreds. He sat at the front of the team bus and as we started to pull away, he punched a hole in the double-paned window beside where he was sitting. We had a six-hour drive to Halifax, and the bus driver told him, "If you ever do that again, you're getting out." Broph looked at him – he gave him one of those long, scary glares – and said, "Listen, buddy. If you say another word, I'm gonna kick you out and drive the fucking thing myself."

JEFF JACKSON: Broph was inconsolable after losses. One night, we were dumped 3-2 at home to Binghamton. He came in the dressing room, which was quite small, and said gravely, "Leave your equipment on." He proceeded to snap every one of our sticks in half with his bare hands. He took off his suit coat – he was a real clotheshorse back then, and his suit must have cost $1,000 – and spent the next ten minutes trying to rip it in half. The room was dead quiet except for the sound of Broph trying to tear up his wardrobe. We were all thinking to ourselves, Geez, we only lost 3-2. He made us go back on the ice and skate another hour without pucks. The next night, we could have lost 8-0, but if we won all of the fights, it would have been okay.

JOHN BROPHY: Being a Maritimer drove me 150 per cent to succeed in hockey because my alternative was sixteen miles out on the Atlantic Ocean, fishing. As soon as I smelled the rink, I was hooked, but one thing you have to remember is that Maritimers were a rare breed in the pros. In my day, the East Coast was shit on by a lot of other Canadians. There was such great prejudice that teams didn't even look out there, even though there were hundreds of players. I got my start playing in a big senior league up in northern New Brunswick, where there were lots of overage juniors. There was a tough guy in the league – I can't remember his name but he was big, French, and red-headed, with a crewcut – and I fought him during my first game and I knocked him out. That's how my reputation began. From there, I went to pro training camp in Baltimore. I had to go through Boston airport to get there, but when they asked me for ID, I didn't have any. All I had were my skates. They asked if I had a driver's licence, and I said, "Mister, I haven't seen many cars, let alone driven one." But he let me go. I approached training camp vowing that I'd never lose my job to another player, and most of my rivals couldn't walk by the time we were done. In Baltimore, I took out another of the so-called tough guys, and the coach told me, "Brophy, don't bother thinking about going home."

FRANK BEATON: One time during an intermission in Hampton, Broph came into the dressing room. I thought we were doing okay — we were only down by a goal — but Broph laid into us. As he spoke, he began tapping his fist on the trainer's table, and getting more animated, he started punching his fist a little harder. He was saying, "You sons of bitches, I am not going to have players who just go through the motions!" He was punching the shit out of this table and his knuckles started bleeding. He did this for ten minutes straight. By the end of his rant, there was blood splattered all over the white table, like something had been hacked off.

JOHN CHABOT: We'd played Moncton in Halifax and had lost at home. The game before, we'd had some disabled kids come down to the room. One of them was a huge Voyageurs fan. Everybody was signing things and patting him on the back and somehow he ended up getting invited back for the next game. He was wheeled into the room after the loss and put near the door. Broph came in ranting and raving and screaming about us being a bunch of invalids. He spotted the fellow in the wheelchair and said, "What the fuck is he doing in the room? We got enough of these fucking guys sitting right here!" He opened the door, put his foot on the back of the wheelchair, and booted him out of the room, sending him across the hallway and into a wall. He yelled at the guy, "Now stay the fuck out!" Then he smashed our weight machine to pieces, ripped the stick holder off the wall, and broke every stick we owned. Then we skated for an hour and a half in front of our home fans.

JOHN BROPHY: Every rink I went into in the minors, they had someone new for me to fight. In places like New Haven and Philly, you never had any idea who they were going to call up. One night in Greensborough, they brought in a bulldozer operator from Sudbury to fight me. There was fifteen inches between his eyebrows, but I took care of him. In New Haven, they brought in Ray Leacock, who was the light heavyweight champion of Canada. On the first shift, he tried to tear my head off, but I'd been anticipating it, so I battled back and sent him home. The worst incident, I think, was a stick-swinging fight with Bobby Taylor, who played for the Argonauts and Calgary in the CFL. He was built like a rock, and he was a better-than-average hockey player. It was a matter of life and death and there's no question in my mind that I tried to kill him. I knew that if I didn't kill him, he was going to kill me, and from the first punch, I was overwhelmed by this crazy feeling. We got cut everywhere. After the fight, Bobby tore the first-aid room apart, so I couldn't even get stitched. Everything was on the floor, so they called an ambulance, where the attendants put clips in my head to stop the bleeding before they could get me sewn up. After leaving the hospital in Hadenfield, New Jersey, the team decided to stop in a bar to get some food, and the first person we saw was Bobby Taylor, nursing a drink with about eighteen patches on his head.

RICK VAIVE: I was nineteen when I played for the Birmingham Bulls. During one of my first games, I heard a rattling sound coming from the trainer's room. When I went to investigate, there was John Brophy in his suit and tie, wailing away at a heavy bag.

FRANK BEATON: For a while, Maritimers had the reputation for being a bunch of hicks and drunks – not just in hockey, but in every walk of life – so there's no way players could keep up with the OHL, QMHL, or WHL. Scouts didn't come east because of this preconception. To get noticed out of the Maritimes the way Brophy did, was really something special. The trail that I blazed was nothing compared to what he had to go through.

JEFF JACKSON: When John Brophy was assistant coach in Toronto, he'd tell us, "You young guys aren't gonna be like these old buggers. It's gonna be different around here when you guys get a chance." He took us under his wing and worked us hard. The next year, when I went to St. Catharines, he was my head coach. He brought us deeper in the playoffs than anyone expected, and I had a good year, way beyond what the team had forecasted. The next year, Brophy became the Leafs head coach. He called me in the off-season and said, "Come to camp in shape, because you've got a job." That was all I needed to hear. John Brophy gave me my break in hockey.

LOU VAIRO: Anatoli Tarasov, the great Russian coach, used to punch his players and hit them with his stick. He'd try to goad them into reacting, and if they looked dirty at him, he'd scream, "Control yourself! You'll never beat the Montreal Canadiens by retaliating!" He preached discipline and team play. He used to talk all the time about conditioning. He said that you don't condition a team to win in the third period; you condition them to win in the first, when your energy and attack is so great that the opposing team has no response.

BOB LORIMER: The Islanders of the 1980s were very businesslike. We had great talent, but everybody knew his role and it was easy to play together. One game, I had a goal and a couple of assists — I only ever scored ten goals in my entire career — and was involved in the play for what seemed like the first time all year. I was feeling good about myself — reporters were crowding around me after the game — but the second they left, Al Arbour came up to me and said, "What the hell were you doing out there tonight?" I asked him what he meant, and he said, "Scoring goals. It's not your job." Then he walked away.

PERRY BEREZIN: After Gord Sherven scored a hat trick for the Oilers, Glen Sather, instead of congratulating him, tore a strip off him: "What do you think you're trying to do? Show up our star players?" Sather's smug, arrogant face was enough to fuel the fire of any team, but he was masterful in the way he put together the Oilers' supporting cast. He protected his star players like no one else. If you came within a foot of Gretzky, you'd have two or three players threatening to kill you. Once, Badger Bob wanted to make a statement, so he started Neil Sheehy, Tim Hunter, and Nick Fotiu in Edmonton. Sather was livid. He blew his top. There was a brawl two seconds into the game, which more or less defined the Battle of Alberta. The gamesmanship was so deep and complex. The time that Mike Bullard was speared in the 1988 playoffs, he was only acting. We had Bearcat Murray [the Flames' trainer] jump onto the ice. He whispered to Mike, "Stay down, stay down. You okay?" Bullard whispered back, "Ya, I'm fine, fine," as he lay on the ice. There were conspiracy theories in both locker rooms on a regular basis.

GARRY UNGER: Tony Hand was playing in Murraysfield, Scotland, a suburb of Edinburgh. My team in Dundee were big rivals with the Murraysfield Racers, who played with us in the Heineken League. The league had made a deal with the Calgary Flames that the British player of the year would get a tryout with the NHL team. Tony Hand won the award at eighteen, and they had a big presentation in Calgary, inviting him to training camp in the fall. That summer I went to Banff and ran into Glen Sather, sitting around a campfire during a pack trip. He said, "Tell me some goofy stories about England." I told him everything I had done and said, "By the way, Calgary's bringing over Tony Hand, the British player of the year." He got this little grin on his face and said, "No they're not. I'm going to draft him." He drafted him for the Oilers just so he couldn't go to Calgary's camp.

BUGSY WATSON: I once said, "Good morning, coach" to Toe Blake at the Forum. Being young and gung-ho, I was at the rink early and thought nothing of it, but he just walked past me in silence. So I sought advice from Big Jean. I asked him if I was in shit with Toe, but he said, "Bryan, let me tell you so we get this straight right now. I've been in Montreal for fifteen years. Last summer on the golf course, I was walking down the fairway and I did the same thing: I said hello. He didn't say 'hi' or 'kiss my ass' or anything. Don't worry about it, Bryan. He treats everyone the same way."

YVAN COURNOYER: Toe Blake was an honest coach. He was demanding, but fair, and he told you what he was thinking. He'd talk to you harshly in the room, but when you read what he'd told the reporters, you were never that bad.

PERRY BEREZIN: Bob Gainey had the most quiet intensity of anybody I've seen. He didn't have to say anything and you were terrified.

BARTLEY KIVES: The Jets' old GM John Ferguson used to get so angry up in the press box that they had to install glass in front of his compartment to prevent him from raining notepads, pens, plastic drinking cups, and other debris on the Winnipeg Arena ice surface.

MIKE PELYK: We had King Clancy coach us one year in the playoffs. I swear that he walked into the dressing room before a game, slapped his hands together, shrugged, and said, "Okay, boys. Just go out there and do the best you can."

BRAD DALGARNO: Butch Goring was the only coach I ever had who called you into his office without making you expect that shit was going to happen. He sat down with guys one on one and asked questions like, "How do you think you've been playing?" and "What can the team do for you to make you a better player?" He defined his expectations, whereas too often in the NHL, coaches make players read between the lines, trying to figure out what they're supposed to deliver. I know that it confuses tons of guys. And unless you've got a great assistant coach, teaching in the NHL stops. It's a self-directed education. They think they only way you learn is if you get sent to the minors.

PERRY BEREZIN: Cliff Fletcher would call you up to his office and instead of intimidating you, he'd ask, "How're things going? How's your place working out? Anything I can do to help?" He actually called me in one day and said, "We've talked to your agent and we want to give you a raise." I said, "No, seriously," but he was being serious. I was living in a world that will never happen again.

NICK FOTIU: Freddie Shero would come in and say things like, "I don't remember where I parked my truck," or "I don't remember which hotel room I'm staying in." He'd walk into the bathroom instead of the dressing room, things like that. He was just playing games, getting people to think he was a gentle, confused guy when he was really a master technician.

PAT HICKEY: When Fred Shero was my coach with the Rangers, he gave us ownership and accountability for the team. In 1979 – the year we went to the Cup Final – he only came on the ice four times; the practices were mostly run by Mike Nykoluk. Twenty games into the season, he announced after a game, "There's a practice tomorrow at ten. Who wants to run it?" I stood right up, and everybody's jaw dropped. Fred let the team be the team. He used to stand behind the bench with a pen and a scrap of paper. I once asked him, "Hey, Fred, what are you writing down back there?" He told me: "Ah, nothing, Pat. I'm just acting here. I'm only making people think that I'm writing something down."

CURT BENNETT: Boomer Geoffrion was my coach in Atlanta. As an expansion team in 1973, we went in to play the Bruins, who'd won the Cup the year before. In an attempt to motivate us, Boomer stormed around the room and shouted, "Over dere in dat odder room . . . who dey got? Eh? Who dey got? Dey got number 4 and 7. Da rest played for da Braves last year!" Anyone who knew the Bruins knew that he was dead wrong, but that was Boomer's thing. He didn't know about tactics, but he knew how to get you going emotionally.

JEFF JACKSON: Before I was an Isle fan, I was a Bruins fan, and Espo was one of my favourites. The reason he traded for me was because, during one game in New York with the Leafs, I was all over the ice stirring things up, and I hit one of the Rangers in front of their bench. Espo, who was the coach, said something to me and I said, "Go fuck yourself, Espo." He yelled back and I got into a "Fuck you" fight with him, right in front of everyone.

Afterwards, he called Bill Watters, my agent, and told him, "I want Jeff Jackson. I like his spunk." When I was traded to New York, the team said they'd send someone to meet me at the airport, but when I landed, there was Espo. He's very typical of a lot of hockey players. He was an icon, but he's also just a guy.

PERRY BEREZIN: Badger Bob was the happiest sports guy I've ever met in my life. He was always on. He must have said, "It's a great day for hockey!" at least ten times a day. You never spoke to Badger because he was a terrible listener. He'd ask you what you had for breakfast, and in the middle of telling him, he'd say, "Oh, you'd better have something better than that. That friggin' Suter, he had cornflakes and water once, what the hell is that?" He'd just go off. He had report cards for us that he handed out every ten games. Some guys didn't like them, but they were perfect for me because I needed constant communication to get better. He'd grade us between 1 and 10, and there'd be tons of comments. Nobody does that any more. Lanny McDonald hated them because he got picked on for things that no one would talk about. I'd get an 8.8 because I played great in my own zone, while Lanny would get a 5 even though he'd scored twelve points. Badger was constantly trying to find the edge. The year we beat the Oilers in 1986, he'd read somewhere – he might have made it up, I don't know – that strawberries helped scar tissue heal faster. He said, "Boys, we gotta load up on strawberries because there's gonna be a lot of scar tissue in this series!" We were laughing at him, but it didn't matter. By the end of the series, everyone was eating a bushel of strawberries because that's what Badger said was going to give us the edge.

Like a lot of rec men's hockey teams, the Gas Station Islanders weren't much to look at. They seemed even less athletic than the Morningstars, which is saying something. Their alleged ace-in-the-hole, scorer Gavin Brown (who'd won a Producer of the Year Juno a few weeks earlier), hadn't even shown up for the game. Not only was his absence a blow to the team's hopes and aspirations, but it complicated things in that we were forced to ice two centremen and three wingers, which meant that I'd have to crunch math while also dreaming up the motivational tricks and strategic hooks required to keep the Islanders competitive. Looking over the team as they strapped on their armour, I wondered whether that was possible.

Dale was the team's least obvious beacon of hope. His brown-black pads, tire-treaded catching glove, sixty-ounce Northland stick, and gaffer-taped chest plate that seemed to provide as much protection as a silk camisole made Dale look like a hockey street-person, someone whose sporting pedigree hinted at a 1974 ball hockey game. But Dale's Sally Ann chic belied his talent. In fact, the Popsicle-stick goalie had once starred for Triple A Niagara Falls, *circa* 1977. That year, his team took part in an international tournament in San Diego, and Dale was the starting goalie, if for a glorious few moments. Things went terribly awry, however, when Dale and his buddies, during a visit to Disneyland, decided to smoke a joint in one of the park's deserted picnic areas. They were besieged by park police, who harangued them before calling for their coaches over the park's loudspeakers. The coaches phoned Dale's parents in Canada and broke the news that their son had brought shame and embarrassment upon the greater Niagara Region. Dale was forced to sit out a month of hockey and was later drummed from the league, derailing his junior goaling career. On the same trip, Dale got into a fist fight with his roommate and suffered a black eye, but the memories aren't all bad. One evening, another teammate propositioned two streetwalkers and bargained with them to service the club at $20 a pop. The players were done two at a time, and Dale remembers he and his buddy on the other bed giving each other the thumbs up for stuffing it to their coaches on at least one illicit teenage front.

I was reminded of Dale's dark and speckled hockey past each time he pulled on his gloves and pads, for they were also dark and speckled, ridden with puck marks that stood out like bullet holes on a car door. Were I Mike Keenan, I would have been on the phone threatening the GM if he didn't get me a proper goalie, but since I'd decided that I was more of a Major Freddie MacGregor type – Chicago's famous Scotsman of the 1930s, who wore a tam-o'-shanter to practice and slid pucks to shooting forwards from his knees – I led the team out of the dressing room and patted our backstop flat on every inch of his gear. It was then that I uttered my first rather coachish command, imploring Dale to "Lead us out there, goaler!" He ended up being the sixth or seventh player to hit the McCormick ice, but no matter. Once the puck dropped to start the game, every Islander knew who they were playing for.

Our opposition for the game was Ottawa's Songbird Millionaires, named for a well-regarded local music shop. No stranger team has ever graced the E! tourney. The previous year, they'd come to the tournament wearing fake moustaches, bowler

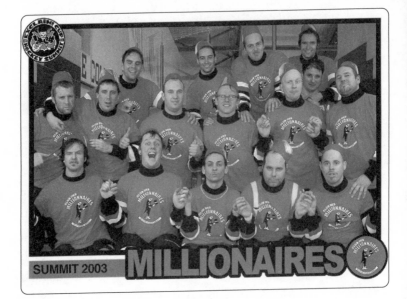

Songbird Millionaires, 2004

caps, candy-striped red-and-black socks and jerseys, and T-shirts with Ottawa 67s socks sewn on as sleeves. They were like a team from the 1930s as imagined by Guy Maddin or Peter Greenaway. Their retro-dandiness was even more exact in 2004: tuxedo jacket jerseys with Roman numerals. More fantastic still was their off-ice dress: tuxedos and tails, top hats, monocles, squirting lapel pins, pocket hankies, and spats. It wasn't until the ceremonial gift exchange that I learned of the Millionaires' inspiration for their style: Millionaires brand sardines ("Fish She Is Very Small"), whose icon is a fish in 1930s formal wear.

During the Millionaires Hootenany performance, a player named the Unknown Wrestler (who was also Guy Carbonneau's cousin) did twenty minutes of stand-up comedy. These were the highlights of his routine:

Q: Why can't you get a drink in Toronto?

A: Because all of the cups are in Montreal.

Q: Why are the Millionaires like the Titanic?

A: They look good until they hit the ice.

Q: Why did the child want to live with the Songbird Millionaires?

A: Because his mother and father beat him. The Millionaires don't beat anyone.

After the Wrestler's act, the rest of the tuxedoed team climbed onto the stage and formed a human pyramid with their goalie – a thimble-sized netkeep named Blake Jacobs – perched atop, holding a Lite-Brite with the numbers 613 – Ottawa's area code – spelled out in purple and green bulbs.

Blake was Dale's match in the vintage of his equipment, but his style was quite different. While the Islander goalie attempted every save as if he were Bernie Parent toeing the puck in the Cup final, Blake leapt at his shots like a cat to a silverfish. One night, after returning to the shed for post-game libations, the small goalie drew a disc of shoepolish and a chamois from his pocket, fell to his knees, and began polishing our boots at the command of another player who was caning him across the back. It was a bizarre scene, bordering on the macabre. It was as unlike hockey as anything I've ever experienced. Which, I suppose, was entirely the point.

JAMES DUPLACEY: Dick Beddoes was a flamboyant and controversial sports journalist who was known as much for his colourful collection of fedoras as he was for his biting satire. Beddoes never walked into a room; that was too pedestrian for him. Instead, he burst upon the scene like an exploding firecracker. When I was working at the Hockey Hall of Fame, he would blast into the library and immediately begin filling the air with outrageous and extraordinary tales of the game as it was in the good old days. Invariably, they'd start like this: "James, I gotta tell ya. So and so did such and such right there and then to you-know-who. James, I know this to be true because King Clancy told me, and King Clancy's been in the game of hockey for over fifty years." For a time, I believed he was relating these tall tales for my edification, but Dick was actually rehearsing a routine he would be presenting later at some sports banquet or roast. One afternoon, Dick flew into the library and without any provocation proceeded to spout a lengthy tale that detailed the immense proportions of Charlie Conacher's penis. He compared its girth to various reptiles, both current and prehistoric, and stated that its length was measured by the rungs on a milk stool. Dick established an on-the-spot thesaurus for the word *penis* that, to my ears, has never been equalled.

Later that week, newspapers across the country were clogged with reports about Dick's performance at a private-school function in Vancouver. It seems that he regaled the students with the same tall tale he had run past me only days earlier, using much of the same detail. Dick's days as a motivational speaker on the rubber-chicken circuit had come to a controversial conclusion. He wouldn't have wanted it any other way.

TIM ECCLESTONE: Jimmy McKenny was our player rep with the Leafs. He was told to go to Chicago for the player meetings during the All-Star break, and was advised to bring his equipment in case he had to play. He got into the game and made a few giveaways, but otherwise, he was unspectacular. In his first game back, Jimmy picked up where he left off, and in the first intermission, Red Kelly, our coach, grilled him about his lack of zone-to-zone comprehension. Jimmy would lug the puck up the ice before he'd pass it, and this really irked Red. [Red always preached moving the puck from zone to zone.] He said, "I watched the All-Star game and noticed that, at one point, Mr. Esposito skated over and the two of you had an animated discussion. He was telling you to pass the puck to the forward out of the zone, wasn't he, Mr. McKenny?" "No, he wasn't, coach," said Jimmy. "He was telling me to check out the broad in the fifth row."

EDDIE MIO: Studio 54 was everything that you've heard about: the girls, the wildness. Pat Hickey, Duguay, Barry Beck, we all went there. I was in awe. It was a great place to be. Ron Greschner moved out and I got his apartment, and I don't think it's an accident that I had my two best years in New York. Barry Beck and I would hang out in the summer and fire trucks would rumble by with the guys yelling, "Hey, Bubba! Eddie!" Nick Fotiu was the mayor of Little Italy back then. We'd walk down the street and people would call him into butcher shops and give him a pound of salami or mortadella: "Here, Nicky, here!" We had a spot called Il Vagabondo that had an indoor bocce court. There was a tradition started by Vic Hadfield and Rod Gilbert where, every

Monday, the team would show up to play bocce. There was no menu either; you'd just order whatever you wanted, and, being Italian, I knew exactly what to eat.

NICK FOTIU: I once put a lobster on [Bill] Goldsworthy's chest while he was sleeping. I got it from the Poseidon Room restaurant in a Toronto hotel. I just walked in, grabbed the biggest one, and hid it under my trench coat. I also used to put baby powder in hair dryers and Vaseline on towels. Once, when I was playing for Calgary, I did about twenty towels. Afterwards, I asked trainer Bearcat Murray, "Didn't anybody complain about the towels?" He said, "No, we sent those to the Vancouver dressing room." I'd rig buckets of water to long skate laces and put them over doors, lockers. I used to room with Steve Vickers, and he'd always put a glass of water by his bed. Once, I got a whole thing of salt and put it in. I drove people nuts to the point that they had dreams about me.

STEVE LUDZIK: The year that Steve Larmer and I finally made the 'Hawks, I decided to have some fun with him on the day of our last pre-season game. If we played well, we were staying with the team; if we didn't, we were getting demoted to Springfield. Because we'd roomed together since junior, I knew that he always got up at around 3:30 p.m. We used to sleep at the old Bismarck Hotel in Chicago, which had small rooms and beds like surfboards. Larms would take his watch off, set the alarm, and phone down for a wake-up call before he fell asleep. While he was sleeping, I changed his watch and the clocks in all the rooms so they'd read 7:30. I got the girl downstairs to agree to phone up at 3:30

and tell Larms, "This is your 7:30 wake-up call." When the alarm went off and the phone call came, he woke me up and freaked out: "Holy shit! We're late! We've missed warm-up!" I had to go into the washroom because I couldn't stop laughing. He was trying to put his pants on in a hurry, yelling, "Ludsy! You think they'd have called us!" After he got dressed, he looked at me with heavy disappointment and said, "Springfield, here we come." I couldn't contain myself any longer. The penny finally dropped and he said, "Ludsy, you fucking sonofabitch."

CURT BENNETT: One late night in Montreal when I was with the Blues, Carl Brewer kept banging on my door to let him in. Finally, I went to open it up, but the door came crashing down. Carl was standing on top of it like King Kong, shouting, "Not even this door can hold me!"

BUGSY WATSON: Doug Harvey told me a story about Marcel Bonin, the old circus performer who played for the Habs in the 1940s. He used to be able to take a bite out of a glass, chew it, and swallow it. He was always doing this for the team. One night, on the train, the boys were having a few pops when the Rocket decided that he was going to eat glass too, just to prove that Bonin wasn't the only one. Course, he cut the fuck out of his mouth really bad. Doug was laughing when he told the story, but that was the Rocket. He was crazy enough to try anything.

JOHN HALLIGAN: Thomas Patrick Barnwell — known around Madison Square Garden as Tom the Bomb — was on the Rangers scene for more than thirty years. He was the ultimate inside guy who did a little bit of everything: helping in the dressing room, handling tickets, fetching beer, and travelling with the team. One of Tommy's unofficial duties was to make sure the players were supplied with post-game beers, especially if the team was departing on a charter flight for a game the next night. Tommy would slip two or three cans of cold beers into the players' travel bags. Tim Horton, who played briefly for the Rangers near the end of his career, was fond of Bomber. Returning from a game in Montreal, the Rangers arrived at the Penn Garden Hotel at around four in the morning. Horton dispatched Tom with a handful of change to get soft drinks for the guys from the soda machine on an upper floor. The machine promptly ate the spare change and produced no sodas. Tom went to the lobby to complain to the hotel's night manager, but Horton – whom many considered to be the strongest man in the NHL at the time – just took the three-hundred-pound soda pop machine, deposited it in the elevator, and pushed the button marked LOBBY. The door opened, the manager saw the machine, and the Bomb got his money back.

BOB LORIMER: After graduating from Michigan Tech, I played in the IHL in Muskegon. In college, I'd flown first class, won the NCAA championship, now all of a sudden, I was making $250 a week. I'd play Friday, Saturday, Sunday, then the next week I'd play Wednesday, Friday, Saturday, Sunday. I'd get on the bus, play on the road Friday, get back on the bus, arrive at four in the morning, play Saturday at home, then get back on the bus Sunday for another eight-hour ride. It was really difficult to get used to. The IHL in 1975–76 was the polar opposite of college hockey. We had a guy on our team named Don Kuntz, a goalie, who was also my housemate. He played the butterfly style back then, but it was considered too radical; everybody wanted a stand-up goalie. He was also a drummer. He used to set up his drums in our house and wail away in the off-hours, creating an incredible racket. The other guy who roomed with us was the team's tough guy – Carlos – who was in a motorcycle gang from Quebec. He kept his chopper in the living room beside the drum kit. He'd start it up all the time to keep it tuned, and with the drums bashing away, we were the loudest house in East Michigan, bar none. One game, we were playing Saginaw in the playoffs. Carlos had been thrown out of the first game because of a bench-clearing brawl, and we knew we were in deep trouble because our tough guy was gone. There was a second bench-clearing brawl, and we didn't know how we were going to defend ourselves until, suddenly, Carlos came flying out of the stands with his street clothes on. I remember it vividly because Carlos always used to keep a deck of cards in his pocket, and as he took flight like some kind of strange superhero, the cards spun out of his pocket and sprayed all over the ice.

STEVE LUDZIK: Dave Farrish lived in a trailer in Moncton, and one night, Larms and I stole his motorbike. We put it in his shower. The next day, Farrish walked into practice and said, "You're never gonna believe what happened to me last night. Five guys came into my mobile home. I had four of them down, but the fifth guy hit me with a block of wood in the back of the head and stole my motorbike." Everybody was following the story with rapt attention, until we started laughing and told him, "Your motorbike's in the washroom, Farrish. We took it."

DON EDWARDS: When my wife, Tannis, and I arrived in Buffalo, Schoney showed up and presented us with this beautiful bouquet of flowers. It was a really nice touch. We had a few beers together and he left. When Tannis and I went out later and looked at our flowerbed, we saw that he'd stripped the garden of every last tulip.

KARL-ERIC REIF: My first time seeing the Sabres play was a 5-2 win over the late Minnesota North Stars in February 1971, Buffalo's maiden NHL season. Gump Worsley started in goal for the North Stars. He was already in his forties, maskless, and wore a drill-instructor crewcut, although it had gone completely grey. We were close enough to reach out and grab the Gumper, and I think my friend tried to wing a peanut or two at him over the glass. Early in the third period — Buffalo had pushed their lead to 4-1 or 5-2 — one of the Sabres walked in on the Minnesota goal with a partial breakaway, and fooled the Gumper with a sweeping forehand-backhand move. As the Aud erupted, no one noticed that Worsley had slumped flat to the ice, lying motionless. The Minnesota trainer and a few North Stars finally dashed over to see what was wrong, and the game was held up for several minutes. The stretcher was called for, and as they wheeled it out from the Zamboni entrance at the far end of the ice, Eddie "the Entertainer" Shack — an expansion Sabre — raced over, leaped aboard, and rode the gurney the length of the ice with a big grin and a wave. As it turned out later, Gump had only strained a groin muscle, so Shack's zany antics weren't quite as inappropriate as they might have seemed.

I wore my long black coat and fedora to the Islanders bench, a 1940s vintage bench general. While the NHL has youngified its coaching ranks over the years, every whistle sergeant looks like an old coach at the same point during every game – during the ritualistic shoe-shuffling skid across the ice from the end of the rink to the players' bench. When it was time for yours truly to take this long walk, one of the players tried to assist me as if I were an arthritic blue rinser crossing a buzzing thoroughfare. But I batted him away, preferring to inch slower than a clockhand across the frosty plain on my lonesome.

Over the course of my walk, I came to appreciate exactly why so many coaches are prone to fiery, rock-crumbling shitfits and macho outrage: it is to compensate for those tender moments when they appear about as comfortable on the ice as Toe Blake in heels. This is to say nothing of how underdressed one feels in a coat and hat while armoured giants (relatively speaking) whiz past you in their RoboCop shoulder pads and pants. Legend has it that Dave Manson once held Mike Keenan against a dressing-room wall with one hand – the other hand was poised for a nose-flattening punch – but you wonder how tempting it would have been for him to simply lay the bastard out in a blindsided, pre-game body slam.

I'm not surprised that arrogance is such a large part of a coach's character, given how I lorded over the players while standing on the bench, a single shoe grooved against the top of the boards. After the game started, I found myself commanding my charges from this perch, hollering through my hands like a Terry Crisp of the beer leagues. I was certainly open to sweetening this routine with moments of philosophical sugar, but the Islanders – perennial third-division bridesmaids – responded to my directions, for they came out fast and hard against the Millionaires and seized the game off the hop.

I carried a clipboard upon which I had scribbled out the lines, and while I occasionally glanced at it to steady the mathematical madness of keeping each unit together during, and after, the penalty kill, I mostly used it like a prop, waving it in the air and shouting, "Protect the hive!" and "Leave it all on the ice, boys!" Before moving behind the bench, I'd never realized how physical coaching is. It's a ligament-yawning stretch to the top of the boards, a sudden excited arm flail, an indignant thrusting finger, an angry-fist-shaking-at-the-referee's-pug moment of apoplexy. Coaching is about perpetually pacing along the bench rubber, your players sitting one hand-tap away from being loosed onto the ice, their numbers staring up at you, imploring you for a turn.

Happy to be the referee's friend whenever he leaned socially against our bench (it wasn't Steve, so I had no personal rapport), I jumped at every opportunity to let him have it when he was across the rink. I also jibed and rode and verbally prodded the Millies (it helped that I knew their names – and collected recordings – well enough to personalize each poke). I begged the heavens for an answer whenever a penalty call went against us, and quietly pressed my fist into my hand with every goal. I was a thrashing bench thespian, using the ice the way Laurence Olivier used the stage.

It was George Collins, our oldest player, who scored first for the Islanders, pinging one under the crossbar after working the defenceman into a perfect screen in front of the goalie. George threw his arms in the air as he curled out of his post-goal turn.

When the oldest player on your team scores, it's usually a good sign, and the Islanders were inspired. The elder Islander had told the team before the game, "My dad played hockey till he was thirty, but quit and then got into all that rich Newfie food. He had a heart attack at forty-eight and couldn't skate another day. So, basically, that's why I'm here." George had lost two teeth during a recent game against Winnipeg, and there was talk that he wouldn't be up for the tourney, but I knew it would take more than a few cracked Chiclets to keep him away from the rink.

The Islanders kept moving the puck and were rewarded with a pair of soft goals that bounced past Blake. And when Dale fell in his crease, only to reach back and steal the puck from a streaking Millie forward – his armour rattling like plastic dinner plates – you knew it would be the Islanders' day. The final score was 6-1, my first victory behind the bench. After taking that long satisfying walk off the ice, someone from the crowd pointed back at the rink. Looking over my shoulder, I noticed twenty blotched, muddy bootprints, a gooey line of steps that connected the points between winning and nothing.

HARVEY BENNETT, JR: My coach in Washington, Tommy McVie, was the ultimate disciplinarian. He ran the toughest practices I'd ever been to in my life. They changed the rules about holiday days in the NHL because Tommy wanted us around on Christmas and liked to practise at all hours of the day. Once, in Vancouver, he had us on the ice at four in the morning. He skated us so hard that guys were throwing up.

MARK NAPIER: My first year in Birmingham with the Bulls was pretty normal. I was twenty-one years old and scored sixty goals. Then John Bassett got sick and handed the reins over to our coach and GM, Glen Sonmor, who immediately traded Vaclav Nedomansky for Steve Durbano. It was the first WHA-NHL trade. He brought in Phil Roberto, Bing Bong Beaton, Ken Linseman. It was sort of nuts. There were five guys on our team who were drawing straws to see who'd get in the first fight. We had a brawl every second night, the kind you've seen and heard about from those days in the WHA. Glen got a little carried away by all of this. One day, he called me into his office after practice and said that he thought it would really be an inspiration if I started fighting out there.

HARVEY BENNET, JR: Another legendary tough guy was John Mariucci, who was Team USA's coach at the '78 World Championships. John was a real character. He was three times my age, but I never would have gone up against him. Sadly, he didn't have a clue about how to coach a team. We were lucky that Herb Brooks was around, because, otherwise, we would have been out-coached in every game. We were about to play the Russians, so my brother, Curt, and Herb came up with something resembling a centre-zone trap, which we ended up implementing un-beknownst to John. The strategy worked and we were tied after two periods. Brooks came into the room before the third, and when John saw him, he threw him against a locker, screaming, "What the hell's going on here? This is my team!" He had no idea what we'd done. We ended up losing by five goals.

STEVE LARMER: Mike Keenan taught you to play for yourself, and for your teammates, because you were never going to please him. Once you accepted that, you were okay. The 1992 Stanley Cup Final was tough on everybody — we lost in four straight games — and, after the first game, Mike came in and tore a strip off us. We'd blown an important lead and he lost it. I've often wondered what would have happened if he'd done the opposite, but I've already thought way too much about that series and how it turned out anyway. For about two years afterwards, I'd be sitting on the bench thinking about it. The coach would tap me on the shoulder and I'd be so lost in thought, I wouldn't know what to do.

BRAD DALGARNO: There's so much that goes through your head when you play in the NHL. Every day in the life of a season, the trainer comes into the room with a sheet that says who's skating with whom, and whether you're going to be on the first, second, third, or fourth line, or not playing at all, which is represented by a black sweater. Drinking coffee or doing your stick, everyone's sitting there quietly stressed. It's like watching a puzzle unfold, seeing this person get that shirt, someone else get moved up, another down. The balance of your career is played out before you every morning. Sometimes you'd find yourself skating with the Black Aces one day, then on the second line the next. It's all mind games, trying to jolt a better performance — or not — out of a player. But you can maximize performances out of fear for only so long.

RYAN WALTER: A lot of people think that NHLers just appear out of nowhere, but the path to your first pro game is never easy and uncomplicated. Weeks before my first training camp, I was playing lacrosse with my brother when I turned and tore a cartilage in my knee. I went down to Washington, they nipped the cartilage in half, and I was in a cast. I missed training camp. I spent a lot of time sitting in a lonely hotel in D.C. by myself while everybody else was at camp in a Hershey. Playing in the NHL was something I'd dreamed about my entire life, and the waiting was just killing me.

BOB LORIMER: Because I was in the bottom third of talent on every team I ever played for, I didn't think too far ahead. I always thought, If I can only play for them for one more year. It was my mantra; a lot of guys who come up from the minors think that. There's massive insecurity for a lot of hockey players — not guys like Denis Potvin, but for most of the rest.

JEFF JACKSON: There's not a whole lot of guys, surprisingly, with tons of self-confidence off the ice. There's great doubt in matters away from the rink. Draft day was nerve-racking, to name one instance. Bill Watters and Rick Curran were our agents. They took us down on the train: me, Andrew McBain, Russ Courtnall, John MacLean, and a few other guys. I was rated in the low thirties and ended up going twenty-eighth to Toronto, which was weird because they hadn't even spoken to me. But I never thought, Hey I'm going to go in the first round. Instead, it was more like, What happens if I go in the fifth? Or not at all? You always consider the worst-case scenario, no matter how real or imagined it is.

MARK NAPIER: Getting traded was one of the hardest things to deal with. When I was moved to Minnesota, I arrived to discover that they already had three great right wingers ahead of me: Dino Ciccarelli, Brian Bellows, and Willi Plett. I seemed destined to be the fourth-line right winger from the moment I got there. I could never really understand the trade from Montreal. I'd pic-tured myself ending my career there, and it really got me down. We had a good bunch of guys in Minnesota, but we never came together as a team. It was a miserable time. You didn't get rewarded for playing well, and you never moved up the ranks if you scored. It was like one long rut. My wife was ready to throw me out by the way it affected me. I did a lot of moping around because you can only reassure yourself and act professionally for so long. There was no one to whom I could vent my concerns, no ear to bend. It was the least joyful time in my hockey career. I remember asking the publicity person if I could visit a local hospital and sign some autographs, and she said, "You'd do that?" I told the guys about it and the next thing you know, the whole team was down there meeting the kids. My saving grace was playing Edmonton in the semifinals and having a pretty good playoff run. It helped me get traded to Edmonton, so I suppose something good came from it.

BOB LORIMER: Before my trade to Colorado, we'd just bought a house in Long Island. I'd talked to my agent about the possibil-ity of being moved, but he said, "Not a chance, go buy your house." Six weeks later, I was gone. For my first exhibition game with the Rockies [after playing four seasons and winning one Cup with the New York Islanders], we were sent out to play at the University of Denver. There were maybe seven hundred people in the crowd. Going from fifteen thousand screaming fans to this was very hard. I remember looking up into the stands and seeing my wife crying.

JOHN CHABOT: The Habs didn't think I took the game seriously enough, so they dealt me to Pittsburgh. When a game would end, I'd go and see my wife whether we won or lost and I'd give her a kiss; to them, that was a sign that the game didn't mean enough to me. I wasn't willing to give hockey twenty-four-hours a day, and I'm still not. When you're out of the rink, there's not much you can do about a loss. I didn't hang with the players; my wife and I were trying to create a life outside of hockey. In Detroit, I was known among my neighbours as the guy who'd come over and help you clean your pool. I wanted to give myself, my family, and my kids a chance to live life away from that glare.

AL MCDONOUGH: It was hard playing on all losing teams in Los Angeles, but it was harder not playing. When your club is in last place and you're not dressed, your confidence starts to suffer. The breaking point for me came during a road trip, when I asked our coach, Fred Glover, "Freddie, am I ever going to get a chance to play on this team?" In my day – I don't know about now – there was an unwritten rule that you weren't supposed to speak to the coach unless you were spoken to, and Freddie responded accordingly. He glared at me and said, "Ah, you rookies. You grumble about this and you grumble about that. You're never happy, are you?" The next day, I was traded to Pittsburgh.

SAM BATTIO: In the old days, you talked to management once: when you signed your contract. It was your moment of glory. Afterwards, they didn't know that you, your wife, or your family even existed.

DEREK SMITH: I was a little shocked when I was traded from Buffalo. The circumstances were unusual because of a prank that Schoney had tried to pull. There were rumours that I was going to be moved, but no one thought they had any substance, so Schoney told Rip, our trainer, to come out and tell me that there was a call for me in the office. Whenever anyone was asked to use the phone in the office, you were either getting traded or being demoted to the minors. So I went in, but of course there was no call, and everyone had a good laugh. The next day, I was at home working when the phone rang. It was 4:45. Scotty Bowman was on the other end, telling me that I'd been traded to Detroit. I told my wife to turn on the TV — Scotty hadn't said who I'd been traded for, or anything — and, at five o'clock, Ed Kilgore came on and said, quite regretfully, "I can't believe the note that's been passed in front of me." I was staggered when he read it: Schoney, Danny Gare, and I were all leaving.

JIM SCHOENFELD: The day I was traded to Detroit from Buffalo, the doctors didn't want my wife to travel because she was eight months pregnant. So, not only was the shock of being traded huge, but all of a sudden the possibility existed that I might not be there for the birth of our baby. Because I'd been a Sabre all my life, there was a great sense of mourning when I got

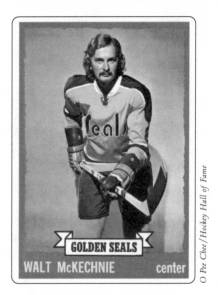

GOLDEN SEALS

WALT McKECHNIE   center

O Pee Chee / Hockey Hall of Fame

to the airport. All of the reporters were there, along with a bunch of fans – people I'd known for a long time – and before you knew it, we were hugging each other and bawling our eyes out.

WALTER MCKECHNIE: In 1973, I could have gone to the WHA, but instead I stayed with the Seals. That summer, I was traded to Boston, and when I went to see Gary Young to say goodbye, I asked him if Boston was going to honour my new contract. I was going to go from $32,000 a year to $65,000, $75,000, and $80,000. Gary got Harry Sinden, the Bruins' coach and GM, on the line, and he told me not to worry, everything would be fine. Two weeks later, I called Sinden to firm up the contract, but he said, "Don't worry, we'll do it at training camp." I went to training camp, but I didn't see him for ten days. Finally, I tracked him down asked when he wanted me to sign my contract, and he said, "Well, Walt, I'm really sorry. My owners won't let me sign any new contracts, so you'll have to play for $32,000."

FRED STANFIELD: I went in seven times to see Tommy Ivan, the Hawks' GM, looking for a $2,000 raise. *Seven times.* We had no agents, so you had to go in there yourself. I went into his office and sat there in front of the arbitrator, who was Clarence Campbell, of all people. I went through some tough times, but I stood up for my rights. I was proud of that. I lost a lot of ice time in the NHL, but it worked out fine in the end. They'd send me down, but I'd score nineteen or twenty goals right off of the bus. They had no choice but to call me up, play me, and pay me.

JOHN CHABOT: Once, the GM in Pittsburgh came to me while I was riding the pines and said, "Why are always laughing? Is there something funny about being benched? You should be pissed off." I said, "Why should I bring my bad attitude to a room when I'm supposed to be helping the team win?" It's been a problem with pro sports in general. GMs want you to live the game at all hours; they think it takes away from your performance if you don't. But the way I see it, your brain works that much better if you have other interests. When I was on the ice before a shift, I could look at the ref and have a giggle; I could talk to my teammates and have a laugh. It's the way I was as a player, but a lot of hockey people can't accept that kind of attitude. They want you to live and die the game every minute and every breath of your life.

JOHN BROPHY: In the old days, coaches didn't tell you if you were off the team. They just didn't hang your sweater in the dressing room. Players today are allowed to be miserable, and it's the coaches and management who've allowed it to happen by not sending guys down, letting them take days off, listening to their bullshit like, "I'm in a slump, they're not using me right, nobody passes me the puck, the system is terrible." For so many contemporary players, hockey has become a game of excuses. Few players play the game for real any more.

13 | SANTA, GORD, AND ELVIS

The Easter tournament, on its own, is quite fulfilling, and not just because it's a great way to get out of going to church. But in 2004, as the first round of the NHL playoffs dovetailed into the E! Cup, even the sickest hockey person's needs were served. The entire weekend consisted of people who smelled of hockey watching other people who smelled of hockey play. If you weren't skating with your own team, or watching another tournament game, you were hit by the buzz of the pro playoffs, taking in Tampa-Islanders on the tiny TV that sat on the middle step of a ladder in the DeLaSalle concourse, or swallowed by Calgary-Vancouver beamed onto a screen the size of a barn door at Studio 99, home of the evening socials. Scattered among the myriad of Leafs fans racked with anxiety over their club's post-season fortunes, the visiting players were just as wound up about how the team they'd left behind was performing in the playoffs.

As a result, most players were an emotionally bedraggled mess. In one instance, the Ottawa Millionaires played a Toronto team in the late afternoon, then rushed out to see the Senators and Leafs wage war. The previous year, I had been on the ice during Leafs-Flyers Game 5, keeping my ear tuned to the sound of a TV parked just above the bench, rushing the puck up the ice into a make-believe swirl of Primeaus, Gagnes, and Desjardins.

This year, I decided to shadow the Leafs to Ottawa during their playoff run. Those who know me from afar might be surprised to learn that this was the first time I'd followed the team to another city, but the notion had never appealed to me. But now was the time to test the luck of the highway. Still, I hedged my bets by first piggybacking on another set of fans' anxiety and enthusiasm before heading off. I stopped in Montreal for Game 4, Habs versus Bruins.

Previously, my most memorable NHL road game had been courtesy of The Tragically Hip's Gord Downie. In 1995, the Rheos were opening for the Hip at the Living Arts Theatre in Philadelphia. Our set ended at around nine o'clock, giving us enough time to catch Philly-Islanders at the Spectrum. Andrew Rourke, our roadie at the time, and I quickly cleared the stage and hailed a cab outside the club, demanding to be delivered to the hockey rink. The day before, in Boston, I'd gone on another sporting pilgrimage of sorts, jumping on the L to visit Fenway Park and Boston Garden, where I stood outside their gates, inhaling the sporting history contained within the old, concrete walls.

Going to the Spectrum, however, was a different kind of pilgrimage. For a Leafs fan like me who'd grown up watching my team pillaged by the Broad Street Bullies, it was the site of much horror and pain. Back in the 1970s, the Flyers were a team of greasy, snaggle-toothed pirates on a bad buzz who'd found a home in the lawlessness and unruly behaviour of hockey. In 1975, the greatest Leafs team of the last thirty years pushed Philly to a seventh game after tying the series in Toronto, but lost 7-3 when Borje Salming fell while pivoting at the offensive blue line, leaving one of the most despised Philly forwards – Don Saleski – to skate in alone and score.

The taxi drove and drove and, after a while, Andrew and I began to wonder whether, like the Leafs teams before us, we were being brought to our demise somewhere in the dark Philly night. We ended up driving through what appeared to be a sprawling industrial lot, and as I poked my head through the partition shouting, "The Spectrum? Where is the Spectrum?", the taxi pulled up in front of Veterans Stadium, home of the baseball Phillies.

"No, not the Vet!" I cried. "The Spectrum. The Flyers! Hockey!" The cabbie rolled his eyes and pointed across the road, where the Spectrum rose above a great set of stairs. Apologizing that we'd ever doubted him, we paid the driver and crossed the street, walking ticketless to the broad glass front of the building. I half-expected the rink attendants to look like Flyers fans during the team's heyday – shaggy-faced, hump-backed, and vaguely Neanderthal – but when we tapped on the doors, an orange-sweatered young black kid named Darnell appeared and asked, "Can I help you, fellas?"

"Ya. How much time's left in the game?"

"About fifteen minutes of the third," he told us.

"Cool. Okay, here's the deal," I said, and told him, in painful detail, all that Andrew and I and thousands of others had suffered throughout the 1970s, concluding my appeal by telling him that we were in town for one night, and that we promised never to return if he could somehow squeeze us into his sold-out rink.

He opened the door.

"Go down there," he said, gesturing down the hallway. "Ask for Chardelle. She'll help you out."

Chardelle was tiny and had gold teeth. She was like the sun to us. We told her what Darnell had said, at which point she looked past us to give him a playful what-for with her eyes. She led us up into the second tier and told us that we could watch the rest of the game on the steps at the north of the rink overlooking Ron Hextall in his black and orange. It was almost enough to make me take back everything I'd said about the Orange Scourge. But then I looked at the crowd. Every fan weighed about three hundred pounds and was hairy-armed, dressed in Eric Lindros sweaters. The Spectrum was the darkest building I'd ever been in, and with the score tied at one, the sound of the crowd – a continuous howl, rising and falling in pitch with each Flyer rush – brought home the fear and horror Leafs teams must have felt in this place during Philly's glory years. At around the twelve-minute mark of the final period, Eric Lindros won a faceoff from Kirk Muller, skated out with the Legion of Doom, and dished to Mikael Renberg, who buried the puck over Tommy Salo's shoulder. The win put Philly in the playoffs for the first time in five years. In celebration, the crowd reminded me of those slack-armed heathens in Mel Gibson's *Mad Max Beyond the Thunderdome*, shouting and howling. After the game, we escaped from the madding crowd, but before jumping into a cab to take us back downtown, I turned to the rink, where a torrent of hairy men were streaming out of the doors. I shouted something I'd wanted to shout in enemy territory for years, "GO LEAFS GO!"

DAN DIAMOND: In 1976, a friend of mine and I hitchhiked to Philadelphia for two second-round playoffs between the Habs and the Flyers. We took the bus from Montreal over the border to Plattsburgh and from there we caught rides to Philly. It took a day and a half and we didn't sleep a wink. We were fried by the time we got to the Spectrum. We had no tickets and the game was that night. We did everything possible to get tickets. When the Black Aces took the optional skate, we talked to them, but they looked at us like we were insane. We knew a girl who'd been in Grade 2 with Orest Kindrachuk in Prince Albert, Saskatchewan, so when he arrived, we yelled, "Hello from Faye!" but, again, nothing. We ran into two floorsweepers from the Spectrum who offered to lock us in a broom closet for fifty bucks, then open the door during the anthem. If we'd have taken that, I think they'd still be looking for our bodies. After a while, we took a break from our ticket hunting and walked around the back of the Spectrum where, near the Zamboni exit, Toe Blake was sunning himself in a chair. We were thrilled to see him. We went up, introduced ourselves – I noticed that he was wearing a 1947 All-Star game tie pin – and immediately started talking strategy: "Do you start the Lafleur line against the Clarke line or do you go with Jarvis-Gainey-Roberts?" After a time, Toe asked us, "Do you guys have tickets for the game?" We told him that we didn't, so he told us to look up Floyd Curry, who was the Habs' assistant GM. We met him an hour before the start of the game and he pulled two tickets out of his pocket, which cost eight bucks. Earlier, I'd called the Flyers' PR department and was able to get a press pass by saying that I was covering the game for the CBC. The Canadiens, of course, won the series in two games straight, and, after watching them carry around the Stanley Cup on Spectrum ice, my friend and I took turns using the press pass to go into the Habs dressing room. It was 120 degrees in there, with sweat raining off the ceiling. They were wildly celebratory, and Dryden was the craziest. Before I showed my pass a final time, a young woman came up to me and asked if I'd give a note to Jimmy Roberts. I told her that I would, but I couldn't resist looking at it first. It had the drawing of a champagne glass with a woman's leg hanging over it and it said: "Jim, thanks for the great time and the tickets. Next time you're in Philadelphia: anything you want!"

I went over to Roberts and told him about the woman and gave him the note. He was naked at the time. He had the biggest cock I'd ever seen.

Gord Downie and his brother, Mike, joined me and a few others on the trip to Montreal. The two of them are incorrigible Bruins boosters. Their obsession with the black and gold is such that, in playoff pools, Gord only picks Bruins. When I suggested during our ride that Gord and Mike follow us on our trail to Ottawa to see the Leafs, the brothers looked at me as if I'd suggested dining on roadkill: "Why would we want to do that?" With the Downies, if it wasn't the Bruins, it wasn't hockey.

Shooting down the 401, we indulged in obsessive hockey talk. To my mind, there's no greater Canadian experience than road-tripping the open highway in the early spring and talking hockey. Still, there were long moments when Gord would fall out of the conversation. Considering the depth of thought in his lyrics, I assumed that he was chewing on a rhyming couplet, perhaps pondering a metaphor, but I was wrong. I looked into the back seat, where he was talking into his cellphone and punching his BlackBerry with his thumb and fingers, communicating with other Bruins fans around the continent. He was whispering things like: "No, Murray's fine. Joe: it's a rib. Is Bergeron playing? You sure? They're looking at a suspension for Ribeiro, aren't they? They're not? Agh! C'mon. They have to." When he rejoined the conversation, he stretched the canvas for the evening's events – who was playing for the Bruins, and who wasn't; what the papers had said in Boston; whether Joe Thornton had walked in unassisted to the building that morning – helping us know the game, as he did, from every possible angle before the first skate scratched the ice.

I'd seen hockey in Montreal before, but never during the playoffs, and never with the Habs up against a team with as deep an enmity as the Bruins. Our seats – secured through some eleventh-hour magic – were high above the visitors' net, behind Belleville's Andrew Raycroft. As it had been for Andrew and me in Philly, it was a stomach-twisting experience for Gord and Mike to wade into a throng of fans who, over the last forty years, had celebrated so much Bruins misfortune, from Don Cherry's Game 7 gaffe in 1979 to Patrick Roy versus Cam Neely in 1988 to Ken Dryden stopping the Bruins in 1971. For the Downies, entering the stands was like walking into the fog of war and sitting among spirits who'd conspired to make the Canadiens the most storied franchise in sports at the expense of their team.

The Bell Centre is a typically enormous – probably too big – sporting bowl, but because the lighting is soft and the mood mellow, it feels less cavernous than buildings in Ottawa and Vancouver. A modest scoreboard, fewer trick lights, and less frenzied pixel strips mean that the oval of ice is the focal point of the building, something that's been overlooked in many brassy new constructs. The pace and tempo of the pre-game theatre had an elevated style too. Despite a beer Zeppelin that wandered loutishly through the air, the tone of the evening was established once the lights were cut and the thumping of war drumming came over the PA. After the players drifted to their benches, two-hundred-foot, red and blue projections of the Rocket, Beliveau, Lafleur, and Doug Harvey swam over the white ice. They were awesome to behold. For the Hab-hater, it got worse: scrolls appeared on the scoreboard listing Hab Cup victories, Hall of Famers, and record holders, a tsunami of achievements unmatched by any team in any sport.

During the game, the fans were as entertaining to watch as the players. I've always had a soft spot for the rhapsodic fan who lives and dies with each home-team stride. This is to say nothing of the Santas, gorillas, Elvises, and bewigged face-painters who enliven the domain of the hand-sitter. It says something about how one views one's participation in the carnival of life when getting ready to go to a game is more than just buying a ticket spat out by a machine; when it's about stealing a bedsheet, slashing it with letters and colours, daubing globs of paint over your cheeks, then pushing your head into a plug of synthetic blue, red, or orange curls. It's about eleven guys engraving *Habs sont la!* on their chests with felt markers, or that quiet man who booked off work early to rent a Colonel Sanders costume for Game 7. Behaving like a goof in public is to do what proper society would rather you not do, which, of course, makes it all the more appealing.

At the Bell Centre, everyone, even people not dressed like Batman, was into the game. Excited fans couldn't stop chewing their fingers as the tension mounted. These moments of fear and doubt — which I experienced at a remove, for I wanted neither team to win — were allayed by every Hab goal. Then, thousands of hands punched skyward, as if the mass of fans was trying to get the upstairs neighbour to turn down his Metallica. Whenever Montreal grabbed the lead, fans worried the clock along with each neon blink, while Bruins goals elicited a low, tonal moan.

Gord's reactions seemed just a bit exaggerated, probably because he and his brother appeared to be the lone Bruins fans in the Bell Centre. Whenever the Bruins missed a scoring chance, Gord's neck tightened and his hands performed karate chops, as if Canada's rock laureate were trying to cleave a plank of wood. Throughout the game, he employed three kinds of laugh: one of disbelief after a wonderful Raycroft save; one of horror after a close Habs chance; and an exultant laugh for each Bruins goal. Whenever they scored, Gord bolted from his chair, tipped his head back, and tickled the clouds with his fingers. Then he phoned every Bruins fan alive to tell them exactly how it had gone down. During the final period, with a disputed Bruins goal under review, Gord took a phone call from a friend who was watching the game at home on television. He told Gord that Mike Knuble's shot had, in fact, beaten Jose Theodore, and while the rest of the

Bell Centre anxiously awaited the referee's decision, Gord bellowed, *"It's in!"* holding up his BlackBerry to the crowd.

Mike, for his part, nervously kept the flat of his palms on his lap, and moved only to pee or celebrate a goal. He was taunted by Hab fans all game long. Whenever Montreal scored, a fan sitting behind him would swing a T-shirt through the air, hitting Mike on the back of the head while pretending he hadn't meant to. After a while, Mike responded by launching some beer over his shoulder after every Bruin scoring chance. And when Glen Murray scored in OT — giving his team a commanding 3-1 lead heading back to Boston — the Downies jumped and frugged and swore into the night, vindicated by the Bees come-from-behind victory.

After the game, we strode through the Montreal rain to Ziggy's, a small, low-ceilinged bar made famous by Nick Auf der Mar, the late city columnist. Someone named Jean presented Gord with a Jose Theodore T-shirt. Over the moon with the Bruins' triumph, Gord announced, "I love *all* goalies!" the polar opposite of "I hate *all* shooters," which the tall goalie had confessed to me after a rec league game. Jean's reaction to the series surprised me. He was loose and happy even though there'd been two ugly Habs incidents in the last two games: a floundering pantomime by their young star, Mike Ribeiro, and a vain attempt by Alex Kovalev to convince the referee that he'd been slashed while skating away from a free puck, a play that had resulted in Murray's breakaway goal. When I asked Jean why he wasn't crying in his glass of 50, he said, "Well, there is still some hockey to be played." It was exactly what I expected from a fan whose team had won so often, but I reminded him, "Yes, but the way they lost . . . there's never been a Canadiens team ever that's lost like that." Mike Downie, who was quite Ziggied by this point, took my criticism of the Habs' play as a slight upon his Bruins, and demanded that I explain myself: "The Bruins? Wha? They won! Whaddya mean it was in a bad way?" The adrenalin, the awful tension, the glorious, redemptive victory in the face of a lifetime of aching defeat had been a potent cocktail for Mike. It was as if the power of the victory — much like the shudder of bad news — was impossible to deal with straight-on. When I finally left the boys at the Hotel Vogue for a late-night drive to Ottawa, neither Gord nor Mike could move from where they were sitting. They'd wrenched every last bit of triumph and celebration out of the evening. This was certainly a good thing, since the Bruins went on to lose three straight, giving way to the peerless Habs in seven crazy games.

JOHN CHABOT: Something about hockey in Montreal is different. People still get dressed up to the nines, and the writers are as passionate as the fans. During my first year, Toe Blake was always in the room. He was elderly, so he'd come up and shake my hand and talk to me because he couldn't remember if he'd done it the game before. Serge Savard was my GM, Guy Lafleur was my winger, and Larry Robinson commanded the power play. My hero growing up was Peter Mahovlich, and when I asked for his autograph, he took me aside and said, "Listen, kid, you really shouldn't do this in the dressing room." It was total hockey culture. The downside, of course, is that I'd get into a cab after a loss and the driver would ask me what the hell was wrong with the team, or the waiter in the restaurant would give me the evil eye. In the summer, I thought I might escape this a little, but I remember spending a half-hour in a restaurant signing autographs on a July afternoon. Hockey is never over for Montreal fans.

BUGSY WATSON: I had a CH on my ass from the time I was very young. Back then, the Montreal Canadiens had feeder teams in Regina, Peterborough, and in Montreal: the Junior Canadiens. I was playing in a high-school tournament when I passed Baldy McCabe, who was standing near the boards just as I laid someone with a check. He was the coach of the Petes and he said, "You're going to be playing for me in a couple of years." He was half-right because I ended up playing for the Petes, only for Scotty Bowman. By the time I turned pro at nineteen, I knew the whole Montreal system and they knew me. Every Sunday, when Peterborough played at the Forum in front of Mr. Selke and Sam Pollock, they knew what they had. There was no nonsense. Scotty was there, Cliff Fletcher, Toe Blake, all these incredible hockey people. The year Sam Pollock took over from Mr. Selke, he brought in Gump, me, Fergie, Terry Harper, Red Berenson, Dick Duff, and Dave Balon: the biggest onslaught of anglophones ever in the Montreal organization. It was a huge change. It was tough for the English to make the team because the Habs had two first-round picks every year and they chose the best kids in Quebec. Because of this, you'd do anything to make the team. Ralph Backstrom was one of the greatest players ever to play junior hockey, but he sat for six years on the bench behind big Jean Beliveau, Henri Richard, Phil Goyette, and Donnie Marshall. It was the same for a lot of us, but just being around the team meant something. One of the greatest experiences of my life was travelling by train with these guys. I remember Gump and Geoffrion and Beliveau telling Montreal stories. The guys never talked about other teams or other players. They talked only about the Montreal Canadiens.

MARK NAPIER: I went from the Birmingham Bulls to Montreal. Beliveau, Henri Richard, and Toe Blake were all still around. It was magical. Being in the WHA made me appreciate the Habs experience, but because I'd played a few years of pro, I was less in awe of the Montreal aura and what it represented. When I came up, Cam Connor, Pierre Mondou, Pierre Larouche, Pat Hughes, and I were all vying for two spots. What made getting in the line-up twice as difficult was that Scotty Bowman never changed it when the team was winning. And the Habs won a lot. It put a lot of pressure on us young players, praying that the team would win whenever we got a chance to play.

CURT BENNETT: Scotty played his guys on the bench like a great piano player on a keyboard, mixing, switching, pressing all of the right keys.

TIM ECCLESTONE: When Scotty Bowman was GM of the Blues, I had to go in before the '68 season and negotiate my contract; there were no agents back then. Scotty wouldn't move from $17,000 a year, so I sat for the beginning of training camp. I went up to his suite and argued that I'd had a pretty good playoff and that we'd gone to the final, but he said, "Not $19,000 (which is what I wanted). The most I'll offer is $17,500." So I sat some more. Days went by and I still wasn't skating. He called me up again and said, "So whaddya think now?" and I told him that I couldn't stand watching: I was ready to play hockey. He filled out the forms and got the contract ready and when I went to sign it, I looked down at my salary: he was paying me $18,500. But that was Scotty.

CURT BENNET: When I was with the Kansas City Blues of the Central Hockey League, we were asked to play an exhibition game against the U.S. Olympic team over Christmas. Only eleven guys showed up, but we played anyway and won 7-3. But I guess we didn't play well enough, because Scotty Bowman barged in after the game, threw all the sticks to the floor, and fired the coach and GM on the spot.

MARK NAPIER: You never knew where Scotty was coming from. He was pretty hard on me and a lot of the younger players. He never approved of my short stick; it really bugged him. One day he called in the entire team and tore a strip off my ass for cutting down my stick. I skated around after that with my head between my legs, then Yvan Cournoyer, who used to have the shortest stick, came up beside me and said, "Thanks a lot, kid. You just took the heat off of me. Scotty's been giving me shit for fifteen years, but don't change anything." From that point on, any time Scotty started to jump on me, I'd look over at the Roadrunner, and he'd wink at me and start laughing.

YVAN COURNOYER: One day Scotty gave me hell for having a different kind of stick. I guess he was upset because I'd only scored five goals with it the night before.

LARRY PLAYFAIR: Scotty and Roger Neilson arrived together in Buffalo. Roger ran the practices and Scotty ran the bench. Roger never raised his voice. He was very matter of fact and forgiving. One thing he told me was, after missing a hit on a player coming down the boards, to throw my stick and crash into the glass and let him think that he was lucky to pass me. Scotty, on other hand, was always barking. I was scared to death of him, but he was unquestionably the greatest coach I've ever played for. One night in 1980, he threw me and another rookie – Mike Ramsey – on to the ice with forty-five seconds to go, with the faceoff in our end. I was nervous and I didn't understand, at first, why he was doing this, but he was just seeing if we could handle the pressure of a playoff-type atmosphere. He'd test rookies like that, always looking ahead, a dress rehearsal for the big dance.

RYAN WALTER: When I got to Montreal from Washington, I knew there was going to be huge pressure. I remember stick-handling on a breakaway and losing the puck in the corner because I was so tight, and the crowd booing me. After we lost in 1989, the city was like a morgue. I went with my wife to the grocery store after we'd lost and people were screaming at me. Still, I learned more about myself as a player and an individual with the Habs than with any other team. Jean Beliveau was there and Bob Gainey was my captain. I sat next to Larry Robinson. I'll never forget Toe Blake being around in 1986. He came into the dressing room wearing his fedora after we'd won a big game and talked to the guys. He sat down next to me and said, "Way to go, Ryan, good job!" Then he looked me right in the eye – I'll never forget the stare – and said, "But don't forget. You've got nothing yet.

Nothing." The whole point of being a Canadien was that if you didn't win the Stanley Cup, you were nothing. Out in Vancouver and other places, fans criticize their team for not going all the way. But the Habs demanded success and all that it did was turn them into the most winning team in the history of pro sports.

YVAN COURNOYER: Getting ready for Canadiens camp, I made a wall to shoot steel pucks against all summer. It was made of hay and carpet and I put it in the garage. Whenever it rained, I'd stand in there and shoot all day long, from the morning until the night. At training camp, I didn't mind the physical punishment. I had cuts, bruises, black eyes, but I loved the game so much that I barely noticed. I had to go out and get a hat, coat, and a suit to wear when I travelled with the team; something you never think about when you think about what it means to be on a team. The coaches watched us constantly – Sam Pollack too – and there was tremendous pressure on me because I felt I was representing the Montreal Canadiens, even if I was only auditioning to become one. Players like Rocket Richard were around at the rink. The first time I met him, he gave me that long, intense look that he's famous for. I said to him, jokingly, "I'm here to take over!" He didn't say anything. He just looked at me with deep suspicion.

RON MURPHY: Phil Watson used to put me against Rocket Richard. To me, he looked like he'd taken some kind of medicine, there was a real glaze in his eyes. I'd simply try to stay with him on the ice. Once, when I got his stick underneath my arm, he ripped it out and, Christ, he burnt me. He burnt both my arm and my side. That was my lesson number one about defending against the Rocket.

NICK FOTIU: In the Stanley Cup Final in 1979, the Rangers beat Montreal in Game 1 at the Forum. After the game, Rocket Richard stormed into the Habs dressing room and cut up the whole team. It must have been really scary. He mocked and lambasted them and they never lost another game.

JAMES DUPLACEY: One afternoon Scotty Morrison, who was president of the Hockey Hall of Fame at the time, called me down from the library to help answer a question that was puzzling Maurice Richard. I'd never met the Rocket, so this was the opportunity of a lifetime. When I arrived in the exhibit area, I noticed Mr. Richard and Mr. Morrison and a few other interested observers discussing a life-sized reproduction of the famous Turofsky brothers photograph that captured the exact moment the heel of the Rocket's skate shattered the supposedly unbreakable glass at Maple Leaf Gardens. The Gardens was the first rink to erect the new Plexiglas protection and, naturally, it was also the first arena to have to deal with it exploding into a million pieces of powdery glass. That picture, which ran in every major newspaper the day after the event, shows the Rocket falling back to earth amid a shower of glass while a bemused Maple Leafs forward named Cal Gardner looked on. "I don't remember much from my playing days," the Rocket confessed, "but I'm sure it wasn't Cal Gardner who hit me that night." Mr. Morrison asked me if I could shed a little light on the subject. I could. I had just finished researching the details of the event and I could identify the guilty party. I explained to Mr. Richard that the newspaper photo had been cropped, but the actual picture was much larger and it had one other Maple Leafs player in the frame, quietly sulking away from the carnage. "You are right, Mr. Richard," I offered. "It wasn't Cal Gardner. It was Bill Juzda." The words hadn't even left my lips when the Rocket erupted, shouting and swearing, "Juzda! Juzda! I hate that guy. I hate Bill Juzda! I hate that dirty, little . . ." His eyes turned from pieces of black coal to blazing fireballs. Suddenly, it was as if the Rocket was back on the ice, on that night, reliving the moment and ready to do damage to anyone he saw who might even remotely remind him of Bill Juzda.

RICHARD HARRISON: Because I'd written *Hero of the Play*, I was asked to write four poems in honour of the game's fantastic four: Howe, Hull, Beliveau, and Richard. Nelson Saunders of the Calgary Booster Club told me the club was going to bring them to Calgary as guests for the Sportsman of the Year Banquet, an annual awards night where the club recognizes the lifetime achievement of one of its own. The banquet, with its star attractions, is a fundraiser for athletic programs all over the city. After the reception, I took my seat at a table of eight in the dining room. The ceremonies would begin after dinner. Two of the people at my table were a father and son who both idolized the Rocket. The son had a photograph of his go-cart, which had been painted bleu, blanc, et rouge with a big number 9 on it. He wanted to get Richard to sign the picture after the celebrations were done. But Richard was very ill, from the cancer and the flight and the medicines. In the brief chat I'd had with him, he'd said his legs were gone from the treatments he'd been receiving. He was tired, and he couldn't stay for the whole event. Before the speeches and the auctioning of his sweater began, he had to return to his room to rest. It was the last time I and almost every one of the eight hundred in the room ever saw him. As he rose from his chair, we rose from our seats. Before he began to make his way to the other end of the huge, dimly lit dining room, he motioned to our table, for the boy to come to him. When the child came back, he was clutching a hockey card and the photo of his go-cart, both signed. Then Richard made his way across the hall, pausing every so often to steady himself on his weakened legs and to acknowledge all of us who were applauding. Then the big doors opened and the light from the hotel shone in the entrance so that when he turned to wave to us one last time, he was a silhouette framed in gold. Then he was gone.

14 | THAT CERTAIN FACEWASH

Both teams switched ends to start the third period. We sucked water, moved the defence down to one end of the bench and the offence up the other, and checked our sticks for holes and skates for cracks. I tried to draw some hope from the masses of fans who were now stacked one atop the other and leaning over the ice, and gazed searchingly at the puck-pocked boards, spit-strewn bench, and the tip of Al's bugle for inspiration. It all came down to whether the Morningstars could stare at 3-1 with twenty minutes left and find any trace of hope in the numbers.

Mark yelled that we should shoot the puck more, but instead of hollering back, "You've been on our asses all year, man!" I told him that he was keeping us in the game and that he was the greatest goalie ever. I told him, "Those guys in white . . . you've got 'em guessing!" before skating to the bench wondering why goalie masks didn't come with zippers. On the pine, the

Morningstars huddled like scullers lost at sea, our faces wan and red, hearts thumping, legs hot with fatigue. Sitting next to me, Tom Goodwin, who'd deflected two pucks past Mark — an unfair fate for the tournament's tireless organizer, let alone someone who's grandpa once played with Rocket Richard — bowed his head while a river of sweat dripped from his shaggy sideburns. Exhausted yet hard-bitten, he gathered himself, stared out at the ice, drew a deep breath, and shouted, "Go get 'em, 'Stars!"

Each Morningstar interpreted Tom's command in his own way. Al hit the ice shrieking; Cheech used a stoned zigzaggery to befuddle the Unyon defenders; Steve checked his opposite as if trying to feed him through the boards into another dimension; and the Chizzler whistled the puck at the Detergent Box whenever he got within thirty feet of the goal. I decided to take another tack in announcing to the Unyon that the third period would be no croquet match on ice. For me, Tom's command meant, "Get out there, Bidini, and hit that fat guy with the ponytail!"

Ponytail and I were more than overdue to engage in a little twist and shout. Were you watching the game, you would have noticed our after-the-pass slashes, the geez-I'm-in-the-vicinity-anyway elbows, a litany of long cold stares while skating to the bench, and the sure-you're-not-hurting-yet-pal? cross-checks whenever the two of us met near the shooting perimeter. You would have noticed that we were the most involved agitators on either side — Johnny and Dutch also pitched in in this regard — and if you hadn't already gathered that there was great unpleasantness brewing between us, you might have even confused it for a weird kind of love.

Our eventual set-to near the beginning of the final period was the result of both teams realizing, suddenly, that the outcome of the game was hanging in the balance. It's always the best sequence in any game – one team, having skated confidently all match, steels themselves for the final thrust of their opposition, who realize, at the same time, that the moment of truth is upon them – and our confrontation was a microcosm of that. Both Ponytail and I felt that if we could somehow get the other to cry uncle, it might portend the outcome of the game.

I am not a fighter, so it was not really a fight. I've lost every fight I've been in – on and off the ice – and since I took Ponytail for being more or less the same kind of decorative scrapper, I waded in without fear of getting pummelled in my home rink. It was, in fact, a great theatrical moment for both of us, played out in front of an enlightened, liberal arts, alt-rock, socialist crowd, no less, whose enjoyment of our mini-bout allowed them a delicious reprieve from their commitment to peace and understanding in our time. Our confrontation started with the puck staring up at us from between our feet. I dug my shoulder into Ponytail's chin, and he reacted with a butt-end to the ribs, which I answered with a groovy slash down his inner calf. A snug headlock gave way to a rib-rattling elbow, and another butt-end was traded with a forearm shiver until we were squishing our gloves into each other's faces, our *nrrrrghs!* and *ohhhgnnns!* and *grrrrrrss!* stifled by the hot, sweaty leather.

Yup, lovers for sure.

After trading facewashes, I hiked an elbow under Ponytail's yap, and, for an instant, I thought I felt the lummox's legs ripple. But as soon as the image of me standing in victory over his limp carcass flashed through my mind, Ponytail carried out what must have been an official Unyon retaliation, slugging me in the bugle with the blunt knuckles of his padded glove. My oft-whomped schnozz absorbed the blow, and I slugged him back, only to see that he'd recocked his punching hand. I recocked mine. Then Steve the Rock and Roll Ref jumped in, tying up our arms and shouting, "Cool it, sluggos!" Making one final lunge for each other, we buried our faces in the zebra's shoulder as he pulled down our arms. The top of our helmets touched, and after plastic kissed plastic and the crowd *yaaoowed!*, we pushed apart, meeting each other's gaze. I smiled, and so did Ponytail. It was an intimate, "Those guys – Brad and Chad, Topping and Chizzler – sure they're pretty good. But who's everybody talkin' about now, eh?" kind of smile. We pawed each other's helmets and skated to the penalty box, where we sat together and watched the beginning of the last ten minutes of the game of our lives.

FRANK BEATON: I grew up on a small one-hundred-acre farm near Antigonish, Nova Scotia. Our family was totally self-sufficient, at least until the town started to come out to us a little bit. The biggest influence in hockey came from my oldest brother, Don. He made sure I had skates and would always shovel the pond. I don't think I skated on an inside arena until I was eleven, and I had to walk three miles into town to do that. The townies would pick on me. There was nothing I could do about it. I'd have my little brother with me, and it killed him to see me picked on. That was the seed of my rage. I made a promise to myself that, one of these days, I'd even the score. When I was fourteen, my older brother Bill bought me a speedbag and put it in the barn. Every day, I came home from school and started hitting that speedbag. I'd hit it for two hours. The local radio station would play rock and roll from 3 to 5 p.m. and I'd hit the bag for a song, then rest for a song. I wanted to become good and dangerous with my hands so that I'd never have to take it from those townies ever again. All of this lurked in the background as I moved up through hockey, and when I went to Sarnia as an eighteen-year-old, I didn't go as a tough guy. I went there because I worked hard and hit hard, skated up and down the wing. I hadn't done any fighting to get recognized to that point, but when I got there, I found certain opponents intimidating my teammates the same way that I'd been picked on in town. These guys needed to get tuned, and now I had the ability to take care of them. After my first fight, everyone stood back and said, "Holy shit! Where did that come from?" All of the rage and bitterness in my life came to a head and was released. From then on, whenever someone would get picked on, they'd look down the bench at me. There were a few times when I rebelled against it and thought I'm not going to do this tonight. I'm going to let so-and-so fight his battles, but I'd get benched. So I persisted, and eventually I got some notoriety and started to get better pay out of other teams.

NICK FOTIU: When I was a kid, my dad took me to see the Flyers play the Rangers at the Garden. I'm no bible freak or anything, but at that moment, God told me, "This is what you're going to do." It was like a religious experience without the religion. I'd never played hockey before. I'd tried figure skates, but the first time I wore hockey skates was when I turned fifteen, right after that game. My family thought I was crazy. My parents asked me, "How are you going to make it over Canadian kids who've spent their entire lives playing the game?" I used to flood fields in Staten Island by opening the hydrants and skating across the ice by myself. I'd get up at three in the morning, pack my duffle bag, head up the street to get the bus, go over the Verrazano Bridge, catch the RR to 57th Street, get off, and catch the train to Coney Island, carrying my hockey bag and a hatchet in the dark just so I could be on the ice at five. Eddie Stankiewicz, who was coaching the Long Island Ducks at the time, wrote me and said, "What I see in you tells me that you're going to make it." His letter meant the world to me.

Lou Vairo cut me from the Brooklyn Stars after I tried out for them. I told him that he was going to regret it, that I was going to play for the Rangers, but Lou said, "The only thing you're going to be doing in Madison Square Garden is selling popcorn." After that, I went to New Hyde Park and played for the Arrows. It was the same rink where the Rangers practised, so I got to know Emile Francis. At that point, I was playing in the Metropolitan League, but the following year, Emile did me a favour and sent me to the Cape Cod Cubs, who were a Rangers/Bruins farm team in the East Coast Hockey League. In one year — my first year of pro hockey — I went from Cape Cod to the top Rangers farm team [Providence Reds] to the WHA. Within twelve months, I was playing against guys like Rosie Paiement and Reggie Fleming, whom I'd watched at the Garden. I could skate, shoot, fight, and I hit everything that moved, but it wasn't until I made the Rangers that I felt like I'd realized my goal. As a kid, I'd been taught by

Rod Gilbert; now I was his linemate with the Rangers. In the summer, my friends would go to the bar, but I'd ask them to drop me off at the rink. It was the middle of June and I'd crawl up into the blue seats, waiting to wake up from my dream.

CURT BENNETT: My dad, Harvey, had been an NHLer, and he passed on certain things that helped my brothers and I survive in pro hockey. Back in the 1970s, it didn't mean much that I was an All-American. As both a college kid and a Yank, I had to earn respect; not like today, where a lot of highly touted kids come out of college. One of the many things my dad suggested was taking karate. The whole idea was learning about how to be tough while not letting anger get in the way. My first camp, I played well, but nothing was happening for me. My dad said, "Remember those karate lessons? Well, it's time you to got into a fight." I fought Moose Dupont twice in one game, and after that, the club loved me. It was the turning point in my career because I'd adapted to what, back then, was considered Canadian hockey.

RYAN WALTER: You needed extreme mental toughness to play in Philadelphia against the Broad Street Bullies. Max McNab, our GM, used to draft players not necessarily on talent, but on whether they could stand up to the Flyers. You'd sit in the dressing room and look around and it would be very quiet. I'd do a mental check and tell myself, If we get into a brawl, this guy's with me, so is he, he's not, maybe him, yes, no, not him, not him for sure. You could feel the emotional state and the level of intimidation the Flyers used. One time, Mike Gartner and I lined up against Bobby Clarke and Paul Holmgren. Even though we were our team's leading scorers, I fought Clarke and Garts took on Holmgren. These days, players like Teemu Selanne haven't had to suffer a single fight in their entire careers. But back then, you were required to prove yourself physically, and even though I had broken wrists, knee surgeries, pins here and there, it was nothing compared to the mental strength you needed to play in Philadelphia. It was literally a feeling of going to war.

HARVEY BENNETT, JR: We had Bob Kelly on the Penguins. He was as feared as much as anybody in hockey. People said that he had heavy hands and could throw a mean punch. When we went into Philly, Bob brought a lot of respect. Once, Gary Dornhoefer put his stick up to Durbee [Steve Durbano] and I suckered Dorny. I knocked him down, then Moose Dupont jumped me, and at one point I was on top of both Flyers, with their hands pinned. It was so loud in the Spectrum. The benches emptied and it turned into a circus, but, as a team, we proved a point because nobody went into the Spectrum and started that sort of stuff. Because we had Battleship Kelly behind us, we felt confident. Schultz and the rest of them knew that if they tangled with Bob, they could get embarrassed. Of course, they traded for Battleship, and that was the beginning of the Broad Street Bullies.

BUGSY WATSON: Pittsburgh in the 1970s had a really tough-assed team. We'd go into Philly and Dave "the Hammer" Schultz would get kicked out in the first minute of every game because he didn't want any part of it. He knew exactly what was coming down. After one particularly nasty brawl, I was traded to Washington, and I had to play Philly ten days later. On the first shift, I ran into Bill Barber. I'd taught Bill in hockey school and really liked him, and as he was down, I said to him, sort of playfully, "Banging and bruising. Hitting. Isn't this old-time hockey great?" He said, quite calmly, "Well, Bugs, you're really going to love this game because we've been waiting to get at you for two weeks now." I fought Holmgren, Schultz, a bunch of others. It was an epic friggin battle: the Flyers versus Bugsy. I was cut up and battered, but I survived.

AL MCDONOUGH: My first game for the Los Angeles Kings was in January 1971 against the Flyers in the Spectrum. I'd already been a pro in the AHL for three or four months – I'd had played in all-Ontario junior finals too – so I thought that I knew what intensity was. When I got to the Kings dressing room, everybody was laughing and kidding and getting along. The warm-up was loosey-goosey, another day at the office. But when I walked into the room after the warm-up, I remember Bob Pulford – who was our captain with the Kings – standing up in the middle of the room and commanding, "Okay. Everybody get ready because we're about to go to war. This is going to be a tough night." From then on, every night was like that. You were a mercenary and it was all business.

WALTER MCKECHNIE: One year in Oakland, our whole season was nothing but brawls with Philadelphia. One night at the Spectrum, a kid by the name of Barry Cummings, who'd been called up from the Salt Lake Golden Eagles, took on Bobby Clarke. As Clarke was skating away, he speared Barry on the forehead and opened him up. The kid went crazy. He chased him to

Philly's bench, where he baseball-batted Clarke in the side of the head and knocked him out cold. The wolves on the Philly bench jumped the boards and went after the kid. Cummings cut two more of them with his stick before they jumped him. We jumped too, but our job was to try to pull the wolves off our player, who was getting savaged. At one point, Bill Barber tried to get his stick underneath the pile, but somebody fell on him and snapped his leg. We all thought that was more than a little ironic.

MIKE PELYK: Doug Favell, who came from Philly, used to say, "These guys are all bullshit. I'm tougher than half of them." You had to have that attitude. We had a guy named Willie Brossart, from the Middle of Nowhere, Manitoba. He couldn't skate or shoot – I'd tell him, "As soon as you get the puck, Willie, give it to me" – but if a Flyer were standing in front of the net, he'd be eating Sherwood and Koho. He told the Flyers: "If anything wearing black or orange ever comes near me, I'm breaking its arm." None of us were afraid, least of all Borje Salming. The first time Shultzie tried to fight him, Borje grabbed his arms and didn't let go. The veins were popping out of the Hammer's head, he was so frustrated at being manhandled.

FRANK BEATON: The meanest guy in the WHA was Gilles "Bad News" Bilodeau. He was not only the strongest sonofabitch I'd ever seen, but he was the meanest. One time, there was a game in Birmingham against Kim Clackson and the Winnipeg Jets. In those days, there were no officials on the ice during warm-up, and when the Jets came on to the ice, Clackson liked to do a big circle in our end behind the net, then come back into his own end. It was his routine. It got to the point, however, that Glen Sonmor said, "Tonight, I don't want anybody coming across our half of the ice," knowing full well what to expect. Everybody was pushing at the door trying to get out first: Dave Hanson, Steve Durbano, Bilodeau, et al. Moments later, we were all on the ice waiting for him. He came over the line and Bilodeau was the first to charge after him. He banged him against the boards, and Clackson turned around to fight. Sure enough, Hanson and Durbano and I came in spearing and punching over the top. Nobody from the Jets did anything. They were all pretending that they didn't see anything. Finally, Clackson held up his hands and skated back into his end. We were pretty happy with ourselves because we'd carried out the coach's orders, and left it at that. The warm-up continued, then all of a sudden, Ulfie Nilsson collapsed in pain at centre ice, holding the back of his leg. Nobody could figure out what had happened. Finally, when Bad News got to the bench, I asked him what he'd seen. He looked over at me and said, "Beater, his foot was that far over the line." He'd broken his stick while spearing Nilsson in the back of the leg.

DAN DIAMOND: At the end of the second period during a Jets game at home, Ulf Nilsson held the puck behind the net as the ref blew his whistle. The players started to skate off the ice, but Curt Brackenbury went up to Ulf, pinned him against the boards, and flattened him. Looking back, Bobby Hull saw what had happened, skated the width of the ice, and sent Brackenbury flying with a crushing hit. The benches cleared and the players fought for forty minutes. Eventually, the police came on to the ice and restored order. Two days later, they did it all over again.

JEFF JACKSON: Scott Mellanby hit me in the jaw at centre ice in Quebec and knocked me out, but my chin hit the ground and I woke up forgetting what had happened. I went off, got stitched, and tried fighting him again. But the scariest moment of my career was when the gloves came off with Joey Kocur. John Brophy was our coach and it was a Saturday night against Detroit. He sent Brad Smith and I out on to the ice about five minutes in, our first shift of the game. He told us to go out there and make something happen. We ran around a little bit, threw some hits. I ran into Kocur, he turned around and looked at me, and I dropped my gloves. As they were falling off, I wondered what I was doing. We squared off. He took a swing and I stepped back and heard it go by my ear. Luckily, I stepped on my stick, fell back, grabbed him, and pulled him on top of me. Needless to say, I held him very close.

TIM ECCLESTONE: We had a tough team in Atlanta: Pat Quinn, Willi Plett, Eric Vail, Curt Bennett, and Ken Houston, who once broke Dave "the Hammer" Schultz's jaw with one punch. One night, we were out drinking when a fan walked up and complimented me on our game. "Now tell me something," he said. "All of those fights: they're fake, right?" I told him, "Listen, buddy, if they were fake, I would've been in a lot more of them."

★

After my set-to with Ponytail, the Morningstars started to come on. "They're starting to come on!" is a phrase used by announcers to describe a team suddenly awakening from its stupor. Chris Topping led us back. Chris did not have Al's sea-snake hair,

Dutch's zombie death face, Tom Goodwin's hockey lineage, or Howie's Howie, but he didn't need them. Where Howie used words like *stoked* and *cheesecake* and *swerve*, Chris started his sentences with "Jeez, I hope you guys don't mind me saying this, but . . ." His single moment of anger came when he fought a member of the Black Windows, who promptly knocked out his front tooth. Not that this did anything to lend Chris's appearance the mark of an unhinged warrior; he got his tooth capped and was the same old 'Star, benignly skating through the opposition while being punched in the head by three defenders stuck to his back.

Because Chris was a tall, square figure – at times he looked like a Georgian door on skates – and because he could stickhandle a dime through a carnival funhouse, opponents were always trying to bag him along the boards. He'd try to avoid getting hit by the defender by slipping along the wall, only to get entangled with the player as if catching him in the spokes of a great, turning wheel. These confrontations resulted either in injury – Chris had ripped apart his knee a few months prior to the E! Cup – or in a penalty, since, on occasion, Chris would crunch the defender with his forearm, even though all he was doing was protecting the puck. But despite his handful of prison hours and Disabled List duty, he nonetheless led the team in scoring and was a constant threat whenever he hit the ice.

Chris is largely responsible for one of my finest rec league memories. It came in overtime during the first game of the 'Stars final against Life: the Nightclub, in which I flung my body along the ice to thwart a slapshot by the goateed lawyer who'd call us cocksuckers two games later. I know the rush isn't on par with

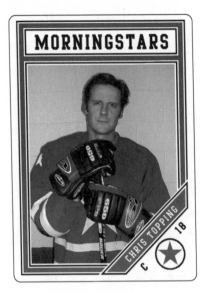

MORNINGSTARS

CHRIS TOPPING 18
C

Hawerchuk-Gretzky-Lemieux, but the puck became trapped in the soft folds of my stomach before I squeezed it out to a safe, empty spot near the edge of the faceoff dot. I scrambled to my feet to pass the puck to Chris, but as I did, I felt myself being pulled backwards by one of the Nightclub forwards. While falling to the ice, I kicked the puck to our winger, but I never went down. I did one of those guy-who-is-almost-too-wasted-to-stand body tilts, then forced myself back on my gravitational axis, racing alongside Chris up the ice. I zipped past a surprised defenceman, who turned to give chase, making it two 'Stars against one Nightclub. The defenceman tied me up as Chris gained the zone, at which point I turned and gently massaged the defenceman in the face, who responded by wrestling me into a headlock. It was from this vantage point that I saw the puck spinning into the top corner of the net. Extracting myself from the player's armpit, I hugged Chris, who had barely enough time to celebrate before the goalie burst from his crease and started punching him with the end of his waffleboard.

On the ice at McCormick, the Unyon, cocooned by the false comfort of their two-goal lead, weakened just enough to allow us to bend their fences. After a faceoff in our own end, Johnny stormed out of the zone, then slung the puck over to Chris, who hurried up the ice. With Cheech moving longitudinally for the first time all game, three of them proceeded against the two Unyon defenders. The first defenceman came at Chris, who displayed the puck before quickly tucking it away, turning the defender inside out. As they moved deeper into the Unyon zone, a second d-man approached, but this time, using the broad side of his shoulder, forearm, and hip to blunt the players' advances, Chris concealed the puck. The defender reached for it, but as he did, Chris slipped past him. In the time it takes for a good idea to become a bad one, the tall, polite Morningstar winged the puck at the net, having occasionally glanced at his linemates to trick the Detergent Box into thinking he might pass.

Chris's shot moved in a class all its own. There was no hang, dip, or sigh to it, none of the tumble through the surprised air that defines most rec leaguers' chances. Instead, it took off like Mighty Mouse with one hand outstretched as it leaped past the goalie's short side. I had just hit the ice after changing shifts with Dutch and heard the bench's exultant roar at my back as I skated toward the goal scorer. Behind the net, fans pounded the glass and cheered. Even Cheech's cameraman had moved his eye away from the viewfinder, further sabotaging his film, I hoped. Mid-celebration, I stole a glance at one half-dressed player whose team was due to play in the next game as he moved away from the glass, skate-stepped to his dressing room, pushed the door open, and shouted excitedly to his teammates that the Morningstars had just made it a one-goal game, and wouldn't you know it, they had a life, after all!

IGOR KUPERMAN: Some talented players exist on a level beyond all others. They see and feel and play the game differently. Take Alexander Mogilny. He was on a junior tryout with the Russian under-fifteen team when he missed the plane to Khabarovsk. The next one was in a week, so he sat around in Moscow, doing nothing. A friend who was practising with the Central Red Army said, "C'mon down to the rink and bring your equipment. Maybe you can skate with us." He did. The Red Army took one look at him and they wouldn't let him go. He'd made the big team at fifteen.

STEVE LARMER: Once, I saw Denis Savard kill a penalty by himself in which he also scored a short-handed goal. It was against the most skilled team of all-time – the Oilers – and he deked around everyone, some guys even twice. At one point on the shift, I just stopped at centre-ice. I just stopped and watched him. At the end of his whirl, he went in and beat Grant Fuhr.

FRED STANFIELD: Bobby Orr was the best player who ever put skates on. He could slow the game down and speed it up however he pleased. I once saw him kill a penalty all by himself, controlling the puck for two minutes. He could do everything better than anyone else in the league: shooting, passing, stickhandling, shot blocking, you name it. Bobby Orr played the game tough; it's why he only lasted nine years. He got hit every game as hard as anybody, yet he'd always take the chance to go through a space nobody else would try and go through. He was clipped, slashed, hit. But he kept coming back, game after game.

RON MURPHY: Even in practice, Bobby Orr would come up with something new. His hands were like lightning. I always said that if he hadn't been a hockey player, he would have made a great boxer. I've never seen a guy get his hands off his stick into a fist quicker than Bobby. He used to drop guys with a single punch. He was a fierce player.

CURT BENNETT: People forget that Bobby Orr had to fight his way into the league. He fought John Ferguson and every other team's tough guy. These days, that does not pertain to any of the league's skill players, let alone their best player, which is what Bobby was.

DEAN PRENTICE: Gretzky was amazing, but Bobby Orr dominated the game when there were just six teams, and a few more later on. Every team was a threat every night. There were no soft touches in his day.

GARRY UNGER: Gretzky was amazing skating laterally, and at getting in the right place at the right time and making sure that other guys were in the right place at the right time too. But when Bobby Orr played, there was him, and then there was the rest of the league. He had another gear that was foreign to every other player, and he was tough as nails. He played defence and he won the scoring championship. Every superstar is different, but Bobby was complete in every aspect of the game.

FRANK MAHOVLICH: Bobby Orr did things that coaches had told us explicitly not to do. I remember feeling a little jealous that he got away with it while other players like me didn't.

YVAN COURNOYER: Bobby Orr was one of the greatest hockey players to ever live. But, it has to be said, he couldn't beat the Montreal Canadiens.

TIM ECCLESTONE: Orr, Gretzky, Lafleur were all amazing, but there was only one Doug Harvey. A lot of people don't remember this, but after Doug Harvey stopped playing for the Rangers, he toiled in the minors. He was down in Kansas City in 1968 and I was up with the Blues when Scotty called him up for the last month of the season. In the seventh game of our series against Philadelphia in the Spectrum to decide who would go on to face Boston in the Stanley Cup Final, Doug was tremendous. He was the first star and I was the second, which really meant a lot to me because both he and Dickie Moore had taken me under their wing. Before Doug passed away, Dickie invited me to come up to Montreal and say goodbye. Jean-Guy Talbot, Henri Richard, Beliveau, and the Rocket all went to the hospital room, and they ordered in a lobster dinner. They did it up just right. It was like a Last Supper, but that's how close teams were back then, and that's how much we all thought of Doug.

BUGSY WATSON: One game while I was coaching in Edmonton, Lee Fogolin threw the puck in from the point. Gretzky jumped in the air, caught it, dropped it to the ice, and backhanded it about three inches over the goalie's left shoulder. So before the practice the next day, I told Fog to go stand at the blue line and I said to Ron Low, "I'll bet you a hundred dollars that Wayne can score on you." Ronnie said, "No way." They tried the same play, and Gretz did the exact same thing, beating Ronnie over the shoulder. It ended up wrecking the practice. It scared the hell out of Mark Messier and the rest of the kids. They'd never seen greatness like that before — no one had. Afterwards, when they were skating around, it was like a goddamned funeral. The whole rink went completely quiet.

EDDIE MIO: The scariest thing about that move was that it had been done the night before and Ronnie Low knew exactly what was coming. He knew where Wayne was going to put it and how. But that's what it was like in practice: something new would happen every time. Gretzky made everybody better just by watching him. B.J. MacDonald — along with Brett Callighen — was Wayne Gretzky's linemate in 1979, his first season in the NHL. They were decent players, but all you have to know about Wayne's genius is that B.J. scored fifty goals that year and Brett about thirty.

PERRY BEREZIN: When you shadowed Gretzky, he wouldn't even try. It was really boring. Mario Lemieux was the exact same way. But if you let your guard down for a millisecond, he was gone. *Bang.* Goal. It would take about ten seconds out of a minute and a half. It was rare that Gretzky was spectacular because what he did was normal. I'd only give him an opening the size of a puck, but even that was too much, because he'd put it there.

JOHN CHABOT: Gretzky would take advantage of every situation. If you were a little lax on him, he'd burn you. But Mario could burn you whether you were lax or not. Mario was a much better one-on-one player. You could put Terry Ruskowski and Warren Young on his wings and Mario would still score 50 goals and get 150 points. Gretzky would find somewhere else to get his points.

GARRY UNGER: The Blues played the occasional exhibition against WHA teams. I faced-off against Gretzky once when he was seventeen and a member of the Indianapolis Pacers. He was so skinny I thought I was going to rip his arms off, but I think he got four points that night and beat us 7-4. It was the same when he went to the NHL. He was so deceptive that you'd think he hadn't had a good night, but when you checked the scoresheet he'd had a goal and three assists. Years later, I got a chance to play with him in Edmonton. The Oilers used to throw their sticks in the middle of the ice after an hour and a half of practice and scrimmage three on three from blue line to goal line. Messier, Gretzky, Lowe: it was never enough for them. They had to keep going and going.

PERRY BEREZIN: I'd broken my ankle and was walking out of the Saddledome one day when Gretzky walked in. I'd never met him before and this was during the Battle of Alberta. I was shocked when Wayne said, "Perry, hey, Perry! How you doing?" I told him that I was okay. He asked me, "You going to be able to get back?" A little bewildered, I told him that I probably would. "Well, I hope so," he said. "Good luck, eh?" I couldn't believe it, after everything our teams had been through. I called my dad and effused, "Gretzky talked to me!"

BUGSY WATSON: The first time the Oilers played in Toronto, forty members of Wayne's extended family met him at the airport. We'd gone in early so that he could do his press, and on the day of the game, every paper had about four or five pages on the guy. Each day, the rink was full of reporters, clamouring to talk to Wayne. I remember saying to Slats [Glen Sather]: "Christ, Glen, if this guy can stand up for the national anthem, he'll be lucky." He only got eight points that night.

JEFF JACKSON: You weren't supposed to be in awe of other teams, but with the Oilers, you had no choice. Sometimes when we'd be killing a penalty, the Oilers would put out Gretzky, Messier, Anderson, Kurri, and Coffey. If you won a draw in your own end, you'd consider your shift a success, even though you wouldn't get the puck out of your zone. Because I played on the second penalty-killing unit, I got to watch their power play before I was thrown up against it. It was insane. Guys would lower the heads on the bench so that the coach wouldn't hear and we'd whisper to each other, "Can you fucking believe these guys?"

BUGSY WATSON: One year, I said to Gretzky that his breakaways had got a lot better, and he said, "Ya. I worked on one-on-one's all summer on the driveway with my brother Keith." After he said that, I thought to myself, All these other so-called stars. I wonder how many of these fucking guys worked on anything over the summer, let alone on their driveway, with their brother?

EDDIE MIO: In 1978, Wayne's first year in Edmonton, he was having a bit of trouble adjusting. He was playing on the fourth line with Ace Bailey and Cowboy Flett. It's impossible to imagine Wayne as a fourth-liner — or having to struggle in any capacity, for that matter — but that's the way it was. In our first game back in Indianapolis — the team that Wayne, Peter Driscoll, and I had been traded from — we stunk the joint out. I was terrible, we were all terrible. The next night, he was benched in Cincinnati. He didn't see the ice for two periods, and we were losing 2-0. I was sitting on the bench because Slats was mad at me, and at one point in the third period he looked up and down at the guys before his eyes settled on the kid, who must have felt about a hundred times smaller than any of us, knowing that he had so much talent and that, so far, that talent had failed him. Slats kept looking at him until Wayne made eye contact, at which point the coach said, "Are you ready to play?" The kid went out and got three goals. We won the game, he became our top line centre, and that was when it all locked in. It was the beginning of Wayne Gretzky as we know him.

JEFF JACKSON: One time, Messier was going back to get the puck. He was winding up and doing his cross-cuts, charging full steam ahead. He had that huge head and body and he was such a force, more so when he was in full flight. I thought I'd read him pretty well, so when he came around the net, I went for it. I caught him with his head down. We collided dead-on. He got up, brushed himself off, and skated away, but I just lay there. It was like I'd been hit by a truck. It took me forever to shake it off. I remember going woozily back to the bench and looking over at the Oilers, who were pointing and laughing at me.

GORD SHERVEN: When I was with the Oilers, I saw what it took to be as successful as they were. They were a tight-knit group, but they had fun. They were all a little different, but they respected each other. You need that respect and commitment to each other to win. Fuhr did his own thing; Messier did his own thing; Glen Anderson did his own thing; but, when they got into that room, there was togetherness as well as respect.

One thing I remember were the practices. I never had as much fun as I did with the Oilers. Sather would set up four or five flow drills — just regrouping, two on ones, three on twos, and, honest to God, there would be maybe two or three bad passes the entire practice. The guys had a blast. The puck was flying, tape-to-tape. It was a thing of beauty. We used to practise at the West Edmonton Mall and there'd be two thousand people there, in the upper and lower levels. It was incredible, free entertainment. You'd work hard and keep moving for fifty minutes. And then slugs like me would have to do a little skating at the end.

15 | THE HOUR OF THE PLATYPUS

I know that winning isn't everything. I know that sport is about playing hard and honouring the name you bear on your sweater; that it's about gaining the respect of your opponent and skating away from the rink knowing you left your soul on the ice. In rec hockey especially, the result should slide away as you re-enter the orbit of family, work, and all the rest of your life that affords you the privilege of pretending you're Cyclone Taylor once or twice or three times a week.

But losing never sunnies a black mood. It never paints hope, joy, and wonder across the face of a kid or infuses a nation with a sense of unity, love, and the glory of achievement in the face of impossible odds. Losing never rewards you for all of those seasons you spent living and dying in support of your favourite teams. Losing won't help you feel vindicated after wasting endless hours foolishly defending your compulsion to unbelievers for whom Dryden is the name of a seventeenth-century English poet. Losing is a fat jerk in a stupid hat who stomps on your Christmas presents and raspberries Santa and hoofs Rudolph in the yarballs. Losing is an idiot. Losing is a lout. Losing should seek therapy and get a life.

Tying, on the other hand, is just right. Or at least it seemed that way as the Morningstars skated into the last few minutes of the game, trailing by just one goal. Sonic Unyon were probably starting to wonder where their Wonder Boys had gone as the red and white rallied in hope of achieving the fairest of all results. This isn't to say that we weren't dreaming of two goals before time elapsed, and when Craig Barnes picked up the puck from his defence position, moved through the middle of the ice, deked past three Unyons, and suddenly found himself alone in front of the Detergent Box, those of us on the bench shot to our feet with excitement, our hearts surging.

Because Craig was the smallest of the 'Stars, we tended not to notice him much. He hadn't played a large part in the game to this point. But he'd been a vital figure the previous year, in a circumstance quite similar to the one in which he now found himself. It was Craig who rescued us during a memorial game played in honour of T's father, Ron Parker, who'd passed away in the middle of last season. I'm not very good at funerals – no one is, I suppose – but we'd gone to the service the day before the game, and it was a moving occasion because so much of it was about the power and beauty of hockey. One by one, friends with whom he'd played for most of his life stood up and told funny and profound stories about goals scored and chances muffed, winning, losing, falling together, rising as a group (after becoming ill, one of his friends had encouraged Mr. Parker to get back soon into the lineup, but T's dad said, "I don't know how the fellows would feel about seeing a guy walking around with a bag strapped to him." His friend reminded him: "Ron, you've seen the kinds of things that walk out of that shower.") The funeral was probably like a lot of services in Canada where hockey is the metaphor used by family and friends to understand the complications of life and death. For the 'Stars, it was one of those times when each player understood where we were headed, and how lucky we were that so little sadness or pain had stricken our team. Our notion of the Morningstars was wonderful, drunken, bruised, wild, rank, glorious, inglorious, and occasionally profound. Teams aren't like families — families allow for darkness inside deep love — because teams reflect simple freedom and happiness. Teams are about strength, truth, and wisdom while allowing you to feel like you're eleven years old. Losing isn't a good way of celebrating this.

Near the end of Ron Parker's memorial game, Craig Barnes grabbed the puck on the blue line and skated through the opposition to score, and now, he was trying to match his end-of-game heroics at the Unyon's expense. All of the feelings we'd had that memorial weekend came back as the small defender — seeming even smaller against the white expanse of the Detergent Box's chest — strode in, pushed down on the puck, and wristed it at the net. Our hearts leapt as the puck climbed through the air, but the Detergent Box hiked his shoulder and stunned the disc. He fell to his knees, trapped the puck with both hands, and looked up. For the first time all game, I could see them.

His eyes.

A few plays later, the Winterbird reciprocated with a save sequence of his own to keep it a one-goal game. I'd given up on an attempt in earlier books to devote a chapter to exploring the role, character, sense of dress, behavioural patterns, and mental anatomy of goalies, but after watching Mark and the Detergent Box play such vital roles in the outcome of the game, I couldn't resist poking around the subject just a little.

I flirted with goaltending a few years back, but the thought of being hit in the throat with the puck terrified me. I just couldn't push the image out of my mind. Despite wearing one of those padded blue mufflers, my hands rushed to my Adam's apple with every shot, which is not the best move when you're trying to protect the net. I enjoyed the mad buzz of action around my net, had great fun sliding across the crease like a kid down a toboggan run, and was more than willing to pretzel my body to try to stop shots zooming at me from impossible angles, but after a while, the fear that I'd be clunked in the throat got the best of me. I packed my hulking equipment away and later passed it to two other players, both of whom relearned the game using my gear and were now backstopping teams at the tournament.

Sometimes I look at Mark in the dressing room, his pads standing beside him, his gear bag immaculately clean and well kept, his mask sitting on the bench like an astronaut's bubble, and I ask, How? What? Why? Baseball catchers are different too, but they get to hit. Soccer goalies are also a breed apart, but even Ricardo, the Portuguese national team's goalie, was asked to kick the winning penalty past Britain's Tim James in the quarter final of Euro '04. But no pro athlete is as distinct from the rest of his teammates as a hockey netkeep. You'd think that rearguards — naturally sacrificing their bodies to block pucks, tirelessly (except when tired) trying to rid the zone of the offence, and generally trying to help the goalie — would win a few points, maybe the odd slap on the pants from the goaler, but no. The only time Mark ever talks to me at a game is to tell me that I'm screening him, or to "watch this guy in the slot," or, "Um, you're, like, crushing my arm," which I'm prone to do as a crease-crasher, drawing pleasure in landing on his poofy chest protector to tamp a puck or subdue an attacker. I've commended him many a time on a particularly acrobatic save, but I don't think he's ever thanked me in turn. For goalies, there can never be enough shots on goal at the other end, which tells you a little about how they feel about other members of the netminders' union. It's not like I've ever implored a forward to crush an opposing team's defenceman, sharing, as we do, in the pain and misery and selfless responsibility that it takes to man the second last line of defence. And while goalies have the same low opinion of every forward who ever lived, you rarely see them hanging out together after games or commiserating about opposing teams. Instead, they glower at each other through their masks, aligned in their hatred of goals, and unified in their suspicion of each other.

Solitude is the goalie's lot. Once you've clamped that heavy mask to your noggin, most of the rink noise is pushed out, leaving room for the music of your breathing. You might think that goalies would relish the moments before taking to the ice and letting the oneness engulf them. But you would be wrong.

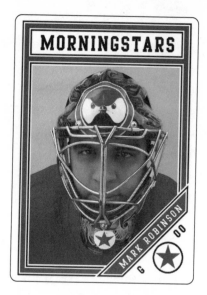

Instead, the Winterbird, like most netkeepers, establishes his inner zone well before he pulls his skates from the bag. Once fully dressed, he sits like a paratrooper about to be dropped over the dark forests of Denmark, psyching himself into a place so still that, when called upon, he attacks and thwarts the puck for threatening his peace.

A goalie's equipment makes it difficult for him not to believe he's the most important member of his team. You simply can't not genuflect to someone who hoists an equipment bag that's twice as wide and heavy as anyone else's. Even the way it shwumps to the floor has a tone of self-importance. It bulges with exaggerated hockey gear, including the jock, which is as big as a bedpan. Once strapped on, the jock must give some goalies a terribly false sense of male sexual power. When I wore one, its size and shape always made it seem more like headgear than a groin-guard, though there was something oddly satisfying – and, I suppose, empowering – about hearing the *plock* of the puck deflecting off it, and not my penis.

Mark's goalie pants could have housed a small family. His catching mitt, like one of those arm-length gauntlets used by attack-dog trainers, ran a three-inch layer of padding from the tip of the finger to the point of the elbow. His blocker (or waffle-board) wasn't particularly oversized – compared to, say, Martin Brodeur's – but once Mark had completed his costume, it looked like a mascot's outfit – perhaps the Pittsburgh Platypus – that had been abandoned halfway.

The goalie mask is what separates the netminder from any other position player in any sport. I've often wondered how goalies would react if a jealous forward decided to equip himself with a similar device. After all, helmets and visors have so inhibited a players' recognition factor that they might as well wear brightly painted cages, giving character to those fourth-line forwards who are so hard to know. Then again, if other players were allowed to wear masks, netminders might lose their unique sense of identity and abandon the game and allow unprotected creases for shooters at all times. Now, there's an idea. . . .

Players sometimes forget the importance of the netminder, in spite of the remarkable costume, but there's nothing like a fast three-save sequence to renew one's appreciation of the position. In Mark's case, his acrobatic backstopping not only held the Unyon at 3-2, but it saved me the embarrassment of having Ponytail score on my shift. The puck was initially thrown at Mark from the left wing, but he poinged it with his blocker to the sideboards, where a Morningstar should have been, but wasn't.

An Unyon player raced over and zinged it at the net, but Mark, coolly playing the angles, kicked it out, this time to the other wing, where a Morningstar wasn't either. The puck landed on Brad's stick, and he fired it toward the net, but missed. After seeing him with the cookie, I'd raced over to his side – had we not previously explored our aggression, I would have chanced a provocative stab in the goolies – so when I looked back to see the puck bank from behind the net directly to Ponytail on the other side, my heart sank.

Mark followed the play side-to-side-to-side, looking through the players' legs like a barn cat tracking a field mouse in tall, waving grass. When the shot came, Mark threw his body sideways at the puck. His pads rose from the ice to form a twenty-inch wall of leather. The Joe Louis found the deep grooves of his padding, but it popped back to Ponytail, who was now surrounded by various 'Stars and Unyons, all jabbing their sticks like eager Musketeers. Lying with his right shoulder pressed to the ice and sensing that there was less than a fraction of a second to react, Mark slithered over and captured the jumping bug before anyone could control it. I threw myself on the goaltender to further protect the disc, at which point the Unyons leapt on me, perhaps realizing it might be their last opportunity all game to do so. "Uh, you're, like, crushing my arm," Mark told me through his mask. Realizing the play was dead, the Unyons grudgingly climbed to their feet. I was the last to stand, releasing our goalie and apologizing to him for the way I'd bounced on his chest protector like a four-year-old on a spring mattress. Mark shook ice shavings from the top of his glove and settled back into his crouch, staring out at a rink filled with morons.

MIKE PELYK: Jacques Plante was a great goalie, but as a team guy he was something else. He was always broke and borrowing money, but he'd never pay you back. One year, we had a bowling tournament and I'd just got my knee out of a cast. I was a pin boy as a kid, so I thought I'd enter the tournament anyway, having played so much growing up. Jacques was also a big bowler, being from Quebec, where everybody plays. We played three games and I shot two hundred each time. Jacques would sit there scowling as I'd hobble up to the lane and shoot on practically half of a leg. Still, I beat him every game and he went home fuming. He couldn't stand losing. He left the party so pissed off at me that I don't think we ever spoke again.

DEAN PRENTICE: When Andy [Bathgate] popped Jacques in that famous game where he went into the dressing room and came back with his mask, he was only doing it because Jacques had tried to bodycheck him when he was out of the crease. Plante was always doing that.

FRED STANFIELD: In the Bruins' first game of the playoffs against St. Louis in '68, I split Jacques Plante's mask with a slapshot and knocked him out cold. He told me later that his mask was tested for 105 miles an hour. They showed me the mask after they'd taken him to the hospital and it was cracked right up the middle between the eyes. Later, Glenn Hall skated up to me and said, "Gee thanks. Now I have to play the rest of the series."

YURI BLINOV: Jacques Plante came into our [Team Russia's] dressing room before the first game in Montreal [in 1972] and sat down with Tretiak. One by one, he told him how to play each of the Canadian shooters. As you know from the score [7-3], it was all very helpful.

DEAN PRENTICE: It was an unusual thing for a goaltender to do, but Charlie "Bonnie Prince" Rayner would stay out on the ice with me and Andy Bathgate and teach us how to be goal scorers. He'd tell us what a goaltender looked for, and what we were to look for. He used to say that when a goalie dropped his shoulder, that's when you went the other way. He gave us so much insight into goaltending, we could have played the position ourselves. We were shooting on him all the time: deking, faking, until we could finally beat him. He was like a father to us. He'd take us around New York and show us the ropes. He loved the Ames Brothers and was always getting tickets to the Roosevelt Ballroom, and once he took us to meet them. It was a great experience for a young kid playing his first few years of hockey in the Big Apple.

DON EDWARDS: I went to the Sabres camp in 1976 and there were six goalies vying for two jobs. They had Roger Crozier, Gerry Desjardins, Gary Bromley, Rocky Farr, Al Smith, and they'd drafted Bob Sauvé. They'd also drafted my uncle, Roy Edwards, who'd retired the year before. I was only the seventh goalie on the depth charts, and because I had no contract with the Sabres — even though Al Eagleson said that I did — they sent me down to Hershey. My saving grace was that I played a lot in Hershey because Bob Sauvé had a contract that guaranteed him a spot on the big-league roster for the first three months of the season. They needed someone to play enough hockey for two goalies until Sauvé was sent down, and I relished the work. I finally got an AHL contract in mid-November and played extremely well, so when the Sabres decided to send Sauvé down, Hershey's coach told Punch Imlach that Sauvé wouldn't see much time between the pipes. Bobby ended up in Charlotte and I kept playing in Hershey, even though Sauvé was the Sabres' prized first-round pick. I threw five shutouts in eight games, and when Gerry Desjardins got hit in the eye, the Sabres called me up. I played Friday night on the road with Hershey, Saturday at home, Sunday on the road again – about a thousand miles of bus travel – and was on a flight Monday morning to Buffalo.

Derek Smith and I arrived before game time, and Al Smith was slotted to play in goal. We took the warm-up, came off the ice, and I sat down beside Al. I wished him good luck, but he looked at me sort of funny. He said to me, "You're playing." Al was always a bit of a comedian, so I didn't know whether to take him at face value, but when he repeated himself – "You're playing" – I knew he wasn't kidding around. After the warm-up, Imlach had made a call down to our coach, Floyd Smith, and told him that he wanted me to play. It was a shock to the players. Skating around to start the game, they looked as if it was a mistake that I was in the net. They were pissed off because Smitty was their buddy. All told, I had about thirty seconds to get ready. Just after Joe Byron sang the national anthem, Smitty jumped off the bench, skated to centre ice, looked up at owners Seymour and Norty Knox – the Sabres owners – saluted them, and yelled, "See ya, Seymour and Norty!" before leaving the ice. He went to the dressing room and quit the Sabres on the spot. That night, I was alone in the nets without back up, but we won 7-3. There were very few high-fives from the players after the game, my first NHL win. Instead, there was a lot of dismay and unrest. They called in Sauvé the next night to back me up, and we beat Chicago 3-0. Two days later, we beat Detroit 2-0, and then we went into the Montreal Forum and beat a Habs team that had only lost eight games, shutting them out 4-0. I played twenty-five of the last twenty-six games that year, my first in the NHL.

DEREK SMITH: I came up with Don Edwards for our first regular season NHL game. When Al Smith skated out from the bench and shouted into the stands, "All right, Seymour, I'll see ya later!" I was amused. I thought it was some kind of routine that he liked to do before every game.

SETH MARTIN: I used to do volunteer shiftwork at the fire hall in Trail [British Columbia], mostly nights. I enjoyed playing locally, but every now and then somebody would call the station and tell me that their goaltender was injured and could I come and play. The calls came from San Diego, Portland, and Spokane. In some cases, I'd drive to Spokane, catch a plane to Portland, and play a game I wasn't ready to play. The travel in those days wasn't great, so when Scotty Bowman went overseas to the World Championships in 1967 and asked if I'd consider coming to St. Louis, at first I told him that I wouldn't, but reconsidered. It all hinged on whether I could get a leave of absence from my job at Cominco, where I was fourteen years into a pension. I was also thirty-four, which was old for a goaltender back then. But I got my leave and went for a year. I played the first six or seven games because, every fall, Glenn Hall would paint his barn and he'd arrive late to start the season. Before I knew it, I was getting shots from Beliveau, Hull, and Mikita, playing with Bobby Plager. But after a year, I went back to British Columbia. I ended up playing for Spokane, where we became the first American team ever to win the Allan Cup.

EDDIE MIO: Windsor [Ontario] Parks and Recreation provided outdoor leagues, and there was a set of goalie equipment that you could use if you wanted to play net. I did and I liked it. Then my mom found an old set of pads for $10, and I started building from there. The priest at Assumption High School, Father Cullen, always had Red Wings tickets given to him by the fathers of American boarders, and sometimes he'd give them to us. The year I turned sixteen, my friends and I drove to the Olympia in Detroit to see the Black Hawks play. We sat way up in the rafters and afterwards tried sneaking in to Lyndell's AC bar and restaurant, which was where the players went after the game. We finally got through, but they caught us. We didn't care about drinking; we just wanted to see our idols. Still, I remember seeing Tony Esposito in the flesh, and on the drive home, I was over the moon. When we got back into town, the night manager of the local rink, Kirkie Scott, let us play from midnight till four in the morning. Many years later, when the Oilers went to Detroit, I told the guys that we had to go to Lyndell's for burgers and beers, because that place represented for me what it meant to be an NHLer.

DON EDWARDS: In the late 1960s, we played with felt arm pads with sponge, a felt belly pad with leather covering, and horsehide goal pads stuffed with kapok and deer hair that weighed a million pounds. The first day of training camp was the worst. The first bruise on your palm would last the entire year. The top of your knees would go too, and eventually you'd crack your kneecap.

JOE DALEY: I was in Pittsburgh and it was the last game of the year. We were playing Philadelphia. Gerry Meehan had the puck in the corner and he fired it at the net. I was playing without a mask and thought I could play it off my chest. As I rose up out of my crouch, I realized that the puck was rising too quickly and on the wrong angle. I turned my face and it drilled me in the jaw. It knocked me from one side of the net to the other. I was on my knees, trying to put my mouth together. The bottom portion of my jaw was now in the middle of my mouth. They hauled me off to the dressing room and I was lucky there was an orthodontist in the stands. He snapped my jaw back into place and bound my head up like a mummy. It hurt like heck but the thing that pissed me off most was that I was going to spend our end-of-season party in the hospital.

EDDIE MIO: Probably the best save I ever made ruined my career. This was in 1984. Bobby Clarke took a pass in the slot from Bill Barber. I did the splits, but my leg went out too far and I heard it pop. I threw my gloves off and writhed in the crease. I'd torn my hamstring in three places. The pain was awful. It set the stage for my downfall, because I came back too early from rehab, wanting to show the Red Wings that I still had it. I played poorly and started questioning whether I had any right to be out there. Because I'd had such a nice career with Edmonton and New York, it was very difficult dealing with these low points near the end of my career. Mentally, I was a basket case. This threw me into disfavour with management and we fought until, eventually, they demoted me to the minors and gave Greg Stefan my job. The next year, I felt pretty good about coming back, but we had the worst team in the league. It was a terrible situation. Danny Gare and I were among the veterans and it was obvious to us that the Red Wings had to revamp things if they had any hope of a future. Three days after the end of the season, a local newspaperman called Danny and me one morning and asked us, "So how does it feel to be released?" My heart was devastated because I hadn't received a phone call from management; still haven't. Everybody wants to leave the game on a high note, but that was the end for me. I tried to catch on somewhere else, but couldn't. It wasn't until years later that I was able to accept the way it ended. But in a way, I still can't.

16 | THE FLIGHT OF THE LUNKHEAD

While it's true that one's performance is connected by a series of details – a puck banked this way off the curvature of the glass, a pass missed here, collected there, deflected off this stickblade, not that one – sometimes hockey just sweeps you into flight. In my case, it might have been a reward for having devoted my recent artistic life to exploring the game at length; saying a few nice things about the late Ace Bailey in an article I'd written for a local paper; or taking eminent broadcaster Brian MacFarlane out for lunch at Sunshine's restaurant in Bayview Village shopping mall in 1998; but with one minute left to play, the score frozen at 3-2, and the 'Stars having been assessed a heart-stopping penalty for too many men on the ice, I became pushed into the game by a greater force.

The play started with Chris Topping leaning in against Brad for a Titanic – well, as Titanic as a rec league musicians' hockey sawoff can get – draw outside our blue line. Steve the Ref spanked the puck flat on the ice and there was a flurry of action, but the disc slipped between the centremen's legs and stopped. Johnny spotted it and scooped it up. He headed for the middle of the ice, but was met by the Red Chevron, who wound an arm around his midriff. I threw up my hands and turned to Steve the Ref: "What the fuck was that, fuck?"

I screamed the question twice more until I realized that Steve was doing me a favour. Instead of reacting angrily, he simply stared up the ice. I got the hint and stared up it too, and saw the puck once again bobble free. Then I did something that is rarely associated with lead-footed, leather-lunged rearguards.

I pounced.

My feet carried me as if I were running from an escaped tiger. I was possessed with a singular purpose, the way a brave (or foolish) soldier might race into enemy fire while shouting at the rest of the charges to follow. The element of surprise worked in my favour too, for it took the Unyon a few seconds before they realized what I was doing, which was wildly taking myself out of position while killing a penalty in the last few moments of the game.

Nonplussed by my sudden flight and trying to redeem himself after a woefully ineffective period, the Red Chevron followed me. He reached in to poke away the puck, but he was met with all the physical intensity of a marginal player speeding toward his chance at glory. I threw an arm in his path and skated off toward the Unyon's zone. The Chev tried bulling through my clothes-line, but I was able to keep him at bay long enough to feel the blue line pass under my feet.

As my skates touched the Unyon's end of the ice, I felt like an explorer stepping onto virgin land; not since my first-period pinch had I skated so far into the Unyon's zone. The Detergent Box neared. I found his eyes. They were strangely soft, blue, unthreatening. I noticed his small features and a wisp of grey hair falling out the back of his helmet. For a fraction of a second I was mildly disappointed that he hadn't looked more like a yellow-eyed primordial puck beast and less like someone who sells nails down at the Home Hardware. I believed I could have him.

I drove to the net.

Because I was dragging the Red Chevron to my right, I'd left myself vulnerable on my left, and that's where a Unyon defence-man appeared and started to slash and whack my stick. I drove and drove — he whacked and slashed — and soon the puck was freed from the comfort of my blade. I lunged after it with the desperation of a man dropping his keys over a cliff, but came up short. The Detergent Box slithered back into the depths of his crease and the puck skipped into the corner. Momentum carried me toward the Joe Louis, but Johnny Sinclair raced into the zone and got to the puck first. He was quickly surrounded by the rest of the Unyon players, and the game became reduced to its most elemental state: nine players fighting to win the puck along the boards. We were a turmoil of red, black, and white; a riot of shoulders, sticks, and helmets screaming as the puck jumped between our feet. Finally, my skate stabbed the Oreo at the base of the boards and held it there. Steve the Ref tweeted his whistle and I looked back at the scoreclock, where a number told the whole story:

30.

As we set up in the Unyon zone – or, rather, as my teammates set up, I took myself off the ice in favour of Tom Goodwin and the Chizzler – I saw that other tournament teams had massed like sentries behind the glass. Fans who'd watched the entire game were regaling those just arriving at the rink, telling and retelling the story of how the Unyon had had their forearm pressed against our throats but, for whatever reason, could not administer the killing blow.

The Winterbird was standing at my shoulder, after coming off the ice for a sixth skater. It's always odd to find your goalie beside you when they've been called from the ice. This usually signifies one of two things: either the game will end in delicious triumph, or it will fizzle out like a spent sparkler. Since most rec league benches are only big enough to accommodate the skaters, it felt as if Mark had pushed his way among us like an obese passenger on a crowded bus. His size tightened the team shoulder to shoulder, pressing us together in a red mass of hope and worry.

Steve the Ref played to the drama of the faceoff, setting the opposing forwards until they were positioned fairly. He turned his head clockwise and back again, peered at the wingers behind him to make sure everyone was where they should be, and then slapped the puck on the ice. Topping won the draw back to the Chizzler. The strong, gentle-faced defenceman steadied the puck on his blade, wound up with perfect form, and fired the puck as a wave of Unyon forwards slid toward him on their stomachs. The Timbit rose just above the black-and-white tide and headed for a letterbox at the top of the net, where it struck red metal and rang it like a bell.

To Sonic Unyon, it was the sound of resistance; to us, hollow hope. We'd hit something while hitting nothing. After kissing the post, the puck jitterbugged in front of the Detergent Box, then leapt safely into the goalie's glove, freezing the game's score. The Detergent Box looked up and appeared more human than ever before: two kids, paved driveway, a yearly theme-park holiday, a life wearied by traffic and heating bills, burdened, perhaps, by a bad business move his wife's cousin had talked him into taking. Climbing to his skates, he let his chest protector settle before pushing his gloves tight to his hands and forearms. He rubbed the front of his pads with the back of his blade. None of his teammates said a word to him. It was as if the Unyon had forgotten about their goalie. For a moment, he was the loneliest man in the world.

Steve blew his whistle and pointed for the players to return to the faceoff dot. It felt like only a fraction of a second had elapsed since the last play, but when I looked up at the clock, there were fifteen seconds left. The Unyon tried changing lines, but thought the better of it, and, for one final shift, Brad, Chad, and the Red Chevron readied themselves for the draw. They circled the dot like cruising sharks, their backs bent, sticks arced over their knees as they nodded to each other, remembering the thousands of last-second faceoff moves that had been drilled into them by coaches and assistant coaches. One silent nod met another as Al shrieked, "C'mon Starrrrrssss!" the spittle flying through his face cage. Beside me, I could hear the Winterbird breathing. All was still. All was alive.

Topping won the draw again, this time less cleanly. But Howie — throwing the length of his body at the Red Chevron — wrested the puck from the Unyon winger and sent it back to the Chizz, who wound up a second time. We rose on the tips of our skates as another wave of Unyons slid toward the blue line. This time, the puck streaked to the low left corner of the net, but not before a square of shinpad fringe or strand of glove lace deadened the disc so that it simply rolled into the goalie's midriff.

The clock fell.

1.5.

JEFF JACKSON: I played in St. Louis for my last year, and one game, I scored a hat trick. Before my third goal, I was killing a penalty and I was really tired. I headed to the bench, but as I did, the puck was turned over, and the guys were yelling, "Go! Go!" My legs were dead, but I got the disc and headed up the ice. Scott Stevens was playing for St. Louis and I could hear him coming from behind. I was running out of steam, but I fired a slapshot at the net. Stevens dove and just missed getting a piece of the shot, which sailed into the top shelf of the net. I'd been sent down earlier in the year by the Pierre Page regime in Quebec, and when the puck went in for the hat trick, I thought, There, take that, you fuckers. That's what you're missing.

TIM ECCLESTONE: My most memorable game happened at the Olympia in Detroit against Toronto, which was also the CBS Sunday-afternoon game of the week. Bernie Parent was in net for the Leafs and Jimmy McKenny was on the blue line. The puck came along the boards and I pushed it past Jimmy. I took it along the left wing toward Mike Pelyk, who dove across at me. I pulled the puck underneath and jumped over him as if running a steeplechase, then went in and fired it past Parent. I got more calls about that goal than any other because of the television exposure. After the game, I was sitting around feeling pretty good when King Clancy came into the room and told me that it was one of the best individual efforts he'd ever seen.

BRUCE BOUDREAU: For the most part, I didn't play a lot for the Leafs. But one game, I was sitting near the end of the bench and we were playing the Canadiens. We were losing 2-1 and I was mostly watching the game. My brother happened to be in the morning paper for something he'd done in high-school sports. It was a big day for him, and because my dad was born in Montreal, it meant a lot to him whenever the Habs came to town. During the game, someone came off and I jumped on. I immediately stole the puck near centre ice, deked out Serge Savard, and threw it over Dryden's shoulder to tie the game. If you ever wanted to see a father looking the very picture of proud, it was my dad after the game. It was the best goal I ever scored and probably my greatest day in hockey.

YVAN COURNOYER: The highs are incredibly high – winning my first Stanley Cup, playing in 1972, playing the great Russian team on New Year's Eve, 1975 – but I remember the lows too. The worst moment of my life came when I retired. I'd had back surgery twice, and the second time, I asked the doctor from the operating table, "Is that it for me?" He said, "I will not say yes, but probably." I tried to go to training camp, and I even scored a couple of goals against Philadelphia, but the following day I could not get up. It took me about five years to get over leaving hockey. As I walked out of my press conference to announce my retirement, I felt like I was walking into a prison.

LARRY PLAYFAIR: During one of my last years at training camp, Pat Quinn was having us do a simple drill and I remember thinking, When did my stickhandling get so bad that I can't move a puck around a set of pylons? I knew something wasn't right. I got traded back to Buffalo and was having a good time, but my coach, Rick Dudley, was let go, and I hurt my back. The team offered me a position in marketing and play-by-play and I accepted, so I had a bit of a parachute when I retired. But two years later, I'd wake up in the middle of the night and think, That guy and that guy and that guy are still playing. That guy was on the bench when I was in Los Angeles, and he's taking a regular shift. Eventually, I called Lindy Ruff – who was playing with the Rangers – and told him that I was waking up in a cold sweat thinking about coming back. I said to him, "You still play. You know what I can do. Tell me, can I still play?" He paused a minute and said, "No." Some people might think, "That dirty bastard, he told his friend he was done." But I needed to hear that. My wife couldn't tell me. Schoney couldn't tell me. I needed the right person to help me shut the door.

JIM SCHOENFELD: The Sabres went to the finals in 1975 – I was twenty-two at the time and they'd made me captain that year – and I had visions of carrying the Stanley Cup around the Auditorium four or five times because we had a young, good team. When it didn't happen in 1975, I wasn't that upset. I thought, Ah, hell, we'll be here next year, and the year after, and the year after that. But we never made it back. You never know how close or far you are to a championship until it happens.

JOHN CHABOT: In my early days in the NHL, I was called a squaw, a chief, a brave. Sometimes people would laugh when they said it, sometimes not. Now when somebody calls someone else a "frog," it's frowned upon, but not back then. I've become more aware of it now. I should have won more trophies in minor hockey, but they didn't want to give it to "the Indian boy." The number I wore through my whole minor hockey career was number 11, and people used to call it "the Indian number" whenever someone else wanted to wear it. My dad thought it was racist, but I wasn't sure; I just thought it was how people were. I got called names, but in hockey, everybody does. It was worse for others. There was a kid named Jerry Thack, from Shebenacadie, whom my dad discovered. He was small, but unbelievably skilled. He could do whatever he wanted on the ice. When I was living in Halifax, he and I would get paired up all the time, but he got caught up in the reserve life of drinking. He was invited to play in the QMHL – he would have been one of the first Maritimers to play there – but he couldn't go because of his drinking. It was almost like a way of life for him, and it still is for a lot of athletes, kids, whomever, on the reserve. The things that I see when I travel to the reserve – and the talent these kids have – it would break your heart.

PERRY BEREZIN: Hockey happens twenty-four hours a day. Most people leave their jobs at the office, but not hockey players.

When you're on vacation in the middle of July, you're thinking about the season. You're wondering about what you're doing to your body, good or bad. I was really comfortable with the sport at the beginning of my career, and a little beyond that. Then one day, as a pro, it kicked in where I was. And then it got really hard. My attitude changed. I was sitting out occasionally, and I started to doubt myself. The business of sport jumped in and complicated things. The doubt and anxiety burned me out and I retired at twenty-eight. I was mentally and physically roasted. Nine seasons. I couldn't do it any more. I didn't want to be living every day not knowing whether I was going to play, or whether I was going to be sent down. (I was only sent down twice for small stints.) I couldn't be on the bubble any more. Every time I got injured, I was that much farther from the edge; when I got sent down, I was beyond the edge. And because I was injured a lot, those feelings were exacerbated. I had groin injuries throughout my career.

One year, we were playing Montreal and I was flying through the neutral zone. I was going to outrace everyone to the puck until I felt a pop in my abdomen. I continued to skate until the pain started to come. I changed, took the next shift, then realized there was nothing there. I wasn't the same player after that. I never came back as myself. Eventually, I went to see Cliff Fletcher and asked to be traded. Coach Terry Crisp wasn't playing me, but Uncle Cliff told me to wait a few months. The irony is that when he called to tell me about the trade, I didn't want to leave. I went to Minnesota, but the Flames went to the Stanley Cup.

GARRY UNGER: You can always be a great player when things are going great. You can always be a great person when things are falling into place. But what makes a person is how they react when things aren't going well. In hockey, you have to learn how to stay positive, because you never know when you're going to be needed. Everybody's sat on the bench and thought, Man, I don't even like hockey, or I'm not sure if I want to play any more. But if somebody goes out of the lineup and you're called in, you better not mess up because you might not play again. Ever. You've ruined the one chance to show the coach that you're ready to go. The players who handle the mental part of the game are those who rise above it. I had to convince myself that even though I was the leading scorer, the St. Louis Blues weren't going to fold if I left them. If you're putting your faith in being a big NHL star, where is your self-worth when you lose all of that, whether you've retired, been injured, whatever? How do you handle standing in line for a restaurant or paying a speeding ticket? You have to answer these questions fast, because you might never answer them at all.

HARVEY BENNETT, JR: I'm a Wendy's franchisee now and I do pretty well, but when you get out of hockey, the trust in your fellow businessperson — or in the world — makes you disappointed pretty quickly. Being called a "backstabber" in hockey or someone you couldn't trust was the ultimate insult, whereas in the real world, it's normal. I still meet some great people, but I met more great people in one year in hockey than I have [elsewhere] in the last twenty.

PAT HICKEY: Hockey was my way of being free. It's like that song "Desperado" by the Eagles: my stick was my six-string on the pathway to freedom.

JOHN BROPHY: If you're not the happiest person in the world when you're playing hockey, there's got to be something wrong with you. Anybody who's unhappy after making the NHL should be shot.

✴

Some things are possible in 1.5 seconds: death, a single "*darggghh!*", the salient note in Jimi Hendrix's "Axis: Bold as Love," winking, realizing there's a strange clucking sound coming from under your bed, Chris Gaines's career, the amount of time it took for "One-Eyed" Frank McGee to get his nickname, transmitting a radio wave, pulling out a hair, and scoring. Yet on that Friday afternoon between the gold and purple walls of McCormick Arena in Parkdale, Toronto, all but that last item seemed plausible. To us, 1.5 seemed as tiny as an ant's eyelash as we laid our stomachs over the boards and tried not to puke, watching the last handful of red and black skaters gather for the game's final draw. One point five seconds wasn't even two seconds. In two seconds, you could paint a desert landscape, invent linoleum, coax King Kong down from a building, write an angry letter to the president of Turkmenistan, or break Wayne Gretzky's seasonal goal total of ninety-two. One point five seconds, on the other hand, was a squashed dream, a pitted plum, a flicked butt, a fart. It was an insult to the very concept of time itself.

For 1.5 to be anything more than pure astral dreck, Chris Topping had to win a third consecutive draw against a player, Brad, who was half his age and steaming mad that he'd let his team down when they'd needed him most. He'd have to pull the

Morningstars, 2004

puck back in one strong – but not too strong – and easy – but
not too easy – lash so that it cut in a perfect diagonal across the
ice to the Chizzler, who would have to slap the puck with authority – but not too much authority – toward a place at the net so
perfect that not any of the five sliding Unyon defenders nor the
Detergent Box nor the 'Stars' manic crease-crashers could stop it.

But sports is odd. We've all walked around spouting stuff like,
"Any team can beat any other team on any given day!" but no one
ever means these things. There are probably less than 1.5 instances
in a sports fan's life where we can remember the impossible
coming true – where athletics defies science and the physical
universe is flipped on its ear. Yet in the breath before Steve the
Ref threw down the puck for the last time, 1.5 seconds forced us

to push hope along like a small shining ship motoring through a sea of despair. It wasn't much to go on, but at least 1.5 seconds wasn't zero.

It wasn't much, but it wasn't nothing.

Getting the puck for a remarkable third time in three draws, the Chizzler shot the puck low, half a foot off the ice on a frozen rope to the net. The Unyon had very little surf left in them, and chose to cordon the front of the net with bodies. The Detergent Box extended his legs so that both skates touched both posts. His gloves shot out, his groin pressed flat to the ice. The puck was alight with real smiling speed. The Detergent Box saw it approach, but he could not find the energy nor the will nor the elasticity to lift himself from his spiderly crouch. Sticks swung, helmets lunged, and skates were kicked out in a explosion of action. The frozen doughnut rippled the net with an exultant wave.

We scored.

On the bench, I grabbed Mark's head and pulled it with my hands as if trying to wrench apart his costume. He pogoed on the spot like a fat owl trying to take flight, shouting, "*Yaaaaaaayyyyyy!*" Fans pounded the glass and hollered to us and it felt like confetti was about to pour from the sky. We chugged across the ice, swearing in singsong — "*Fa-o-uh-uck!*" — as the Unyon skated off the ice, slamming their sticks, punching doors, and yelling at the referees. Overhead, the rink's ceiling lamps shone like a hundred brilliant suns.

As we came off the ice, we were high-fived and back-slapped and patted on the head by friends and strangers and a mass of players waiting to take to the ice. The next day, the only thing anyone at the rink or the Hootenany or the various hockey klatches around town could talk about was how the Morningstars had tied the game with .001 seconds left to go, and were you there? and did you see it? and could you ever imagine a better finish to a hockey game? Ugly with sweat — and knowing, to a man, that we would lope through the rest of the tournament before bowing out in the semifinals to another more motivated and conventional team filled out by real hockey players — we trooped into the dressing room feeling joy, pride, and relief. We sat there until the rink attendants came and asked us to clear the room, and as I stuffed my gear into my hockey bag and rolled it toward the door of the arena, I knew that even though I'd been involved in one of the great games of my life, the only thing that really mattered to me once the door swung shut behind me, was that I'd return to walk through it again.

APPENDIX

Exclaim! Cup participants
(* denotes division winner)

2004

Boom*
Bovine Sex Club
Capsule Music
Dufferin Groove*
Edmonton Green Pepper All Stars
Edmonton Green Pepper Gong Show
Gas Station Islanders
Guelph Three Gut Feelings
Halifax/Dartmouth Ferries
Hamilton Sonic Unyon Pond Squad
Hockey Lads
Jokers
London Fog
Long & McQuade
Montreal Ninja Tune Wicked Deadly Karate Chops

Morningstars
Ottawa Songbird Millionaires
Peterborough Pneumonia*
Sgt. Rock
The Fruit
Vancouver Flying Vees
Verses Magazine
Victoria Humiliation
Winnipeg Wheatfield Souldiers

2005
Boom*
Bovine Sex Club
Capsule Music*
ChartAttack Hack
Dufferin Groove
Edmonton Green Pepper Gong Show
Fluid Living Arseholes
Gas Station Islanders
Halifax/Dartmouth Ferries
Hockey Lads
Jokers
La Hacienda Flying Burritos
London Fog
Long & McQuade
Montreal Ninja Tune Wicked Deadly Karate Chops
Morningstars
Nightmares
Ottawa Songbird Millionaires

Peterborough Pneumonia
Porcupines
Sgt. Rock
The Fruit
Vancouver Flying Vees
Victoria Humiliation*
Winnipeg Wheatfield Souldiers
Guelph Three Gut Feelings

ACKNOWLEDGEMENTS

The Morningstar photos featured in the book were taken by Simon Evers, and the cards were laid out by Stephen Cribbin, whose company, Cribwin Trading Cards, will happily square your mug for a tidy fee. The photo of Tyler Stewart, Chris Murphy, et al., was snapped by my sister, Cathy Bidini, while Deborah Taylor captured the image of the masked Winterbird. Regards go to the Sonic Unyon Pond Hockey Squad for providing the dark to the Morningstars' light, and to Alan Muir, Mark Keast, 90th Parallel, and House on Fire Productions, the *Toronto Star*, Rheostatics, CBC Television, and the *New York Times* for keeping me in pen nibs while I wrote. Acknowledgements also to Jim and Chris at Kwik Kopy on College, (Mary) McCormick Arena in Parkdale, Kong Njo, the Russian Nomad crew, Tom Goodwin, Gas Station Islanders, Mark, Hal, Pete, and Eric Mattson, the NHL, NHLPA, and NHL Alumni, and Cafe Faema on Dupont. Thanks go to Glen Hall, Bill Ranford, Ray Miron, Lanny McDonald, Dennis MacDonald, Stu Hackl, Ira Gitler, Jeff Z Klein, Dennis Murphy, Brad Smith, Mike Antonovich, André Brin, and Andre Lacroix — all of them gave me their time, but I was unable to crowbar them into the player/commentator chorus. I'd like to blame my editor, Dinah Forbes, or my agent, Dave Johnston, for this – I'd blame my wife, Janet, and kids, Lorenzo and Cecilia, if the shoe fit – but it was up to me to make their stories work. It was also my job to paint the Morningstars as they appear staring across from me in the dressing room or at my shoulder on the bench; should they take exception to their portraits, they must know that I wrote this book with nothing but love in my heart, which is tattooed with a big pointy star, and bleeds red and white.

Please write:

Dave Bidini
PO Box 616, Station C
Toronto, ON
M6J 3R9
Canada